THE NEW BEATS

the new
beats

Exploring the Music
Culture and Attitudes
of Hip-Hop

S.H. FERNANDO JR.

PAYBACK PRESS

Published in the UK in 1995 by Payback Press
an imprint of Canongate Books Ltd
14 High Street, Edinburgh EH1 1TE

Published in the USA by Doubleday
a division of Bantam Doubleday Dell Publishing Group, Inc.
1540 Broadway, New York, New York 10036

All photos by Jeremy Dawson except for those on the following pages:
p.11 (Richard Bailey, 1988), p.103 (Peter Dokus), p.126 (Mario Castellanos), p.142 (Susan Now),
p.20 (David Corio), p.78 (George Hirose, 1988).

Lyric permissions appear on pages 293-94

Book design by Terry Karydes
Chapter opening photo-collages by Jeremy Dawson

British Library Cataloguing in Publication Data
A catalogue record for this book is available on request from the British Library.

ISBN 0 86241 524 1

For Sid & Siromi

789.4 FER

781.69 FER

contents

preface

Having not grown up in New York, I was among legions of youths whose earliest encounter with rap was a bouncy, danceable twelve-inch by the Sugar Hill Gang called "Rapper's Delight" (Sugar Hill Records, 1979), a single that announced the debut of an art form—worldwide. Weaned on the progressive rock and funk in my older brother's and sister's record collections, as well as the pop of the day, my love of music was just developing, and this jam made an indelible impression on me. I remember taping it off the radio, playing it, rewinding it, playing it more, and being able to recite most of the nonstop rhymes. Little did I know at the time, however, that rap and "Rapper's Delight" barely scratched the surface.

Rap was not the novelty or fad that the media made it out to be, rather part of a whole inner-city culture that manifested itself in such varied forms of expression as break dancing, graffiti, slang, and fashion. The term "hip-hop," used as far back as Malcolm X's day to describe the dance parties of his youth, suddenly became relevant to my youth when the Sugar Hill Gang were going off about: "With a hip, hop, the hipit, the hipidipit, hip, hip, hopit, you don't stop. . . ." That peculiar term was appropriated by Bronx deejay Afrika Bambaataa to describe a thriving culture that originated in the ghettos of his borough. But, of course, I was unaware of it all. I just knew what I heard on the radio—Grandmaster Flash, Funky Four Plus One, Kurtis Blow, Bambaataa's "Planet Rock," and Newcleus's "Jamonit." Thanks to the influence of my older siblings, my musical tastes were rounded off by the sounds of David Bowie, Bob Marley, Parliament, Talking Heads, and The Clash.

It was not until high school, while I was entrenched in punk, new wave, and reggae, that hip-hop really delivered one to the head, opening up perspectives beyond the music and into the culture of the streets. In 1983 Run-D.M.C. burst out of the underground with such singles as "Hard Times," "Rock Box," and "Sucker MCs," a defining musical moment in my life. To me, Run-D.M.C. represented the most original, alternative, supercharged music I had ever heard. As it turned out, their big-beat-blasting sound also recalled the raw feel of hip-hop parties in parks and community centers in the Bronx.

Stripped down to the barest essentials—voices over a staccato kick and snare—this music held an awesome, hypnotic power that lured you into the flow of Run and D.'s rhymes. Even though all they were talking about was themselves, and the outlook, desires, and realities of the average urban kid on the street, they did it with unmatched style and attitude. This duo from a middle-class neighborhood in Queens spared the gimmicks and outlandish garb that were the norm at the time and just got down to hard rhyming. In the process, they inspired a whole slew of other rappers who followed. Run-D.M.C. ruled for years, taking me into college with the phenomenal *Raising Hell*. I thought that things could get no better.

But hip-hop could and would only grow and progress under the guardianship of Boogie Down Productions, Eric B. & Rakim, Public Enemy, and EPMD, four groups that shaped my college years. Although my first love was reggae, which I beamed out across the Boston area from WHRB in Cambridge, hip-hop shared time on my own turntables. Also, after finishing my reggae show, I could go back to my dorm and check "Street Beat," hosted by Jon Shecter and Dave Mays, who, along with DJ Def Jeff from Roxbury's Almighty R.S.O. crew, kept the beats pumping in Boston. Jon and Dave went on to start *The Source*, "the magazine of hip-hop music, culture, and politics."

It was during my undergraduate years that the idea for this book originated. There was little documentation of hip-hop culture on par with a book like Stephen Davis's *Reggae International*, which laid bare the roots, culture, and consciousness of the Jamaican sound. I envisioned doing a similar treatment with hip-hop, which I had practically grown up with and which meant much more to me than simply entertainment. Though rap had always been perceived as a passing fad, years after "Rapper's Delight" I realized that it had clearly broken into a whole new commercial sphere, and that young people of all races and socio-economic classes were embracing it—and being profoundly influenced by it.

The New Beats is the result not only of a year and a half of continuous research, interviews, and writing, but also of a long-time love affair with the music. Some people consider music as purely entertainment, when, in fact, it is one of the most intimate reflections of a culture. Like other modes of artistic expression, music also offers a direct insight into the soul, and connects those who have traveled the same paths. *The New Beats* is my attempt to capture the essence of what I have seen, heard, and felt along the way.

S. H. Fernando Jr.
Brooklyn
September 1993

acknowledgments

All my love to my family for their guidance, faith, and support: Ammi, Uncle Cyril, Sid and Cynth, Siromi and Alain—I couldn't have done it without you all. Special thanks to my agent, Marlene Connor, and my editor, Charlie Conrad, for giving me this opportunity. Also, maximum respect to Sam Freedman for getting me started and Phyl Garland for her support. Big Up the Dub Posse, who accompanied me on countless musical odysseys, Jack Hornady, and Jeremy Dawson for the visuals. Can't forget Jon Furay.

A big shout out to all the people in the industry who helped make this possible: Jon Shecter and *The Source* (Stay Real), Bill "the Mack" Adler and Roberta "the Macktress" Magrini (nuff, nuff respect), the entire staff of the late, great *Set to Run* (Leyla Turkhan, Max Ernst, Ian Allen, Devin Roberson, Miguel Baguer, Sue Mainzer, Charlene English, Chris Chambers, Chris Reade, Aimee Morris, Ursula Smith, and Lesley Pitts), Brad Balfour and the Funk Archives, Michael Gonzales, Dennis Wade, Jeff Stewart, Anne Kristoff, Phyllis Pollack, Michelle Murray, Chrissy Murray, Deborah Mannis-Gardner, Tracey Miller, Audrey Fontaine, Neale Easterby, Patrick Moxey, Ian Steaman, Karen Sadler, Estela Rizzuto, Jackie Bunch, Wayne Garfield, Archie Ivy, Mercedes Lewis, Roceania Williams, Paula Bradshaw, Meredith Harwood, Beth Ann Buddenbaum, Jerry Heller, Heidi Robinson, Wesley Cullars, Paul Stewart, David Lionheart, Dan Charnas, Shelli Andranigian, Lisa Vega, Jasmine Vega, Marcus Bryant, Orlando Aguillen, Row, Leslie Cooney, Mike Ross, Rick Ross, Marty Schwarz, Derrick Godfrey, Mai Huggins, Sharon Owens, Big Phil and Barbara at Two Friends, Bernard Alexander, Wesley Powell, Greg Jessie, Kirk Pascal, Steve Egerton, Marguerite Lorenz, Bill Stephney, Valerie Sennett, Marco Alpert, Larry Troutman, the "Funky Man" Dave Lee, Brad Taylor, Colson Whitehead, Schenk, Nick Spooner, Janine Amber, Peter Jarvis, Joe Doughrity, Susan Now,

David Corio, Murray Elias, Jack Schwartzberg, Steve Barrow, and Henry Chalfant.

Extra strength to all the artists who stay true to hip-hop—especially the ones who contributed their voices to this book: Erick Sermon, Parrish Smith, Dray and Skoob of Das EFX, Chris Charity and Derek Lynch of Solid Scheme, Redman, K-Solo, Sam Sneed Anderson, Kris Parker, Kenny Parker, Paul "Large Professor" Mitchell, Rob Swift, Dr. Butcher & the X-Men, Ivan "Doc" Rodriguez, "Prince Paul" Houston, DJ Mark the 45 King, Afrika Bambaataa and the Mighty Zulu Nation, Jazzy Jay, Crazy Legs, Futura, Cold Crush, Red Alert, Kid Capri, Ultramagnetic MCs, Diamond, Lord Finesse, Showbiz & Andre the Giant, Fat Joe Da Gangsta, Dres and Lawnge of Black Sheep, Gang Starr, Cypress Hill, Poor Righteous Teachers, Jamalski, Daddy-O, Double X Posse, Chi-Ali, Pete Nice, Paris, Masta Ace, Kool G Rap & DJ Polo, Biz Markie, Pete Rock & C.L. Smooth, Run-D.M.C., Boss, OFTB, Eazy E., DJ Quik, Dr. Dre, the D.O.C., Yo-Yo, Kam, Da Lenchmob, Tone Lōc, Too Short, Paris, MC Eiht and Compton's Most Wanted, Sir Jinx, Beastie Boys, Eric Sadler, Roger Troutman, George Clinton, David Nelson, George Porter, WAR, Chris Frantz, and Tina Weymouth. Also to Public Enemy, Eric B. & Rakim, Schooly D., Ice-T, A Tribe Called Quest, De La Soul, Jungle Brothers, Snoop, Daz, Kurupt, Rage, Jeru, Geto Boys, Wu Tang Clan Leaders of the New School, Brand Nubian, Nice & Smooth, Digital Underground, Naughty by Nature, Puba, Queen Latifah, MC Lyte, Awesome Two, Salt-N-Pepa, Shanté, Slick Rick, Above the Law, King Sun, Beatnuts, Fu' Scnickens, and all the hedz who are running things in the underground . . .

Thanks to the publications that helped me along the way: the mighty *New Review of Records*, Sacha Jenkins and *Beatdown*, Hoagy and *Dub Catcher*. Also Steve Hager's *An Illustrated History of Rap, Breakdancing and Graffiti* and David Toop's *Rap Attack 2: African Rap to Global Hip-Hop*— two essential texts, and other influential works like *Cut 'N' Mix* by Dick Hebdige, *Reggae* by Howard Johnson and Jim Pines, Stephen Davis's *Reggae International, Subway Art* by Martha Cooper and Henry Chalfant,

Tougher Than Leather and *Rap Portraits* by Bill Adler, and Nelson George's *The Death of Rhythm and Blues*.

I would also like to thank three people who contributed to this project in one way or another, but could not be here to see it—Gad Johannes Schuster, Fernando "Kid Fresh" Marti, and Dr. J. B. DeSilva. I think of you often. Rest in peace.

This book was overseen by H.I.M., who makes all things possible.

WoRdSoUnD
is
PoWeR

introduction

From its raw rumblings in the Bronx to a sound that has saturated suburbia, hip-hop has triumphantly emerged from the underground to take its place in the mainstream of popular culture. Although it has taken almost twenty years to reach this level of mass exposure, the movement now stands as a multimillion-dollar enterprise and a dominant cultural force that continues to grow. Soaring sales of rap records and an increasing presence on the pop music charts attest to only part of the phenomenon. The pervasive influence of hip-hop extends to television, film, advertising, fashion, the print media, and language itself. But transcending all these, hip-hop represents a culture with deep roots that has exploded onto the mainstream and expressed itself via rap music.

Rap evokes the drums of Armageddon, but from the gangster fairy tales of N.W.A. (Niggers With Attitude) and Ice Cube, "The Nigga Ya Love to Hate," to the rampant black nationalism of Public Enemy, its appeal to the youths of the nation rivals even that of rock 'n' roll. While addressing the hopes, dreams, and frustrations of America's minorities, rap is the music of a whole generation, breaching barriers of race and class. In 1992, the Recording Industry Association of America (RIAA) reported that 11 rap albums reached platinum, selling over one million units, while 23 had gone gold, with sales exceeding 500,000 units. The joint category of rap and r&b dominated the revenue shares, grossing roughly $700,000,000 for the recording industry. Among the top sellers were the familiar names—N.W.A., Ice Cube, Public Enemy. But the ranks had also grown to include newer talent such as Das EFX, Naughty by Nature, Cypress Hill, Kriss Kross, and Arrested Development.

On the visual front, *Yo! MTV Raps* and Russell Simmons' *Def Comedy Jam* are cited as two of the most popular programs on cable TV, while the commercial networks cater to the youthful hip-hop nation with such shows as *The Fresh Prince of Bel-Air, In Living Color, Martin*, and the *Arsenio Hall Show*. On the big screen, a new wave of black film—including *Boyz N the Hood, New Jack City, Juice*, and *Menace II Society*—depict the reality of the ghetto to a rap soundtrack. McDonald's, Coca-Cola, Sprite, and Nike routinely use rap to sell their products. Even the Pillsbury Doughboy is rapping. In addition to *The Source*, which has been committed to covering the entire realm of hip-hop since 1989, and Time Warner's *Vibe*, a recent entry in the media convergence on the art form, rap has commanded the attention of countless fanzines and upscale glossies—*GQ, Vanity Fair, The New Yorker*. In the midst of such commercial success, it is often easy to overlook, or forget, where this creative tide of expression originated—the streets.

Rap bloomed in the depths of the ghetto, a place characterized by overarching poverty, violence, and crime. Though currently reflecting a diversity of lifestyles, opinions, and feelings, rap responds directly and indirectly to the trials and tribulations of life at the bottom, and for the most part remains true to the gritty reality of the streets that produced it. The raw creativity, however, has been honed into a precise art by a generation of young blacks whom I refer to as the New Beats. Reminiscent of the jazz-influenced writing of the Beat Generation, who challenged the literary conventions of the 1950s, the New Beats are shaking up today's society with rhyme and rhythm. They create dialogue, and often controversy, while testing the boundaries of art. Though the voices are varied and the topics endless, at its most basic level rap represents communication, instruction, and expression—all relayed through music. This music links a black community, really a burgeoning nation, that is progressing to a new level of self-awareness through the basic elements of word and sound.

The New Beats explores the complexities of hip-hop's words, sounds, images, and attitudes. Though I strived to be as comprehensive and in-depth as possible, I soon discovered that the realm of hip-hop exceeds all easily definable limits. Each chapter, I found, could have been a book in itself, so the challenge was to be as representative as possible and to represent what was real. The first portion of the book provides a detailed historical context, linking rap with the earlier forms of black music that influenced it. Discussing the relationship between hip-hop music and culture and the social and political forces that spawned them, I then step behind the scenes of the industry today to examine rap as a business and to view the business from an artist's perspective. Finally, I focus on the music itself, speaking with artists who not only explain their motivation and inspiration but describe what their lyrics mean and how the music is assembled. I present hip-hop as a serious art form so that readers will be able to judge it on its intrinsic value.

'Frank depictions of sex and violence, the liberal use of harsh language, and a celebration of lawlessness found in some rap have fueled notions that, across the board, the music is crude, obscene, and lacking in artistic merit. However simplistic this summation—in its total disregard for a wealth of exciting, innovative sounds with positive messages—rap's controversial side certainly sells records and commands the most attention. Especially within the black community, there has been a backlash against that brand of outlaw, or "gangsta," rap that fulfills the worst racial stereotypes, and justifiably so. After all, the black experience in 1993 encompasses infinitely more than drug dealing and drive-bys. While I won't attempt to defend the gangsta rap genre, I will say that rap is essentially rebel music, made by people who have been cast as the outsider. The consumers of rap—overwhelmingly male teens—relate to rebelliousness, and record companies, in their push for profit, package and sell it to meet a demand. At the same time, reality is a very prized commodity in the field of rap, and rappers who are not authentic, no matter what they portray, are guaranteed to fade faster than an old pair of blue jeans. Despite all the hype, rap does not thrive on negativity.

The New Beats tells of the uplifting of the African American—a story that has as much to do with such engineers of social change as Marcus Garvey, Malcolm X, and the Black Panthers as it does with popular music. Though the term "slavery" conjures up a brutal past, many blacks continue to struggle under the yoke of mental and economic slavery, languishing in a substandard public education system and trapped in the self-perpetuating despair of the ghetto. The hope and promise of the civil rights era appear empty today as affirmative action and necessary social programs have been eroded during the administrations of Reagan and Bush. Meanwhile, drugs, crime, poverty, AIDS, unemployment, and teen pregnancy plague the black community as never before. Rap speaks not only of these problems but of the larger issues of being black in America, where race remains a weighty issue.

On another level, *The New Beats* relates a human drama of individual achievement that firmly bases it in the American saga. Hip-hop has infiltrated the mainstream because creativity is a commodity. From Miles Davis to Michael Jackson, blacks, more than any other minority group, have achieved great success as entertainers, leaving numerous contributions in their wake. The thriving arts and entertainment fields have been the hallmark of American culture as well as our most visible export to the world, and black artists have created their own niche within it, as a route to fame, fortune, and respect. As the economic climate in this country worsens and prospects diminish, music in general—and rap in particular—represents a real and accessible route out of the ghetto. Black youths, denied the traditional avenues of progress, have taken their destiny into their own hands in order to improve their situation. Rap creates not only artists but businessmen.

Rap is both startlingly new and yet firmly tied to the past. In order to fully understand and appreciate it, one must be aware of its heritage. From the blues to gospel, jazz, rhythm and blues, rock, and soul, there is a thriving tradition of black music in America, of which rap represents the latest chapter. As Nelson George writes in *The Death of Rhythm and Blues*, "In retrospect, rap or something like it should have been predicted. Each decade since World War II has seen the emergence of some new approach to black dance music. The 1940s brought forth rhythm and blues, and the 1950s rock 'n' roll, the 1960s soul, the 1970s funk and disco. Something was due in the 1980s, though the contemporary tastemakers of r&b conspired to hold off the inevitable."[1] As cultural heir to this wealth of sounds, rap owes much to the body of music that preceded it.

In general, black American music may be viewed within the larger context of the African diaspora, during which blacks were forcibly thrust into slavery and brought to the Americas and the Caribbean. Though the effects of this tumultuous event can never be fully understood, a legacy of suffering characterizes the history of the African in America. Dispossessed of their land and liberty, the slaves fought to preserve their native culture and identity as they became assimilated "citizens" in an alien land. This new breed of African tried to make sense out of life in a society that oppressed him, and drawing from his own heritage, expressed himself through music.

"Each phase of the Negro's music issued directly from the dictates of his social and psychological environment,"[2] writes Leroi Jones (Amiri Baraka) in *Blues People*. Thus the blues, the first form of African-American music, offers an intensely personal depiction of suffering. Similarly, gospel music, which was rooted in a dependency on Christianity, reflected the view that the church was the rock of salvation. Phyllis Garland, in *The Sound of Soul*, further fleshes out this concept, writing, "While spirituals might have been sung by slaves closer to the big house of the plantation who got a secondhand whiff of Christianity, the devil songs and their derivative blues were more likely to have been shaped by the substance of field slaves and their descendants who were compelled to remain closer to what we might call the nitty gritty. . . . The blues must be regarded as intense, highly personal and telling depictions of the human condition expressed with cutting candor."[3] This description also applies to many of the dark tales expressed in rap, suggesting that some segments of society are still singing the blues.

Despite the celebrated sophistication of jazz and white America's complete appropriation of rock 'n' roll, black music in America has never received the credit it deserves. During the jazz age, for example, white bandleaders such as Paul Whiteman (lionized as "The King of Jazz") and Benny Goodman (similarly called "The King of Swing") completely overshadowed the crucial contributions of their black contemporaries, Edward Kennedy "Duke" Ellington and Fletcher Henderson. The same holds true for rock 'n' roll, in which Elvis is simply regarded as "The King," although his style and many of his hit songs came from black artists or song writers such as Big Mama Thornton and Otis Blackwell.

Like other forms of black music, rap also has had to combat perceptions of it as crude, simple, and barbaric "jungle" music. Garland writes, "For the same reason the black man's story has not found its way into accepted textbooks on American history, his music has been excluded from supposedly comprehensive studies in this field. Always his music has been segregated from that deemed worthy of designation as art."[4] This brand of cultural racism, fueled by a lack of understanding, intolerance, and a failure to delve deeper into the art form and the culture that produced it, continues to this day.

The mainstream press—slow to pick up on rap in the first place—has been guilty of biased and uninformed reporting, as evidenced by some of the first articles about rap that appeared in *Time* and *Newsweek*, in 1990. Speaking like someone denied his daily dose of Geritol, *Newsweek* writer Jerry Adler observed "the thumping, clattering, scratching assault of rap—music so postindustrial it's mostly not even played, but pieced together out of pre-recorded soundbites,"[5] attempting to discount rap's musical merit and artistic value. The implication: This is not real music. The article also played right into racist notions that equate black with evil, implying that rap is "scary."

A similar appraisal was offered in *Time* by Janice Simpson, who said, "The lyrics, a raucous stew of street corner bravado and racial boosterism, are often salted with profanity, and sometimes with demeaning remarks about whites, women, and gays. The fact that they are delivered by young, self-consciously arrogant black men in a society where black youths make many whites uneasy doesn't help either."[6] In describing rap as inherently offensive and antagonistic, and contributing to white fright, the article almost seemed to suggest that the black youths causing such a stir should shut up. Both articles also condescended to their subject, discussing rap with a kind of the-natives-are-getting-restless cultural bias that showed shallow reporting and plain ignorance.

Elsewhere, in a November 1991 article in *The New Republic*, a more detailed analysis of rap fell way short of its mark. In "The Real Face of Rap," David Samuels made the facile observation that suburban white youths comprise rap's biggest consumer market. This is as true today as it has been throughout history: Whites have always been the main consumers of black culture—if only for the simple reasons that there are more whites than blacks in America and that the whites hold greater economic resources. Obviously, racial issues permeate music just as they do practically everything else in our society. To really delve into rap, the honest, intimate expression of a marginalized underclass, one embarks on a journey into realms beyond music.

America stands in the midst of a renaissance of black culture, propelled to a large degree by the energy of hip-hop. Though we still grapple with many serious problems, no other time in history, save the jazz age or the sixties, has generated the electricity, sense of newness, and consciousness that abound in this musical movement. *The New Beats* provides a living document of these times, as well as the most comprehensive survey of hip-hop to date.

the
new
BEATS

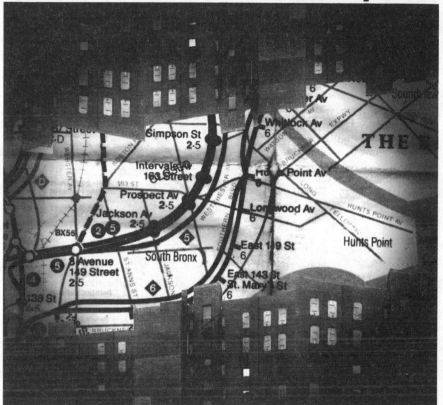

ChApTeR 1

Return of
the Boogie Down

It is difficult to describe New York's South Bronx without invoking a host of clichés: "America's worst slum," "the epitome of urban failure," "a city of despair," "the ghetto of ghettos," "a blemish," "a cancer," "a constant reminder of neglect." On a 1980 campaign visit, Ronald Reagan likened it to the firebombed German city of Dresden after World War II. Many residents of the lower borough—an area of roughly twenty square miles in the southernmost portion of Bronx County—simply call it "Vietnam." To try to put such intense poverty, crime, and drug infestation into words may evoke extremes, but the South Bronx is an extreme place. Statistics cannot convey what a ride on an uptown subway or, better yet, a walk through its streets reveals. The South Bronx is probably the last place in the world where anybody would wish to live.

This was not always the case. In the fifties, the Bronx's proximity to Manhattan and its thriving real estate market of elegant apartments made it another rung closer to the American Dream for Irish, Italians, and Jews fleeing the Lower East Side. By the sixties, however, a new wave of black and Puerto Rican pilgrims, who had missed out on the postwar prosperity, faced an area in transition. When construction of the Cross Bronx Expressway began in 1959, businesses and factories relocated, pulling with them whole middle-class communities to the borough's northern reaches. The value of housing naturally plummeted and slumlords slithered in, providing no real services but milking their properties for any small profit they could get. As the seventies approached, arson became a convenient way for landlords to collect on insurance and a means for desperate welfare recipients to escape increasingly squalid conditions for priority in public housing. As the Bronx erupted in flames, street gangs and junkies ushered in a horrible wave of crime.

In the midst of this overwhelming negativity and decay, an explosion of creativity—an earnest expression of the sufferers—rose above and conquered this seemingly insurmountable environment. Manifesting itself in such forms as rap music, break dancing, and graffiti writing, the cultural movement popularly known as hip-hop spread with the ferocity of the fires, proving that the South Bronx was not some land of the lost. The currency of youth, hip-hop transformed a ghetto into a gold mine—not tangibly, but in the spirit and pride it ignited in every kid who ever attended the early "jams" in parks and community centers. Though the South Bronx still remains an area devastated, a certain legendary aura pervades the streets of what is respectfully known to many as the "Boogie Down."

It's just another Friday night in December, and radios from New York, New Jersey, and Connecticut are locked on Kool DJ Red Alert's mix show on 98.7 KISS-FM. Though he doesn't usually entertain on-air guests, tonight Red keeps some very good company—the single most important figure responsible for transforming the Bronx into the Boogie Down. For most of the youthful listeners, the smooth, powerful voice of Kool Herc is unfamiliar. Others, however, are no doubt enjoying flashbacks to the days when this legendary deejay rocked parties by spinning percussive snippets of records, known as break beats.

Though he's been out of town for some time, Herc, the man who started it all, is seeping out of the speakers, reaching out to infinitely more people than he ever did back in the day. At age 38, he's like the world's hippest granddaddy as he relates hip-hop's early history to the legion of beat fanatics who are tuned in to the show:

The first place I played was 1520 Sedgewick Avenue—that's a recreation room—matter of fact in my apartment, yunno. Like the Pied Piper, the rats came out of the bricks to dance. (Red: How much were your parties back then?) Twenty-five cent. Twenty-five cent. Then it went to the recreation room, then we gave a block party, one time, annual block party. When you come down the block that cleaned up, you know Herc gonna play some music, and 'um, I couldn't come back to the old ranch no more, I had to go to a place called the Twilight Zone. And then I used to give flyers out over by the Hevalo, and my mans would tell me to step off. I said, "One day I'ma be in here." So I gave my first party at the Twilight Zone, it was raining, the gods was raining down on me. Everybody came down from the Hevalo, wondering what was happenin'. They said, "Herc is playing down the block." "Who's Herc?" "That's the guy you chased away with the flyers from outside." And from the Twilight Zone I went on up to the Hevalo. . . .

From there he moved to a spot called the Executive Playhouse, on 173rd Street in the Bronx, as well as playing numerous high schools, community centers, and parks. Assuming his native Jamaican patois, he continues:

My muddah roots come from St. Mary [a parish in Jamaica], yunno. A man named George inspirate I from Jamaica, yunno, and he lived 'pon Victoria Street, yunno, and used to come with the big sound system. It was devastating 'cause it was open air, when it rained that's the dance. . . . I did a lot of things from Jamaica, and I brought it here and turned it into my own little style. . . .

Clive Campbell emigrated to the Bronx from Jamaica in 1967, when he was 12 years old. Though a "Yardie" (Jamaican) down to his avid appreciation for soccer, which was not even a consideration on the garbage-filled lots of the Bronx, he soon adapted to the ways of his new home. As a student at Alfred E. Smith High School, his physical prowess—whether in lifting weights, running track, or playing basketball—earned him the nickname "Hercules," which he shortened to "Herc." In 1973, when his sister Cindy needed music for her birthday party, his deejaying career was hastily launched. Hooking up two clunky turntables in the recreation room of their Sedgewick Avenue housing project, Herc played some reggae, but found the crowd's taste more suited to funk.

The only thing better than dancing to James Brown's "Give It Up or Turn It Loose" was letting loose on the "break" parts, when just the instruments jammed. The break was a sonic orgasm, the climactic part of a song, but the only problem was that it was too short. Herc remedied the situation: Using identical copies of a record, each on a different turntable, he cut back and forth between the desired break, actually creating his own extended version—a continuous beat that he called the break beat. It was pure adrenaline, and the people loved it. Soon, Herc was buying records just for their instrumental breaks.

DJ Red Alert, who never missed a Herc party, says, "Kool Herc was the type of person that he was not really a mixologist, but he was a person who learned to gather together a certain type of record, from all different bases—rock 'n' roll, blues, jazz, whatever it is, folk—and just use one little certain part of a record, and just keep repeating it over and over and over. Even some of the disco records that used to go downtown, he used to play uptown, but then again, he used it in a different form."

"Apache," a song originally written by Cliff Richard and the Shadows in 1960, and covered by a Jamaican disco group, the Incredible Bongo Band, was one mega-hit that Herc "broke," or popularized, in 1974. Red Alert calls this tune "the national anthem for all B-Boys," a term originally applied to break boys, who developed their own form of stylized dancing during the break beats (today the term is used loosely to describe devotees of hip-hop culture). Other "jams" that Herc spun included "Listen to Me" by Baby Huey, "Get Ready" by Rare Earth, and "Do What You Gotta Do" by Collage. As the originator of break-beat music, Herc came to prominence in the West Bronx between 1974 and 1975. To stymie potential competition, he jealously guarded the names of his records, often soaking them in water to remove the labels.

One person he couldn't fool, however, was an Adlai E. Stevenson High School student known as Afrika Bambaataa. Since 1969, Bambaataa, a resident of the Bronx River projects, a massive complex sandwiched between 174th Street and the Cross Bronx Expressway, had been a member of the notorious Black Spades street gang. But instead of hanging out or getting involved in crime or turf wars, he had a passion for buying records. Partly inspired by his mother, his eclectic tastes ran the gamut from the rock of the Rolling Stones, The Who, and Led Zeppelin to such r&b/soul as James Brown and Sly Stone, to the African sounds of Miriam Makeba, Manu Dibango, and Fela Kuti, to Latin, calypso, and classical.

At the time, disco was the sound booming from the systems of popular deejays such as Kool DJ D and Disco King Mario in the Bronx and Pete "DJ" Jones, Flowers, and Maboya in Brooklyn. "When I heard what he [Herc] was playing," says Bam, "I had all those records that he was playing as beats. I liked what he was playing, it sounds funky, and I got all that shit at home, so I'm gonna start playing—you know, once I come out and get my system—I'm gonna start playing that too."

Upon graduating from high school, Bam received a "set" of twin turntables from his mother. Though he had deejayed on other people's sets before, he threw his first real party in November 1976 at the Bronx River Community Center. "Once I got my set, everybody was buggin' out," recalls the man who became known as "Master of Records" for his wealth of rare sounds. Bam might start off with the theme from "The Munsters," taped off his TV, switch into some James Brown, and rock just the beat of the Rolling Stones's "Honky Tonk Woman" for a while, before bringing in the Herman Kelly Band's "Dance to the Drummer's Beat" or something even more obscure. "Hip-hop is all types of forms," he explains. "The music itself is colorless, 'cause you can't say, I don't like r&b, I don't like heavy metal, when half the shit that's out comes from all the different styles of records that's out there. So those who don't have a true knowledge of hip-hop, the true form of it, then they just speak from ignorance. You know, the hell with r&b, the hell with jazz, the hell with this, but hip-hop included all these musics to take a beat, a groove, a bassline."

Like his musical tastes, Bam's ideological influences ranged from the Black Panthers, the Nation of Islam, and Malcolm X to the NAACP and Martin Luther King, Jr. He also identified strongly with James Brown's "Say It Loud, I'm Black and I'm Proud," Sly and the Family Stone, John Lennon, and, like a true product of the sixties, Woodstock. As a teen he also saw a film called *Zulu*, starring Michael Caine, which affected him significantly. A depiction of the legendary battle between British troops and the Zulu tribe in southern Africa in 1879, it shows the British emerging seemingly victorious before they are suddenly outnumbered by a whole mountainside of Zulu warriors, who spare them. The name Afrika

Bambaataa, meaning "affectionate leader," comes from the nineteenth-century Zulu leader who guided his people to victory. Following this example, Bam set about building his own Zulu nation—organized like a gang but unified through music.

His prototype was the Organization, which started out as the Bronx River Organization but grew to encompass adjacent areas such as Castle Hill, Soundview, and the Patterson and Forest projects. "But when I seen that hip-hop started rising with myself and Kool Herc," he explains, "I decided to switch the Organization, after a two-year run, into the Zulu Nation. Then, once the Zulu Nation came out, it was basically just a break-dance crew—the Zulu Kings and Queens and later the Shaka Kings and Shaka Queens. And then as it progressed, years after, it became more than that." Coinciding with the demise of street gangs in the mid seventies, the Zulu Nation harnessed the energy of the emerging hip-hop scene, to include rappers, break-dancers, and graffiti artists. While less structured crews carried on the legacy of the gangs, competition in the various street art forms superseded the violence that had once ruled.

Dueling deejays would usually set up opposite each other at a park, high school, or community center. Sometimes they took turns, seeing who

AFRIKA BAMBAATAA WITH KISS-FM'S PRINCE MESSIAH.

could attract the biggest crowd. Often, the battle was a free-for-all in which the deejay with the loudest system blasted out his opponent with sheer wattage. Jazzy Jay, an early Zulu Nation deejay, recalls the time that Bam and Herc locked horns at the Bronx's Webster Avenue PAL (Police Athletic League) in 1977:

> So we came off our turn, Kool Herc was setting up, so we went over our time, right. Kool Herc still wasn't set up 'cause, yunno, he don't sweat hooking shit up. So Kool Herc setting up, his time's supposed to be now. We still playing, so, fuck it, we just gonna play. So Kool Herc got set up, he said, "Ah, Bambaataa, could you please turn your system down." So Bam's getting all gassed by all the Zulus—"Yo, fuck that nigga, Bam! We got his ass! Throw on them funky beats!" So Bam passed me some shit, I slice that shit up. Herc said [louder, in a more booming voice], "Yo, Bambaataa-baataa-baataa, turn your system down-down-down." Fuck you! Niggas getting on the mike cursing. Now Kool Herc, he said [even louder], "Bambaataa-baataa-baataa, TURN YOUR SYSTEM DOWN!" Couldn't even hear our shit. Whoa! We started reaching for knobs, turning shit up, speakers started coughing and shit. And he came on with "The Mexican." You ever hear "The Mexican" by Babe Ruth? It starts out real low—ba doom, da-doom-doom, da-doom-doom, ba doom, da-doom-doom, da-doom-doom. By about sixteen bars into the song, we just gave up, turned off all the fucking amps. Turned everything off. And the drums didn't even come in yet. When the drums came in, all the walls, just like VROOM, that was it. Everybody was looking at us like, yo, we should have listened to Kool Herc.

Anyone who has ever experienced Herc in session makes reference to his crushing decibel level. Jay adds, "Nobody ain't never thought of playing no records like he was playing before that. And all of them shits was sitting in your house—all your mom's old and pop's old records. Soon as Kool Herc started playing, every motherfucker started robbing his mother and father for records."

It just so happened that Joseph Saddler's father was a huge record collector. Another Bronxite of Jamaican descent, Saddler, a.k.a. Grandmaster Flash, played a seminal role in the development of break-beat music. As an electronics major at Samuel Gompers Vocational High School in the Bronx, Flash perfected the art of mixing and punch phasing, in which a certain musical phrase or vocal snippet from one record could be quickly "punched" in over the other record as it played. Both techniques simply required headphones and a mixer with a monitor switch that allowed a record to be precued to a precise spot.

Disco deejays like Brooklyn's Pete "DJ" Jones, who had graduated to Manhattan clubs by then, were already familiar with blending records with a cross fader, which allowed them to segue from one record to the other in a seamless flow. After observing Jones and practicing on his set, Flash went out and got a SPDT (single-pole, double-throw) switch and installed it on his mixer, allowing him to hear what was playing on each turntable through a pair of headphones. Herc didn't use headphones until much later, but cued by eyesight, which sometimes resulted in sloppy mixing. Though Flash couldn't compete with the sheer power of Herc's massive system, he was determined to beat him with his technique on the "wheels of steel."

In order to develop a following,

JAZZY JAY HANGS AT HIS UPTOWN STUDIO IN THE BRONX.

Flash started spinning in abandoned buildings in the South Bronx. Around 1976, he moved to various outdoor locations—the block-square parks that sat among housing projects and abandoned dwellings throughout the lower Bronx—where people would flock from all over the area to hear him and his partner, "Mean Gene" Livingston. Gene's brother Theodore, who was only thirteen when he used to practice with Flash, is credited with the innovation called "scratching," whereby the record is manually spun back and forth while the needle rests in the groove. The potentially irritating noise created (which, incidentally, resembles the sound of an African instrument called the *sekere*) was used as an instrument of percussion, punctuating the sounds on the other turntable. The technique was, of course, soon imitated and perfected by the ever-increasing number of deejays on the scene. Flash, meanwhile, surpassed Herc's popularity, packing small Bronx clubs like the Back Door and numerous high schools, before rocking a crowd of three thousand at Harlem's Audubon Ballroom on September 2, 1977. The era of the deejay peaked around 1978, and gradually the spotlight shifted to those controlling the microphone—the MCs.

When Herc originally started spinning break beats, he would drop phrases like "rock the house" or call out the names of certain people who were at the party, just like the microphone personalities who deejayed back in Jamaica. "At the time, it was just mixing," says Bam, "and if you didn't feel like mixing, you just say 'Get down, down, down, down . . .' and the echo would override everything, and by the time, you know, another beat or groove was going and people was just 'Oww!' " As mixing demanded more of his attention, however, Herc put his friend Coke La Rock on the mike to coax the dancers on and give the party more of a live feel. In the parks, especially, vocal entertainment was often necessary for crowd control to soothe any tensions that might lead to violence. Taking their cue from popular disco deejays of the day such as Eddie Cheeba, DJ Hollywood, and

Frankie Crocker, who carried on the rhyming jive used by black radio jocks of the 1950s, MCs (mike controllers or masters of ceremonies) dropped only the hippest, most up-to-date slang to keep the party bubbling.

Once again, as with most facets of the early hip-hop scene, any hint of creativity or innovation was pushed further by someone else. Following simple phrases like "Yes, yes, y'all, and ya don't stop!" or "Throw your hands in the air and wave 'em like you just don't care"—standards that are used even to this day—Flash progressed to: "You dip, dive, and socialize / We're trying to make you realize / That we are qualified, to rectify / That burning desire to boogie." He rapped it himself before drafting a couple of friends to do it for him. Though hesitant at first, Keith Wiggins (a.k.a. Cowboy) and the Glover brothers, Melvin (Melle Mel) and Nathaniel (Kid Creole), soon began writing their own lines and rhyming on the mike. The Three MCs, as they were called, formed the core of the fabulous Furious Five.

GRANDMASTER FLASH AND THE FURIOUS FIVE (*l to r:* Kid Creole, Melle Mel, Flash, Cowboy, Rahiem, Scorpio).

Grandmaster Flash and the Furious Five set the trends in the Bronx, inspiring numerous others to put the pen to paper in an effort to get a name and outdo the next man. Rhyme battles became the norm, and Grand Wizard Theodore (Livingston) and the Fantastic Five, DJ Breakout and the Funky Four, and the Treacherous Three were among the crews fighting for microphone supremacy. Bam, meanwhile, also maintained several groups, including SoulSonic Force, Cosmic Force, and the Jazzy Five—among the first groups to tour regularly around New York, New Jersey, and Connecticut. Before the thought of putting out records had even entered the game, bootleg tapes of live performances circulated from the Bronx to other boroughs and beyond. Jazzy Jay recalls, "I mean, we had tapes that went platinum before we was even involved with the music industry." Blasting from gargantuan boom boxes, these sounds soon caused the uninitiated to take notice.

Rap's sudden explosion from the underground occurred quite accidentally, when Sylvia Robinson, a former singer and co-owner of the Englewood, New Jersey–based Sugar Hill Records, heard one of these bootleg tapes and decided to make a rap record. A club bouncer named Hank was rapping along to a performance by Bronx rapper Grandmaster Caz while working at a pizza parlor near Robinson's home. Immediately intrigued with what she heard, she approached Hank about being the third member of an outfit she was putting together called the Sugar Hill Gang.

Reflecting on that incident, an intent-looking Grandmaster Caz says, "Now instead of saying, 'Nah, that ain't me, I don't rap, but I work with these dudes who rap, this is them, I can bring 'em,' he didn't do that. He [Hank] said, 'Yeah, I'm down,' and then came to me like, 'Yo, they want to make a record.' So wha's up? He said, 'Well, they only need one more person, they got two and they want me.' And I said, 'Yeah, well, go ahead, man. What choo need?' Threw my [rhyme] book on the table, yunno, 'cause I figure if you get put on, you put us on. As you see, it didn't work out that way."

Released in July 1979, "Rapper's Delight" by the Sugar Hill Gang (Big Bank Hank, Wonder Mike, and Master Gee) sold over two million copies worldwide, largely as a novelty hit that recycled the disco-flavored backing track of Chic's "Good Times." Lyrics like "With a hip, hop, the hipit, the hipidipit, hip, hip, hopit, you don't stop" also helped popularize the term "hip-hop," which was supposedly coined by Bronx rapper Starski the Lovebug. Caz, who received neither credit nor compensation, describes the record as a "watered-down" version of Bronx rap because of its disco flavor.

"It's like if Greg Louganis is gonna dive, right, and then Greg Louganis's cousin gonna come dive right after him," he says, chuckling. "You know what I'm saying, it's like he might have dove, too, but that ain't diving. So it was like that kind of thing, and it didn't represent what MCing was, what rap and hip-hop was. It didn't represent what it truly was, but mainstream and nationally, it was everyone's first taste of what hip-hop was."

Though "Rapper's Delight" was technically not the first rap recorded—it was preceded by "King Tim III (Personality Jock)" by Brooklyn funk outfit the Fatback Band—many contemporary rappers outside New York, indeed, credit it as being their first exposure to the art form. Overnight, Sugar Hill Records emerged as a rap powerhouse, eventually attracting and releasing the now legendary sounds of Grandmaster Flash and the Furious Five, the Funky Four + One More, Spoonie Gee, and the Treacherous Three (Kool Moe Dee, L.A. Sunshine, and Special K). Following closely behind were labels like Bobby Robinson's Enjoy and

THE COLD CRUSH BROTHERS (*l to r:* **Easy AD, Kay Gee, Charlie Chase, Grandmaster Caz, and JDL**).

Paul Winley Records, which released Afrika Bambaataa's first wax, "Zulu Nation Throwdown, Part 1," in 1980, as well as a break-beat anthology series known as *Super Disco Brakes*.

Grandmaster Caz eventually made good with a highly influential, immensely popular crew known as the Cold Crush Brothers, which included deejays Tony Tone and Charlie Chase, as well as Easy AD, the Almighty Kay Gee, and JDL—all veterans of the early rap scene in the Bronx. With their elaborate routines, synchronized dancing, and flashy costumes, Cold Crush set the standards of showmanship and performance when they came out in 1979. JDL explains, "See, we came from the origin of hip-hop, when it wasn't a money thing. It wasn't a political structure that the record company builds around hip-hop. It wasn't about getting paid and all that. It was about something you loved. It was something we did from the heart. So, therefore, if you doin' something you love, you gonna do it to the best of your ability."

Competition, again, separated the champs from the chumps, and as Caz bluntly states, "It's like I don't care if God, Moses, Abraham, and Jesus come down here to battle us, we bustin' they ass, you understand what I'm saying? So I don't care who show up or who don't show up, whoever shows up is getting smoked, okay?" He recalls one supposedly "friendly" jam at his alma mater, Roosevelt high, that was only billed as a battle to attract more people. Pulling up in Charlie Chase's beat-up station wagon, and wearing street clothes, Cold Crush encountered their opponents, the M&M crew, stepping out of a limo clad in tuxes. "They did routines that was off of our routines, dissin' us in front of the crowd," says Caz. "They had a radio, like a little cassette recorder, and they had a little scenario hooked up, and someone was listening to it and it was a tape of us, and then they took it and threw it on the floor and smashed it, and start doin' they stuff." AD adds, "They left us with like five minutes to perform." Without even changing into stage outfits, Caz says, "We just snatched the mike, threw on Billy Joel, 'Stiletto.' Whenever you hear 'Da-doom-doom, the Cold Crush,' " he chants, "that's it. All we had to do was throw that on and the whole crowd went wild." To be the "flyest" MC or the "dopest" deejay meant being a ghetto celebrity, and hip-hop fever was afflicting more and more as it spread into the eighties.

Harlem World (located at 116 Street and Lenox Avenue in Harlem), the Disco Fever (one subway stop from Yankee Stadium), and T-Connection (located on Gunhill and White Plains roads in the Bronx) were uptown's epicenters of rap during the formative era known as the "Old School." According to Jazzy Jay, "The T-Connection was the home base of all rappers. All of those contests, the battle of the DJs that you see that's held at the [New] Music seminar and all that shit, it started at the T-Connection. All of it, you know what I'm saying? And that's where Tom Silverman got his whole idea from. It was Tom Silverman, out of a whole three to four thousand black kids partying, sweating in this one club, Tom Silverman and his wife would be the only two white people in the whole club. But they had mad juice, you know why? They were Bambaataa's guests."

As a college student, Silverman published a small magazine called *Dance Music Report* that capitalized on the late seventies' disco craze. When he heard about Bam, an introduction was arranged through a mutual acquaintance. Silverman was getting ready to start a record company, and he wanted Bam, a trendsetter on the turntables, to be involved.

Around the same time, an Englishman named Malcolm McLaren, most noted as manager of punk rock icons the Sex Pistols, came to check out the runnings uptown. He invited Bam and the Zulus to open up for the new-wave band Bow Wow Wow at the Ritz (formerly Studio 54). "New-wave people were the first of the white people to accept the music," says Bam. "I guess 'cause both was coming up. It was almost like a family thing. Like punk rock was an opposite, but had a relationship to hip-hop 'cause it was radical. We was against the disco that was happenin', we had the funk back 'cause they wasn't playing James, Sly, or Parliament no more. The new wavers and punk rockers didn't like what was happenin' in rock and tired of disco too and shit."

With their initial exposure at the Ritz, Bam and crew moved into downtown venues such as Negril, the Mudd Club, the Peppermint Lounge, and Danceteria, where they attracted a broad spectrum of people. Finally, their downtown following swelled to such mammoth proportions, facilitating a move to the Roxy, a converted roller rink on West 18th Street. Drawing capacity crowds of three to four thousand, the Roxy proved to be a night-clubbing mecca where regular Joes rubbed shoulders with the likes of Mick Jagger, Rick James, and Madonna. As depicted in the movie *Beat Street* (1984), it also provided an arena for break-dancing showdowns between such well-known crews as Rock Steady and the New York City Breakers. The Zulu deejays—Bam, Jazzy Jay, Grandmixer D. ST., and Afrika Islam (who started the first hip-hop radio show, "Zulu Beats," on WHBI-FM, 105.9, in 1981)—alternated nights at the Roxy, which became their exclusive domain. Whoever was not spinning on a given night was paid $500 not to spin somewhere else.

During May of 1982, Bam, who had been responsible for breaking so many records at the Roxy that were subsequently being programmed on black radio stations like KISS-FM and WBLS, created his own sounds, a twelve-inch called "Planet Rock." Released on Tom Silverman's fledgling Tommy Boy label, the record sold over 620,000 copies in the United States alone before going on to become an international hit. The technologically sophisticated, electro-funk of "Planet Rock" revolutionized dance music, and its popularity took Bam and his group, SoulSonic Force (comprised of himself, Jazzy Jay, Mr. Biggs, Globe, and Pow Wow) around the world. According to Jazzy Jay, who had never been on a plane before, "I think it was, like, '83 when 'Planet Rock' really like exploded and we were all over the place. Yo, I recall it was one month when they logged up all the flights we took, we took 111 flights in like a month and a week."

Prior to that, Bam; Grandmixer D. ST. and the Infinity Rappers; graffiti artists Dondi, Futura 2000, and Fab 5 Freddy; and the Rock Steady Crew all participated in the first-ever hip-hop tour, sponsored by French radio station Europe1. "When I say the word "hip-hop," explains Rock Steady member Richie "Crazy Legs" Colon, "I'm including every element—the graf, the dance, the music, everything, the rapping. And after we came back, we had a big party in the Roxy, and during one of these shows, the people from Paramount Pictures came down, and they saw us there, and after the show finished, they said, We want you in our movie. And, ah, we did the movie, we did *Flashdance*, which was cool."

Besides making Jennifer Beals's cut-off-sweats-hanging-off-the-bare-shoulder look into a fashion statement, the movie turned millions of kids worldwide on to break dancing. Strangely enough, this early element of hip-hop culture had all but died down in the Bronx by about 1979, but was revived through the efforts of true B-Boys like Rock Steady. "See, the whole thing when hip-hop first started," says Crazy Legs, now 26, "was the music was played in the parks and in the jams for the dancers, and those dancers were B-Boys. And when those break [beats] would come on, it would be like, 'B-Boys, are you ready?' And a B-Boy very specifically was a break boy, not a break-dancer; that's media terminology. So B-Boys were the guys that walked around with their bell-bottom Lees rolled up to the side, and the graffiti piece on the other side, with the 69er Pro Keds, and, yunno, you were a B-Boy."

Legs' first exposure to breaking came through his brother Robert and then, later, his cousin Lenny Nuñez, who brought him to an outdoor jam on Crotona Avenue in the Bronx when he was only ten. Here he experienced the full range of hip-hop culture—MCs on the mike, people "B-Boying," and graffiti artists comparing their black books (portfolios) and "tagging up" on any flat surface. "You know, it was a form of recreation," he says. "A lot of these people didn't really have the money to join any of these community centers around the way as far as like baseball, softball, boxing, things like that."

Break dancing actually began during the gang era, and as the music worked its spell, it provided an alternative means to stomp an adversary with one's own style, finesse, and personality (though breaking battles also sometimes ended in fights). But like rap and graffiti, breaking was primarily a means of expression. In one of the first articles on it, appearing in the *Village Voice* in 1981, Sally Banes wrote, "Breaking is a public arena for the flamboyant triumph of virility, wit, and skill. In short, of style. Breaking is a way of using your body to inscribe your identity on streets and trains, in parks and high school gyms. It is the physical version of two favorite forms of street rhetoric, the taunt and the boast."[1]

While the art form was already highly rhythmic, Rock Steady introduced an acrobatic element with gymnastic moves like the continuous backspin. Formed in 1977, the crew's original membership included the top dancers from other crews (ghetto celebrities like Jimmy D., Jimmy Lee, Jo-Jo, Mongo Rock, and Spy). Legs had to battle Rock Steady leader Jimmy D. to secure a spot. During the early eighties, they used to skip school and practice for hours in the park at West Ninety-eighth Street and Amsterdam Avenue, which they renamed "Rock Steady Park." Lacking any formal training in dance, Legs says, "The only place I'd say we learned moves from, which was universal for a lot of dancers, was karate flicks on Forty-second Street, 'cause those movies are filmed the best, you could see the movement of the whole body." Though a fad to the mainstream, to committed artists like Crazy Legs and Rock Steady, break dancing, which they brought out again at a performance at Lincoln Center in the summer of 1992, remains a vital part of hip-hop culture.

Graffiti, or aerosol art, also experienced an explosion of hype and critical recognition in the early eighties, when it moved from the subway trains and ghetto walls to the trendy galleries of SoHo. Two films of this period—Henry Chalfant and Tony Silver's documentary *Style Wars* (1983) and Charlie Ahearn's low-budget feature *Wild Style* (1982)—faithfully document this thriving renegade art scene. In the latter film, graf writer Lee Quinones, playing himself, defined the artists' credo: "You gotta paint and be called an outlaw at the same time," referring to the late-night tactics of breaking into train yards to do a "burn" or a "piece," which the rest of society considered vandalism. Graffiti was movable art, transmitted citywide by the communications network of the subway, and a means to garner some fame and respect among other writers. Though the works of such famed writers as Crash, Daze, Dondi, Lee, and Zephyr grace the transit system no more (the last train was buffed in May 1989), graffiti shows up in galleries, on clothing, and, of course, on the street.

Besides "Planet Rock," the other big song to come out of the Bronx in 1982 (before Queens rappers Run-D.M.C. stole the show in 1983) was "The Message" by Grandmaster Flash and the Furious Five. The first rap to break away from boasting and deal with reality, it described the hopelessness of the urban condition:

> Broken glass everywhere
> People pissing on the stairs
> You know they just don't care
> I can't take the smell, can't take the noise
> Got no money to move out, I guess I got no choice
> Rats in the front room, roaches in the back
> Junkies in the alley with a baseball bat
> I tried to get away but I couldn't get far
> 'Cause the man with the tow truck repossessed my car
>
> Don't push me 'cause I'm close to the edge
> I'm trying not to lose my head
> Ah huh huh huh huh
> It's like a jungle sometimes, it makes me wonder
> How I keep from going under

The person in the song, however, seems lucky when compared to Lawrence Krisna Parker, who at 17 lived out on the streets, sleeping on trains and eating out of garbage cans. Spirituality in the form of metaphysics provided his only salvation. "It's a philosophy that says that nothing you see is real," explains a hulking Parker, better known to rap fans as Kris or Blastmaster KRS-ONE (an acronym for Knowledge Rules Supreme Over Nearly Everyone). "It's here only because you create it. You bring the bad into your life, you bring the good into your life, you create your environment by the way you think." Kris left his Bronx home at 14, he says, to prove this philosophy to himself.

"And I really believed the fact that, yunno, if you keep telling yourself you

want to be this or you're going to be that, then you'll do it. And that was pretty much what I was about," he continues. "Every day I'd wake up, and I wouldn't say I'm the greatest rap artist in the world, I would say that I am rap music period. I am rap. I'm not a rap artist, I am rap. Everybody's trying to do what I am." At the moment, however, survival mattered the most, and Kris worked odd jobs, stole, and even tried selling marijuana—pounds of it, to be exact—for which he was busted and incarcerated for six months.

His life changed, however, when at 20 he decided to check himself into the Franklin Armory Men's Shelter in the Morrisania section of the Bronx. "I'm all into myself spiritually, but physically it was terrible. It was like my clothes was fucked up. I couldn't take a shower every day, wasn't eating properly," he says. "So I said, Let me go in the shelter and mingle with people." Soon he was leading a small gang called the ICU Rebels—Intelligent Criminals United—and ruling the shelter with an iron hand. "The system's nothing like you see on TV, of course," he explains. "There's mad prostitution going on, drug rings, all that type of shit. Sleep with one eye open unless you had juice."

Kris's juice came from the rhyme wars he had with other rappers in the shelter. "We used to battle by beating on the bathroom walls. So I used to always do 'The Bridge Is Over' beat and 'Criminal Minded' beat, those were the beats I had in my head. Nobody ever heard that in their life," he recalls. "And the kids in the shelter were like, yo, that shit is dope. So I would rhyme, beat on the wall at the same time kicking rhymes, and I would break my shit down, do all kinds of things and take these other MCs out."

One of the shelter security guards told Kris that he should look up his cousin, a kid by the name of Ced Gee (Cedric Miller), who lived in the neighboring Claremont projects. The SP-12 drum machine/sampler had just come out in 1985, and Ced was probably the only kid in all the Bronx to own one. Through booming laughter, Kris says, "He was the mack. He was the muthafuckin' man, you don't even know. He was the man in the Bronx 'cause he had an SP-12." Kris hooked up with Ced, and shortly afterward they did a song called "Advance," with Kris rapping: " 'Every generation after every generation / The American nation still hit with starvation / The exploitation, the new sensation . . .' I was just freakin' it." At a time when boasting was the norm, Kris's conscious rhymes set him apart from the crowd.

Meanwhile, back at the shelter, he butted heads with a new social worker and recent college grad named Scott Sterling, four years his senior. "He was saying that all you homeless shelter muthafuckas is bums anyway," recalls Kris. "You'll use tokens to smoke it up, drink it up, shoot it up. I was like, 'Fuck you, you house nigga, sitting behind the desk, wannabe.' So we arguing back and forth, finally he realized that I was kicking lyrics. Actually, I told him, 'You probably never been to a club in your life.' He said, 'See, you don't even know me, I deejay at Broadway RT. I see all you rappers and you come a dime a dozen.' So we calmed down after a while, it was like, you kick rhymes? Word? What, you a deejay? Word? So we was like, oh shit."

When Kris accompanied Scott to the club called Broadway RT (later known as Broadway International), on Broadway and 146th Street, he was shocked to find everyone pushing demos on DJ "Scott La Rock" to play them at the club. Realizing Scott's clout, he took him up on his offer to do some stuff together seriously. It turned out that Scott already knew Ced, so the two of them worked together programming beats and sampling funky slices of James Brown with the SP-12. Kris provided concepts, which he developed into lyrics, as well as contributing his bathroom-wall beats. When they were ready to record, Scott put up his own money for time at PowerPlay Studios in Queens, and they emerged with an album they called *Criminal Minded*. The whole process took roughly one month.

Boogie Down Productions (BDP), a group that proudly proclaimed their Bronx heritage, was in effect.

Shopping for a record deal at Sleeping Bag Records, for whom Kris and Scott had already done a single called "Success Is the Word" under the name 1241, they were turned down. Will Socolov and Juggy Gales, who ran the label, weren't interested, saying, "It sounds like nothing we've ever heard before," which was certainly true. Next, they approached Mr. Magic, a deejay at WBLS. "He dissed us stupidly," says Kris. "He said, 'Yo, you muthafuckas is bums, the Juice Crew is the shit,' this, that, and the other. So we were like hurting. Shit was like, damn, Mr. Magic just dissed us. Yo, fuck that, though, we tha shit, he's a muthafuckin' fraud. So I went back and wrote 'South Bronx.' "

Just as "Apache" epitomized the old school era of break-beat music, "South Bronx" became the anthem that paid tribute to the borough that started it all. With its James Brown hook, it also ushered in a new era of hip-hop sampling. The song answered Queens rapper MC Shan's hit "The Bridge," which told the story of a crew of rappers called the Juice Crew, who were produced by Marlon "Marley Marl" Williams, Mr. Magic's sidekick. "South Bronx," which challenged, "So you think that hip-hop got its start out in Queensbridge? / If you pop that shit up in the Bronx you might not live," came out on an unknown independent called B-Boy Records.

"B-Boy was a pornography ring," says Kris, "and what they used to do was put ads in the papers, saying, 'You want to be a star? Come down, girls over 18.' So girls used to come down and get fucked, literally. So we answered an ad in the paper to Rock Candy Records and Filmworks," which was located at 132nd Street and Cypress Avenue in the Bronx. "We got up there and met Bill Kamaro and Jack Allen," Kris continues. "These muthafuckas was cold gangstas. It was like, yo, we took one look at the scene and knew they was fucking up. So I hit 'em from the hip. I was like, 'Yo, man, we know y'all need a place to get legit, and we'll just do our music and funnel moneys and shit, and make you legitimate by having a record company—all this fucking money you have floating around, yunno'—'cause they was into everything."

By 1986, Kris was already building a reputation for himself at uptown spots like Devil's Nest, as well as at downtown's Danceteria, which had open mike Thursdays, and Union Square's Underground. Scott's connections with DJ Red Alert brought BDP into the radio war between Mr. Magic's show on BLS and Red Alert and Chuck Chill-Out's show on KISS-FM. "South Bronx" blew up all over the country with minimal promotion. Shipping out COD orders through UPS, they took in up to $20,000 a week. Due to the questionable business practices of their partners, however, Scott and Kris were hardly seeing any of the money. Kris says, "I used to hear my shit on the radio every day; I was like mopping floors and sleeping on the train. I did Union Square, ripped it down to the floor, and then got on the train, down the D train and went to sleep. They never paid us nothing, but we'd see the money coming in, and we'd have to put it in the B-Boy Records account. It was wild, yunno, it was a learning experience."

Meanwhile, Marley Marl and the Juice Crew answered "South Bronx" with "(South Bronx) Kill That Noise." Kris went to Marley, saying, "Don't do this, man, don't do it, just let 'South Bronx' go out, don't fuck with us, man, you don't want it," but he didn't listen. "So we pulled out the gat—went *prrrrrrrrrrrrrr!*—his shit was over. That shit was dead. Nobody wanted to hear from them, nobody wanted to see them," says Kris, describing the musical slaughter. BDP came back with probably one of the most ferocious diss records of all time, "The Bridge Is Over," unique at the time for its fusion of reggae and hip-hop. Once again, the Boogie Down Bronx was running things.

Boogie Down Productions suffered a serious setback in August of 1987, when Scott La Rock was gunned down outside the Highbridge Garden Homes on University Avenue in the Bronx in a senseless street dispute that did not even involve him. For his attempts to squash a "beef" (dispute), between 16-year-old D-Nice and another youth, who had accused D-Nice of dating his girlfriend, Scott took bullets to the head and neck. Kris, however, refused to quit invoking the name and spirit of his partner all throughout the groundbreaking *By All Means Necessary*, released by Jive Records in 1988. This album featured the single "Stop the

Violence," written by himself and Scott; the title was subsequently used by a coalition of rappers against violence (the Stop the Violence Movement, spearheaded by Kris, released the very successful "Self-Destruction" in 1989). Kris also wrecked all previous rap stereotypes with "My Philosophy," in which he says:

> Some MCs be talkin' and talkin'
> Tryin' to show how black people are walkin'
> But I don't talk this way to portray
> Or reinforce stereotypes of the day
> Like all my brothers eat chicken and watermelon
> Talk broken English and drug selling
> See I'm intelligent and teach you pure facts
> The way some act in rap is kinda whack
> And it lacks creativity and intelligence
> But they don't care 'cause their company's selling it . . .

This record became an instant classic, propelling Kris, the Horatio Alger of the Bronx, on to a prolific career.

Many classic rap albums, in fact, surfaced between 1987 and 1988. Rap from Long Island hit hard with Public Enemy's *It Takes a Nation of Millions to Hold Us Back*, Eric B. & Rakim's *Paid in Full*, and EPMD's *Strictly Business*. On the West Coast, N.W.A. sprayed shots of harsh reality with *Straight Outta Compton*. While all these records went on to sell hundreds of thousands of copies and establish some of the heavyweights of rap, in hindsight there was at least one glaring oversight: Ultramagnetic MC's *Critical Beatdown*.

Released in 1988 on Uptown/Next Plateau, a label known for the more r&b sounds of Al B. Sure!, Guy, and Bell Biv Devoe, *Critical Beatdown* combined the hardcore attitude of the old school with abstract rhymes and busy, distinctive grooves that seemed to be beamed down from outer space. The group's first demos, in fact, included such titles as "Space Groove" and "Something Else." All four members—Kool Keith, TR Love, Moe Love, and Ced Gee—grew up in the Bronx and were exposed to the hip-hop scene as it was beginning. "When rap came out," says TR Love (Trevor Randolph), "every group sort of had their own technique and style. Furious Five had their style, Funky Four had their style, Treacherous Three had their style. Everyone was innovative." Such was the credo they followed when putting together *Critical Beatdown*, an album that Bomb Squad member Eric "Vietnam" Sadler credits as being very influential during the production of Public Enemy's *It Takes a Nation of Millions to Hold Us Back*.

Despite their respect in the underground—cultivated through a slew of singles that came out prior to the album—Ultramagnetic MCs never received the serious recognition they deserved. Their dilemma mirrors the problems facing much promising talent that, for some reason or other, gets left behind. They consider themselves lucky, however, "because we're sort of like an Energizer battery—we keep going and going and going," says Ced Gee. Ultramagnetic's second album, *Funk Your Head Up* (Mercury), was released four years after their seminal debut, and they attribute the long time-lag to problems on the business side. "A lot of Bronx groups had a chance, but bad business was their own fault," says Kool Keith (Keith Thornton), explaining the demise of the Bronx rap scene in the late eighties. Ced adds, "But the Bronx ain't dead, there's still thousands of kids out there."

ULTRAMAGNETIC MCS (*l to r:* Ced Gee, Kool Keith, TR Love, Moe Love).

ANDRE THE GIANT
(*2nd from left*)
OF SHOWBIZ &
A.G. CHILLS WITH
THE "GOOD
FELLAZ" FROM
PATTERSON PROJECTS.

The low-rise red-brick buildings of the Patterson projects probably look the same today as they did during the heyday of the Boogie Down Bronx, when hip-hop oozed from the streets like hot tar on an August afternoon. Immortalized in BDP's "South Bronx," these projects and neighboring Eighteenth Park played host to some of the early jams, to which neighborhood kids flocked to see the names who are now legends. "Grand Wizard Theodore, Flash, and all them, Cold Crush, all those used to come here," says Andre the Giant, 21. These are the streets where he and his partner, Showbiz, were indoctrinated into hip-hop.

Showbiz, 22, started deejaying after witnessing Flash perform in the middle of the basketball courts here. "He was the man, yunno," says Showbiz. "He wasn't in the public eye, like parents and stuff know him, but everybody who was out on the street. Just like the main drug dealer, everybody know this guy. They know he the man. That's how Flash was."

With a highly successful EP (*Can I Get a Soul Clap*) and debut album (*Runaway Slaves*) behind them, Showbiz and A.G. represent the next generation of Bronx rappers. Influenced directly by the pioneers of the art form, they take the legacy they have inherited very seriously. As A.G. explains, "The Bronx is where everything started, so, yunno, a lot of Bronx rap has something to prove and, yunno, show 'em that this is where it started. We representin' where we come from." They are not alone, either, but part of a burgeoning Bronx scene that includes such respected artists as Lord Finesse, Black Sheep, Diamond, Fat Joe Da Gangsta, Strickly Roots, and a host of unsigned underground talent.

Showbiz and A.G. met while working on Lord Finesse's debut, *Funky Technician* (Wild Pitch) in 1990. Like any self-respecting Bronx rapper, Finesse can freestyle his head off. "I'm in command y'all, won't fall, I stand tall / Smack niggas up like Puerto Ricans playin' handball / 'Cause I'm scoring mine, never kickin' boring

FAT JOE DA GANGSTA GETS AMBUSHED FROM BEHIND.

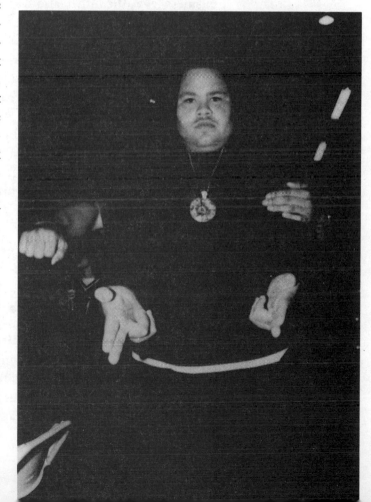

rhymes / I'm living larger than my dick in the morning time. That shit comes natural," he says in between bites of fried chicken. Freestyle evokes the same braggadocio and one-upmanship on the mike that has existed in the Bronx since day one. On *Funky Technician*, A.G. cuts his teeth on "Back to Back Rhyming," which was produced by Showbiz, and "Keep It Flowing," produced by Diamond.

After that project, Showbiz & A.G. recorded a five-song demo, which they pressed themselves, selling about 5,000 copies from the trunk of Show's car and in mom and pop record shops. The buzz they created on the streets eventually led to a recording deal with Payday Records. On a business level, then, they also owe a lot to their predecessors. "See, that's how Flash come in again," explains Showbiz, who learned "by watching him rise and watching him drive a BMW, and then he don't have it after a while. I know these guys sold massive records, but where's their money at? Yunno, so I'm like, there's something goin' on. Then I started hanging around people like Greg Nice from Nice & Smooth. On the business level, he taught me a lot."

The Bronx, it turns out, is a really small world. Fat Joe Da Gangsta, who recorded his debut for Relativity Records, also got his first break through Greg Nice, who used to let him freestyle at shows with Nice & Smooth. Joe also grew up in the Forest projects with Diamond and Showbiz, who produced his album. "I was there when niggas used to die in the parks all the time just to go hear music," says Joe. "Robberies and all that, that was part of the game and shit, but it was dope, you know, and I loved it."

Joe, Diamond, and Showbiz & A.G. all recorded their albums out of Jazzy Jay's studio, a small but cozy 24-track studio located in a second-story walk-up next to the law offices of Jacoby & Meyers in the northern Bronx. "I do this for the brothers, you know what I'm saying?" says Jay, who charges only $40 per hour. "We ain't set up with the high prices like downtown, so the brothers can come in here, and get stuff accomplished, with the degree of professionality that they want without having to spend a whole bunch of loot.

"A lot of studios have came up and folded in the time I've been operating," he continues. "A lot of big studios, too. We're still here, and you know why? It's 'cause we believe in this. And it ain't all about the money. If I ever got any problems, shit ain't goin' right, I can call my people, and they'll come and bail me out. You know why? 'Cause I do my business that way. I take care of my people, and in turn, it takes care of me, you know what I'm saying? You look at my groups, all my groups is jumping the fuck off right now. Show and A.G.; Diamond's jumping off, Finesse is doing his thing, Puba's doing his thing, Nubians is doing they thing, my boy Skeff [Anselm] is doing his thing. And it's like when I see that, all of the work that I put into this is never gonna go to vain, 'cause as long as there's brothers doing their own thing, it's like me doing my own thing, you know what I'm saying?"

Back on the Red Alert show, Diamond's "Best Kept Secret" plays in the background as Herc waxes poetic:

. . .Tougher than tough, no bluff, 'cause maybe I got the musical stuff. That's some of the rhymes from brothers in Jamaica like U. Roy and Big Youth, you know what I'm sayin'? And I am a big youth, 'cause I'm still the oldest living B-Boy. . . . Everybody out there, man, stop killing one another, man, it's just us, you know what I'm saying? We got something that came through me, you know what I'm saying? It's black gold, ghetto steam, that's what hip-hop is, man. Like Miriam Makeba said, "All I do is play my patty, patty sound," yunno? All I want to do is have fun. We can use it, man, to get what we want, man. Anything you want, man, you can use it to the music, you can get it. . . .

recommended
listening

1. Sugar Hill Gang, "Rapper's Delight" (Sugar Hill Records, 1979).
2. Various, *The Great Rap Hits* (Sugar Hill Records, 1980).
3. Grandmaster Flash and the Furious Five, "The Message" (Sugar Hill Records, 1981).
4. Afrika Bambaataa and the SoulSonic Force, "Planet Rock" (Tommy Boy, 1982).
5. Boogie Down Productions, *Criminal Minded* (B-Boy, 1987).
6. Ultramagnetic MCs, *Critical Beatdown* (Next Plateau, 1988).
7. Tim Dog, *Penicillin on Wax* (Ruffhouse/Columbia, 1991).
8. Lord Finesse, *Return of the Funky Man* (Giant, 1992).
9. Showbiz & A.G., *Runaway Slaves* (Payday/London, 1992).
10. Fat Joe Da Gangsta, *Represent* (Relativity, 1993).
11. Strickly Roots, *Begs No Friends* (Friends Connection, 1992).

ChApTeR 2

Rap's Raggamuffin Roots

Though earthquakes are unheard of in Manhattan, the sonic boom produced by powerful car stereos sends tremors through the concrete that are felt for blocks. Shaking the asphalt like thunder from below, the ubiquitous jeeps—or mobile discos—hurl shock waves of bass and beats, rap's signature sound, into the urban soundscape. Rap, however, is not the only music reliant on this primal thud. The last few years have seen the emergence of another sound that has infiltrated the pop charts and had a measurable effect on rap: Dancehall reggae, the long-unheralded pop music of Jamaica, has swept northward with the ferocity of a tropical storm, pumping from the jeeps and moving crowds at dance clubs from Los Angeles to Paris, Toronto to Miami—not to mention Brooklyn and the Bronx. Like rap, dancehall is raw, bass-heavy, lyrically loaded, frenetic, and above all, extremely danceable. With rap's mainstream success, dancehall is finally getting exposure that is long overdue.

While rap is the successor to other forms of black American music that preceded it—primarily funk, jazz, and rhythm and blues—Jamaican reggae also figures prominently in its development. This cross-cultural connection is not difficult to appreciate considering the elements that rap and reggae have in common. Both emerged from an environment of oppression and reflect the culture, attitude, and sensibilities of the ghetto. They are both rhythmic forms of music, favoring the bass while disregarding such formal elements as chord structure and tonality. Both also represent an extension of the African oral tradition of the *griot*, or storyteller, who recited the history of his tribal community—sometimes to the accompaniment of talking drums. The Jamaican tradition of "toasting" (or deejaying), which involves speaking over recorded music, in fact preceded today's rap, and as rap embraces reggae, it also acknowledges its roots.

The fairly recent hybrid of rap and reggae represents the latest stage of an ongoing relationship between these two musical cultures. Now there is almost a free mixing of mediums on any given rap or reggae release. Take, for instance, "The Jam" from Jamaican artist Shabba Ranks's major-label debut, *As Raw as Ever* (Epic Records, 1991). Born Rexton Rawlston Fernando Gordon, Shabba has been toasting since the age of 14. He first made a name for himself with 1987's "Live Blanket," whose success afforded him the chance to leave Jamaica and tour the eastern United States, Canada, and the United Kingdom. Following a string of international hits—including "Get Up, Stand Up and Rock" (Jammys), "Wicked in Bed" (Digital B), and "Roots and Culture" (Digital B)—this deejay (as Jamaican rappers are called) sensation combines his talents with Blastmaster KRS-ONE, of the trendsetting rap outfit Boogie Down Productions, in "The Jam." The song illustrates the natural harmony between rap and reggae, combining a street-tough drumbeat, throbbing dancehall bass, and raps by KRS-ONE tightly interlaced with Shabba's fierce, rhythmic chats. A tremendous breakthrough for a reggae release, the album sold over five hundred thousand units, bringing dancehall to daytime radio and the *Billboard* pop charts, as well as winning a Grammy.

According to Murray Elias, former head of artists and repertory for reggae at Profile Records, the hip-hop label that released Run-D.M.C.'s ground-breaking debut in 1984, "If you go to Jamaica today and you look at like, you know, what the kids are into, they don't want to be Bob Marley," the legendary Jamaican performer who brought international recognition to reggae music. "Most of these kids are now born after Bob Marley died. I'm sure everybody knows who he is, but it's like kids don't want to grow up to be Elvis anymore, they don't want to grow up to be the Beatles, they want to grow up to be something that's happening now. They want to grow up to be Shabba." Within reggae music today, says Elias, "Shabba is the Bob Marley of the nineties."

Though Shabba is not the first Jamaican dancehall artist to be signed to a major label—Lieutenant Stitchie recorded *The Governor* for Atlantic in 1989, and Eek-A-Mouse did *U-Neek* for Island in 1991—he is probably the most successful to cross over to date. The reported advance of $300,000 he received upon signing with the Sony Music conglomerate that owns Epic was unprecedented for a reggae performer. Shabba's success has also opened the door for other popular Jamaican artists, such as Supercat, Tiger, Mad Cobra, Buju Banton, Chakademus & Pliers, and many more.

Though international fame and commercial success have taken him a long way from his humble beginnings in the impoverished Sturgetown in the parish of St. Ann, Jamaica, he acknowledges in one of his hits, "I know me roots and culture." Shabba is only the latest in a long continuum of Jamaican deejays who pioneered an art form that provided the blueprint for today's rapping. Among his early influences, he cites such popular Jamaican deejays as Charlie Chaplin, and his "greatest inspiration," Josey Wales, both of whom deejayed for Kingston's Daddy Roy Sound System, which was run by Jamaica's most famous and best-loved deejay, the legendary U. Roy.

Jamaican Roots

U. Roy hails from a different era of Jamaican music—when up-tempo ska, followed by the slower, groovier rock steady, were the dance beats of the day. Ska, with its characteristic shuffle rhythm and prominent use of horns, was a distinctly Jamaican take on American r&b. Around the mid sixties, it gave way to the more bass-heavy rock steady, which slowed down the sound significantly, paving the way for reggae.

People know U. Roy as "The Originator," not because he was the first to toast, but because he created a distinct style—the modern dancehall style—that had never been heard before. Speaking rhythmically over the music, he used his voice as another instrument. U. Roy was an innovator, and his unique vocal technique inspired many a deejay to follow him.

Born Ewart Beckford, he grew up in the sprawling, corrugated-iron-and-wood shantytowns of Kingston, where he lived with his grandmother. The era of his youth in the sixties was best remembered for the rough "rude boys" (or ghetto youths, now called raggamuffins) who ruled the streets, relying on crime and hustling to survive. Despite the anemic living conditions in this rugged environment, music flowed plentifully from the numerous mobile sound systems that always played.

The early sound systems, or "sounds," were the domain of young entrepreneurs who set up large speakers, a radio, a turntable, and an amplifier and played records in public at every opportunity. Filling a demand for r&b imported from the United States, these sound systems first appeared in Jamaica in the late forties and played in both town and country. They gained prominence, however, after Jamaicans won their independence from Britain in 1962. To a people who loved music, but could sometimes ill afford a radio, the sound systems served a vital role.

"The folk tradition in Jamaica is well documented," says Orlando Patterson, professor of sociology at Harvard University and a Jamaican. "Jamaicans had a rich folk life." This included a musical—especially percussive—tradition, which was a part of the African heritage preserved since slavery.

The sound systems provided a community service for the common people, playing selections not typically found on either of Jamaica's fledgling radio stations—RJR (the British-run, Radio Jamaica Rediffusion) and JBC (the Jamaican Broadcasting Corporation)—both of which catered to the island's elite. The sounds also passed on news and announcements, and during the bitter electoral battles of the seventies between the Jamaican Labour Party and the People's National Party, they became politicized, endorsing candidates.

Playing a "blues dance" became the sound system's forte. Dances occurred nightly at a prearranged outdoor spot, which was surrounded by the sound's massive homemade speakers. Solid enough to accommodate the bone-crushing sound of the bass, these wooden hulks enveloped the dancers with sound. While the selector cued up the records and played the popular tunes of the day, the deejay, whom everyone came to see, announced selections and coaxed the dancers on from the "control tower," usually an elevated position behind the amplifiers and equipment. Mimicking the style of U.S. radio deejays—personalities such as Douglas "Jocko" Henderson, Vernon "Dr. Daddy-O" Winslow, and Clarence "Poppa Stoppa" Heyman—who could sometimes be picked up from stations like WINZ and WGBS in Miami, he introduced songs employing the latest jive. This crucial live element greatly enhanced the experience of dancing to recorded music.

Young Ewart, using the moniker U. Roy, started his career deejaying for a sound called Dicky's Dynamic in the mid sixties. From there he moved to Sir George Atomic, then Coxsone's Downbeat (owned by famed producer Clement "Sir Coxsone" Dodd), before finally coming to King Tubby's Hometown Hi-Fi, based in the Waterhouse section of Kingston. It was through his association with Tubby (Osbourne Ruddock) that U. Roy enjoyed the most success, propelling him to legendary status as a deejay.

Impressed by U. Roy's live work, Duke Reid, a sound system operator who had also branched out into studio recording at his own Treasure Isle Studios, approached him to record some songs between 1969 and 1970. Reid wanted to make some "specials," or exclusive acetate pressings, for his own sound system using U. Roy's voice-overs. He employed King Tubby as his studio engineer.

It was becoming standard practice in this era of primitive, two-track recording—with the vocals on one track and the rest of the band on the other—to reserve the B-side of a record to test sound levels during recording. This instrumental B-side became known as the version, and in experimenting with it, Tubby stumbled upon something new. By manipulating the tracks in the studio, he discovered the possibility of making new versions of a song in which the vocals phased in and out over an instrumental track that could be dropped out altogether or brought forward. The new technique was called dubbing, a recording term for copying or making doubles of a tape, and appropriately, the purely instrumental version became known as the dub.

As Tubby explained to writer Stephen Davis in *Reggae International*, "I had a little dub machine and I used to borrow tapes from the producers and mix them down in a different fashion. You see I used to work on the cutter for Duke Reid and once a tape was running on the machine and I just drop off the voice y'know it was a test cut. Well we take some of these test cut and carry them home and the Saturday we was playing out and I said alright I going to test them 'cause it sounds so exciting the way the records start with the voice, the voice drop and the rhythm still going."[1]

When Tubby brought these dubs to the dance later on, they were played over and over by popular demand.

The songs dubbed on that fateful night in 1969 included "You Don't Care," a rock steady hit by the Techniques, as well as music by the Melodians and Phyllis Dillon. Tubby's sound system boasted custom echo and reverb facilities, which were unique at the time, and the combination of all the elements had a staggering effect. Tubby, the selector, primed the crowd with some straight vocal cuts, concluding with "You Don't Care." As the song faded, he put on the new "specials"—heavy, acetate "dub plates" made from the master tapes. To the crowd, the song seemed to start again, but this time the opening vocals echoed hauntingly and then phased out altogether as a two-ton bass dropped. U. Roy wandered in and out of the "riddim" (patois for rhythm), adding his own live complement of rhythmic scat, singing, spoken words, demented shrieks, and rhymes.

Cutting each version with echo and reverb, the songs could be dubbed differently each time. The plunge created when the vocals suddenly vanished and the bass and drum rhythm came forward pulled the ground from beneath the feet of the thrilled dancers, who had heard nothing like it before. Dubbing also deleted much of a song's original vocals, creating space for a skillful lyricist to throw his own catchy words and phrases on top of the rhythm at the appropriate moments. This early form of rap became known as "chanting 'pon the mike," toasting, or deejaying. Thus, in the discovery of dub, a studio innovation, Tubby had opened the way for the deejay to really flaunt his lyrical style over recorded music.

U. Roy's first two recordings for Tubby were "This Station Rule the Nation," in which he chanted, "This station rule the nation with version," followed by "Wake the Town and Tell the People." Occupying the one and two positions on both the RJR and JBC charts, they were, literally, the toasts of the town. Five or six weeks later, U. Roy went into the studio again to record "Wear You to the Ball." Upon release, the song immediately topped the charts, pushing "Rule the Nation" to number two and "Wake the Town" to number three. Having the three most popular songs in Jamaica at the same time established U. Roy's reputation.

In the introduction to "Wear You to the Ball," a Paragons classic, the group sings "I'm gonna wear you to the ball tonight, put on your best threads tonight" over a lilting rock steady melody. No sooner is this line delivered than U. Roy cuts in with "Did you hear what the man said, baby. Said be your best 'cause this is a musical test," delivered in a half-spoken, half-sung toast. Then, in time with the "riddim," he speaks in patois that is almost unintelligible to the non-Jamaican ear before returning to a half-sung toast. A snippet of the Paragons returns, "Though those other guys put you down, you'll wear my cro . . . own," adding some variation. As an echo prolongs this last high note, U. Roy slides back into the mix with perfect timing and continues his lyrical flow. He breaks up the toast along the way with high-pitched "Ahhhh's!" and a "Chick-a-bow-wow-wow."

Toasting, a precursor to modern-day rapping, revolves around precise timing and knowing the rhythm well enough to weave in and out of it. It also involves originality and having a distinctive style or toast to share with the audience. When younger deejays come to U. Roy today and ask his advice, he says, "Be sure that you're not running away from the riddim or the riddim's not running away from you and you'll have it."[2]

When U. Roy was coming up he was inspired by a deejay called Count Machouki, who may be considered the true originator of the deejay style. Starting off at Sir Coxsone's Downbeat and eventually joining Prince Buster's sound system, Machouki changed the role of the deejay from someone who just introduced records to a true microphone personality and the main attraction of the blues dance.

Interviewed in *Reggae and African Beat*, U. Roy said of Machouki, "Well, he was a man who I used to love to listen to . . . whenever you been to a dance and been listening to this man it was like, ya know, you never hear anybody like that before. This man phrases his words, in time, he doesn't crowd the music when he's talking or things like that, so you can always hear what the vocalist got to sing and this really was a man who I used to say, I'd like to be like this man."[3]

Machouki was plying his trade for Sir Coxsone's Downbeat around 1957, when r&b from New Orleans was especially popular. Top-ranking performers such as Fats Domino, Amos Millburn, Louis Jordan, and Roy

Brown were among the favorites because, as author and cultural historian Dick Hebdige noted in *Cut 'n' Mix*, "The relaxed, loping style of their music seemed to cater to the West Indian taste for unhurried rhythms. In fact, the r&b produced in the southern states of America tended to be much less frantic than the music coming out of the black ghettoes of the north. The southern stuff almost had a Caribbean tinge."[4]

Among the crowded and competitive field of sound systems at the time—King Edward, Sir Coxsone, Duke Reid, V Rocket, Prince Buster, King Tubby, and Jah Love—Sir Coxsone and Duke Reid were considered to be the best. Music evolved into such a serious business for them that they frequently traveled to the United States to keep their sounds supplied with the latest American hits. These records became the exclusive property of the sound system, and to discourage the competition from getting wind of the new titles, the records were often soaked in water to remove the labels (a practice Kool Herc adopted later on in the Bronx to ensure that other deejays could not easily discover the source of the break beats he was playing).

When he started deejaying, Machouki, interviewed in *Reggae, Deep Roots Music*, recalled, "A deejay was a man who was responsible for conduct and behavior, and what goes on inside the dance hall. And we used the music as a message to control the hearts and minds of the people, and utter—we didn't realize then that word is power, and the words that we used really could control people.

"We could actually talk to the audience and everybody was happy, y'know. We didn't have to really be singing on the records to keep everybody happy. We just make utterances before a record, introduce the artists, give an idea of the message the artist is going to give you. And sometimes when we listen to the record and find that music is wanting, we would inter-serve something like 'Get on the ball . . .' and cover the weakness in the record. It was live jive and it really made people feel happy."[5]

Machouki's jive, which included phrases like "Live the life you love, and love the life you live," and "Whether you be young or old, you just got to let the good time roll, my friend," could only be heard live at a blues dance. His protégé, Sir Lord Comic, however, took the style one step further by recording a toast, thus making him the first deejay to put his voice on vinyl.

In addition to the skill and popularity of the deejays, the sound systems also built their reputation on the quality of music they played. By the late fifties, however, the U.S. r&b that was so popular began to give way to rock 'n' roll, which did not have much of an audience in Jamaica. Influenced by r&b and the Jamaican folk music called mento, which combined Latin-flavored rhythms and a European chord structure, local musicians began producing their own sound.

With the development of this homegrown sound also came an interest in recording it—not surprisingly by the same men who had run the sound systems. In 1959, Clement "Sir Coxsone" Dodd and Duke Reid topped the list of fledgling producers who were among the first to employ local session musicians to record instrumentals called "rudie blues," Jamaica's answer to r&b. Dodd's success in this arena spawned the seminal Studio One label, sometimes called "Coxsone University" or the Jamaican Motown, which churned out some of the island's most scorching hits throughout the sixties and seventies. Reid started the equally regarded Treasure Isle label.

The early domestic recordings, which could not be heard on the radio, became ammunition in "sound clashes," as sound systems vied for popularity. The upbeat, shuffle rhythm that characterized the new sound inspired the jerky movements of a dance called the ska, which became the name for Jamaica's dominant music of the sixties.

Sir Lord Comic, a street dancer, or "legs man," attended all the dances before ascending to the ranks of ska deejay. His breakthrough came during Christmas 1959 when the regular deejay for the Admiral Deans sound system fell ill and he was asked to cover. His first words to the throng of partygoers were, "Now we'll give you the scene, you got to be real keen. And me no jelly bean. Sir Lord Comic answer his spinning wheel appeal, from his record machine. Stick around, be no clown. See what the boss is puttin' down."[6]

In 1966, Comic recorded a tune called "Ska-ing West," probably the first deejay toast on vinyl. Over a simple ska/rock steady groove, he drops random phrases such as "Adam and Eve went up my sleeve/and they didn't come down till Christmas Eve," along with some demonic laughter, to liven up the festivities. This record conveys much of the feel of a blues dance and shows firsthand how the deejays entertained the crowd.

Following on the heels of this record came other songs in which a deejay toasted over a "riddim." King Stitt, another deejay who worked for Coxsone, recorded three toasts for producer Clancy Eccles between 1968 and 1969—"Fire Corner," "Vigorton Two," and "This Is the Days of Wrath (Lee Van Cleef)"—all of which were hits. In "Fire Corner," Stitt says, "No matter what the people say/these sounds lead the way/it's the order of the day/from your boss deejay/I King Stitt/up it from the top to the very last drop . . ."

In 1970, U. Roy emerged as the deejay of note, and his unique combination of scat, chat, rap, and singing spawned a whole host of imitators and a whole new genre—the dancehall style—within reggae music. He inspired the likes of Dennis Alcapone, I. Roy (Roy Reid), and Big Youth (Manley Buchanan), who in turn influenced others who have kept the tradition of toasting alive and well to this day in Jamaica.

A true innovator, U. Roy pushed the boundaries of the art not only by his style but also by taking toasting from the realm of nonsense to a higher level of political, social, and cultural awareness. As he adopted Rastafarianism—the mystical philosophy that deifies the late Emperor Haile Selassie of Ethiopia and is based largely on the teachings of Jamaican activist Marcus Garvey—his lyrics came to utilize more Rasta iconography. Rastafarianism, in fact, became a very potent influence in Jamaican music during the seventies, and U. Roy set the tone in the dancehall, shouting down Babylon (the establishment) and lacing his toasts with biblical imagery and references to Mother Africa.

Although the sound system, the deejay, and dancehall music were all important facets of Jamaican culture by the early seventies, the only exposure the rest of the world had to reggae was largely through Bob Marley, the Trenchtown prophet whose conscious "roots" music propelled him to international stardom later in the decade. Backed by the unmatched musical talents of the Wailers, Marley was a Rasta missionary, preaching to the world the doctrines of love, positivity, truth, and awareness over a sticky, seductive groove.

The roots reggae of Marley and other powerful Rasta voices such as Burning Spear, the Mighty Diamonds, and Culture was dominant, and in fact defined reggae for many, but this was due largely to their success outside of Jamaica, in places like the United States, Europe, Japan, and Africa. Dancehall was still more of a street form of reggae and not as accessible to non-Jamaicans. According to Columbia dancehall artist Supercat, "With Bob Marley's roots, rock reggae, where there's slow version and slow words, you could easily listen to what Bob Marley's saying in English. The deejay in the dancehall is more like broken English, which is patois, and so it's like the Cockney slang from London. So if you don't understand a lot of these words and the terminology these guys use, you know, it's very hard for you to catch on."

SUPERCAT
STRETCHES OUT
OUTSIDE
HARLEM'S
LEGENDARY
APOLLO THEATRE.

New York Stylee

Dancehall was, however, nurtured by the significant population of Jamaican immigrants in the United States, Canada, and Britain. London, in particular, the destination of countless Caribbean immigrants in the early sixties, provided fertile territory for a domestic recording industry, which still plays host to the cutting edge of reggae. Toronto, Paris, Miami, Brooklyn, and the Bronx were not far behind.

"Jamaicans are among the most traveled people in the world—even more so than the average American," according to Professor Orlando Patterson, "and this has been going on since the 19th century. They are widely dispersed, and constantly moving back and forth." The result of this migration, he says, is their "exposure to different cultures, where they try to reproduce it locally." Like other immigrants, they also bring a part of home to their new surroundings.

Such was the case with Clive Campbell (Kool Herc), who emigrated from Kingston, Jamaica, to the West Bronx, New York, in 1967. Well acquainted with dancehall culture and sound systems, he built up his own mighty sound by 1974, consisting of twin turntables, a Macintosh amplifier, and massive Shure speaker columns that accommodated tremendous decibels—just like the sound systems of his native land. Known as the Herculords, he and his crew started spinning at house parties in the West and South Bronx. Instead of playing reggae, however, Herc had been influenced by the musical currents in his new surroundings, where they favored the hard-driving polyrhythms of Latin salsa and the funk of James Brown.

Like the early Jamaican deejays who added a crucial live element to the party, Herc spoke over the records, favoring the latest Bronx slang over patois. Eventually, though, the speed and precision required in spinning small sections of break beats demanded his total attention, so he employed MCs, rap's equivalent of the Jamaican deejays, to take over the microphone duties. While Herc was cutting up the wax on "the wheels of steel," his MC would whip the crowd into a dancing frenzy with words, in the same manner as the dancehall deejay.

KISS-FM's Kool DJ Red Alert credits Herc's MC, Coke La Rock, as being the very first MC. "He always used to say one verse: 'You rock and you don't stop.' And he used to always shout out people names, say, 'Rock on my mellow.' So this man had really developed something that a lot of people couldn't understand, but you know like they always say, once you form something, the generation you start with will grow with you and follow from there."

Kool Herc and Coke La Rock were to the fledgling hip-hop scene what King Tubby and Daddy U. Roy were to dancehall in Jamaica. Musically, Tubby made the most of the limited capabilities of two-track recording and the custom echo and reverb facilities (which are now standards) to pioneer dub. Herc, on the other hand, employed twin turntables and a few seconds of a record to introduce the break beat, which is the equivalent hip-hop riddim that is rapped over. However simple these respective techniques might appear in hindsight, at the time they were on the cutting edge.

**KOOL DJ RED ALERT
AND
PRINCE MESSIAH
CLOWN AROUND
INSIDE
KISS-FM'S STUDIOS.**

The similarities between the two innovations are unmistakable. Dubbing breaks down elements of the song—drum and bass, vocals, guitar, keyboards—allowing the isolation of individual instrumental tracks. The emphasis, however, is always on the repetitive bass and drum rhythms. Similarly, Herc's use of the break beat provides an early example of sampling, a standard practice in hip-hop today in which a beat or musical phrase is isolated within a song and "looped" (repeated continuously) using a sampling machine. Herc, of course, sampled his beats manually on the turntables. The use of dubbing and sampling allows one to arrange prerecorded sounds in new patterns, providing the musical foundation—the bare bones of beat—over which the deejay or rapper practices his/her art.

In Jamaica, dancehall embodied vital aspects of daily life and ghetto culture, and testing one's skills on the mike evolved into a folk art. Through lyrical poetry set to a beat, the forgotten denizens of the ghetto had found a medium through which to express themselves—and they were being heard. With the continued success of Bob Marley, any sounds emanating from Jamaica attracted the attention of such record companies as Island and Trojan, both owned by Englishmen. As a result, dancehall began its slow diffusion into the more mainstream markets of England and Canada.

The island's recording industry itself had also developed fully by this time, and Kingston supported a thriving music scene. Unlike the album-oriented U.S. market, however, Jamaicans favored singles—seven- and twelve-inch (disco) formats suitable for sound systems, as they included a dub or version along with the vocal cut. Whenever a popular riddim surfaced, deejays would make their own version of it by toasting on the dub. No payment to the original artist or producer was necessary due to Jamaica's lack of copyright laws. At a dance, one typically heard version after version of the same riddim with different deejays toasting on top. The dance fans devoured it. A demand for the choice riddims also led to the release of compilation albums that contained multiple vocal versions on the same riddim.

Jamaican music in America was largely confined to college radio and the Jamaican enclaves of New York, Miami, and Los Angeles. In the early eighties, however, reggae collided with rap in Manhattan's downtown clubs. Murray Elias, who used to spin at Club Negril on Second Avenue in Manhattan, a venue run by promoter Ruza Blue, says, "Before the Roxy, the trial thing was [Club] Negril, and that was the first reggae/hip-hop connection and also the first downtown hip-hop connection. Then it just blew up later, once she got Bambaataa and met the real B-Boys in the Bronx and busted it out at the Roxy."

Though Negril and Danceteria were among the first downtown venues for hip-hop, the Roxy quickly became the center of the scene during the early eighties. According to Red Alert, an early member of Bambaataa's Zulu Nation, "When we was in the Roxy during the time of '82, '83, we had one of the biggest crossover crowds ever come. I mean, it was nights on a Friday we averaged 3,500 people in there, and there was no such thing as advertisement. We just had a flow of people." From tourists to celebrities, people were drawn by the excitement of something new taking place.

"You felt comfortable in there," says Red. "You had crazy-looking people, to cool-looking people, to it doesn't matter. Whatever nationality it was—put it this way—for what dictation that Michael Jackson doin' with his new record, *Black and White*, is what we doin' in our music form too. We were showin' that we could join everybody together and listen to music. That's what the whole point was."

Onstage were three DJs behind the turntables (Red Alert among them), and ten MCs "rocking the mike," as well as a group of break-dancers known as the Zulu Kings and Zulu Queens. Together they comprised a mighty sound system—the Jamaican dancehall, New York style. From the shanties of Kingston to the tough streets of the Bronx, to the trendy clubs of downtown Manhattan, ghetto music was breaking into a whole new commercial sphere, and breaking the barriers of music as well.

Bambaataa and his group, the SoulSonic Force, subsequently signed with Tommy Boy Records, and in 1982 they recorded a tune called

"Planet Rock," which explored new aural landscapes. Using the techno-pop melodies of "Trans-Europe Express" (by the German electronic music outfit Kraftwerk), a subterranean, synthesized bassline, the rhythm track of Captain Sky's rap record "Super Sporm," and various other snippets, Bambaataa, with Arthur Baker and John Robie, constructed a huge hit. The song conjured up a dark, ominous mood, raising havoc on the dance floor with a robotic voice exhorting, "Rock, rock with the Planet Rock. Don't stop." The space-age sound of "Planet Rock" also influenced other popular songs of the time, including Herbie Hancock's break-dancing classic, "Rockit."

Meanwhile, in the sun-drenched Caribbean, dancehall music was slowly coming into its own as the most popular form of reggae in Jamaica. With the death of Bob Marley in 1981, roots music had lost the voice of its leader. "It was in the years after Marley died," observes Murray Elias, "that whole Rasta, conscious school of reggae was really undergoing turmoil. Without Marley, there was like what's next? And really what was next was dancehall."

The Champion Sound: Reggae/Hip-Hop Fusion

Dancehall music was the sound of the party. Like disco, it had more of a hard, driving beat, which distinguished it from the slow, staggered feel of other reggae. In *Cut 'n' Mix*, Dick Hebdige writes, "By the late 1970s the [roots] music was starting to become predictable and closed in upon itself. . . . Reggae would only be renewed and refreshed if it was combined again with other forms of music. Ska had begun as a hybrid sound: a mix of r&b, mento, jazz, gospel, Pocomania and burra rhythms. And if it was to survive into the 1980s, Jamaican popular music would have to go back to its source in the mix."[7]

Influenced perhaps by the techno sound of such records as "Planet Rock" that came from the United States, as well as new technology in the form of the Casio electronic keyboard, Jamaican producers started incorporating these elements into their own music. Just as drum machines and synthesizers had revolutionized hip-hop, making the music more of a producer's art, technology also made it possible for one man—instead of a band of session musicians—to create all the instrumental tracks for a song. Dancehall producer Prince Jammy (Lloyd James) was among the first one-man bands in Jamaica.

"I would say that what we call the modern era of dancehall," says Elias, an avid fan of the Jamaican sound, "came in 1985 with the '[Under Me] Sleng Teng' record by Wayne Smith, which was really Prince Jammy. And that was really like the first massive drum machine record where the drum machine replaced live musicians in the studio. It was even more, or even less, than a drum machine. What that record really was, was a very simple Casio, a toy Casio. Like this big." He spreads his hands about two feet apart. "The whole track was one setting, the drums, the bass, was one setting on that Casio. That was the biggest record of the year, and being the biggest record of the year, that changed the sound.

"Jamaica's music industry," he explains, "is probably laissez-faire capitalism at its purest. The taste of the market has such an immediate influence on the production of records. I mean, like the next day, you know, the next trends will be in the store. It doesn't take a month or three or four. It literally happens overnight in Jamaica because everybody makes records. There's no such thing as contractors in Jamaica. It's very easy to do something and get it into the stores in a day or two."

As one of the biggest all-time hits in Jamaica, "Under Mi Sleng Teng" derived its appeal from the hypnotic, programmed groove, over which Wayne Smith talks about smoking *ganja*. Its modern sound spawned countless versions by other artists, including "Buddy Bye" (Jammys, 1986) by Johnny Osbourne, "Small Horsewoman" (Witty's, 1986) by Shelly Thunder, the hip-hop/reggae fusion of "Trash 'n' Ready" (B-Boy, 1986) by Sound Dimension and "Na Touch da Just" (Sleeping Bag, 1988) by Just-Ice. The first two selections are included on an album called *Sleeping Bag's Reggae Dance Hall Classics* (Sleeping Bag, 1986), compiled by Elias while he worked for that label. These songs, with their close approximation to hip-hop beats, were the first dancehall hits to get played in such New York clubs as the Paradise Garage, Devil's Nest, and Latin Quarter.

Specializing in dance music, the now-defunct Sleeping Bag Records' roster included such artists as singer Joyce Simms and Mantronix, the rap/dance duo. Recognizing the growing underground following of dancehall, however, they released *Reggae Dance Hall II* in 1988, which contained two of the biggest dancehall hits of 1987, Admiral Bailey's "Big Belly Man" and Tiger's "Bam Bam (Tiger in the Dance)." Already big in the Jamaican communities of the Bronx and Brooklyn, dancehall had finally crossed over with its exposure in the downtown clubs—just as hip-hop had done in the early eighties.

Elias has been tracking the rise of dancehall in New York since his days as a club deejay in the late seventies. "I've always had the feeling in my mind that reggae was club music, and was black club music," he says. Outside the Caribbean community, however, white audiences have always been reggae's biggest audience, especially in the case of Rasta-inspired roots music.

The rise of dancehall has changed all that. "What I always thought would happen," he says, "you know, in terms of like the acceptance of black American kids accepting reggae music—in 1985, I came to the conclusion that it was a certainty."

As Elias moved to Profile Records, he was able to convince owner Cory Robbins, who was looking to expand his hip-hop label into something new, to focus on reggae. The result was the *Dancehall Stylee* compilation, released in 1989, which continued Elias's efforts to publicize the biggest dancehall club hits of the year. Volume two followed in 1990 and included two massive hits—"Wicked in Bed" and "Roots & Culture"—by rising star Shabba Ranks. Each compilation sold about 70,000 copies, which Elias describes as "phenomenal" for a reggae album.

The impetus for this sudden surge of interest in dancehall came from the street—what was playing from the B-Boy's mobile sound system, the jeep. Red Alert seconds this notion, attributing dancehall's appeal to American blacks "because it's more a street form."

Rapper KRS-ONE says, "The reason American blacks, or Africans trapped in America, are getting off on reggae is because they now are getting an understanding of what reggae artists are saying. The artists are becoming more clear, concepts are coming out. The American audience is getting into dancehall because dancehall artists are, you know, coming to New York, hanging out with rappers, seeing what the audience is about, and they rhyme according to that." He adds, "Once you realize what you're listening to, you get into it, and I think the kids in America are finally getting into what it is they're listening to. And it got heavy bass, hard snare, and somebody rhyming fast."

KRS-ONE, Elias, and Red Alert credit Shabba Ranks for the newfound popularity of dancehall. In addition to his solo hits of 1990, Shabba also teamed up with dancehall artists Coco Tea and Home-T to do "Everything You Go Away" (Music Works), "Don't Test Me" (Music Works) with singer Deborahe, and "Twice My Age" (Pow Wow) with Krystal, another singer. All three of these songs were certified hits.

"Shabba is a ghetto youth," says Elias. "Kids in America and Jamaica realize that he's about them." Red Alert grounds Shabba's popularity in the fact that "he caters to a street form, and also, it's about his unique style." He adds, "In the N.B.A. there are so many bad ballplayers, but it took Michael [Jordan] to break in an edge. You gotta have one person to break something through, and that's what's up."

Red Alert, who has been programming hip-hop at KISS-FM since 1983, added dancehall to his show around 1988. What started off as a 20-minute dancehall segment on his Saturday night session, which runs from nine to midnight, has expanded to occupy the first hour. Introduced to reggae through Bambaataa, Red was further exposed to it while on tour with Boogie Down Productions in 1988. BDP took the stage to J. C. Lodge's unforgettable "Telephone Love" (Music Works), which ruled all dancehalls and clubs worldwide for almost a year after its release.

BDP and another rap group called Masters of Ceremony both cut reggae-influenced songs around 1986—BDP's "The Bridge is Over" and MoC's "Sexy"—and Red realized that there was a definite interest in the

Jamaican sound. He explains, "It's like one hand washes another. Here it is: Kool Herc wash their hands bringin' in hip-hop. Here it is bringin' it back, people like KRS-ONE, Masters of Ceremony, bringin' back the reggae influence."

"The Bridge Is Over," from BDP's debut album, *Criminal Minded* (B-Boy Records, 1987), was among the first examples of reggae/hip-hop fusion. Over a simple piano melody based on the popular "Boops" rhythm (by dancehall artist Supercat) and a staggered drum machine beat, KRS-ONE toasts a Jamaican-style patois rhyme:

> The bridge is over, the bridge is over, wah-da-by-by
> The bridge is over the bridge is over, hey-hey
> You see me come in any dance with a spliff of sensi
> Down with the sound called BDP . . .

KRS-ONE returns to patois to tell of the brutal death of a crack dealer in "9mm Go Bang."

On each of BDP's releases to date, the fusion between rap and reggae becomes ever more apparent. *By All Means Necessary* (Jive, 1988) features the dancehall-inspired "Stop the Violence" and "T'cha T'cha." Following that in 1989 was *Ghetto Music: The Blueprint of Hip-Hop* (Jive/RCA), in which the songs "Bo! Bo! Bo!," "Jah Rulez," and "Hip-Hop Rules" skillfully combine thumping dancehall basslines, hip-hop's streetwise drumbeats, and the patois toasts of KRS-ONE.

"Jah Rulez," in fact, uses the "Stalag" riddim, an old Jamaican favorite most associated with a 1985 dancehall classic by Tenor Saw called "Ring the Alarm" (Techniques). This riddim also drives Shabba Ranks's "Roots & Culture," (Digital B) and is used again in true rap/reggae fashion by Fu-Schnickens, who do an updated version of "Ring the Alarm" (Jive/RCA, 1991).

The album *Edutainment* (Jive/RCA), BDP's 1990 release, continues in the group's commitment to reggae. KRS-ONE threads the fine line between B-Boy and rough raggamuffin as he alternates between fast and slow, Bronx slang and Kingston jive. The four reggae-influenced tracks include "100 Guns," "7 Deejays," "30 Cops," and the title track, "Edutainment," which samples an early ska tune by Don Drummond called "Man in the Streets."

BDP's *Live Hardcore Worldwide* (Jive/RCA, 1991), recorded in New York, London, Paris, and Tokyo, presents the rawness and energy of the live hip-hop show, and also features KRS-ONE toasting some of his own rhymes, Jamaican style, over dancehall beats. Finally, *Sex and Violence* (Jive/RCA), their 1992 release, carries the hip-hop/reggae connection to new levels: It has the street feel of a Jamaican sound system playing a party for B-Boys in the Bronx.

KRS-ONE, known as "The Teacher" within the hip-hop community because of his college lecture tours and commitment to conscious rhymes dealing with safe sex ("Jimmy"), education ("You Must Learn"), violence and police brutality in the community ("30 Cops," "Stop the Violence"), and other pressing concerns, has not only been on the cutting edge of hip-hop but has also always been aware of rap's raggamuffin roots. "I just think reggae is another hip-hop style, and I've made it my business from back in '85. I said, well, you know the new style is hip-hop/reggae—that's something we personally fused together."

Explaining the relationship between hip-hop and reggae, KRS-ONE says, "Well, it has to do with history, and when you realize that all black people are African, all over the world, no matter what they call themselves, they're African." He points to the slave trade as the force that created various splinters of African culture all over the world. "Most people that have genes that lie in Africa have a love for bass, heat, domineering kinda 'boom, boom, bah.' That's in every African worldwide, and I prove it every year, every time you come out with the 'boom, boom, bah,' everybody worldwide, starting with every black person worldwide, can relate. Reggae is no different. Reggae started off like rap started off." In promoting the fusion of rap and reggae, KRS-ONE has worked with some of reggae's brightest stars—including Shabba Ranks,

Ziggy Marley, and veterans Sly & Robbie, whose 1989 *Silent Assassin* LP (Island) he produced.

As the Riddim Twins, the drum and bass duo of Sly Dunbar and Robbie Shakespeare backed up almost every reggae performer of note throughout the 1970s. They were the pulse of Peter Tosh's Word, Sound and Power band, as well as the musical genius behind the bionic reggae of Black Uhuru, which won reggae's first Grammy award with 1983's *Anthem* (Mango/Island). Under their own Taxi Gang label, Sly & Robbie crossed over to other types of music during the eighties, writing and producing songs for Grace Jones ("Pull Up to the Bumper"), Mick Jagger ("Don't Look Back"), and Gwen Guthrie ("Padlock"). They also released solo albums, *Language Barrier* (1985) and *Rhythm Killers* (1987), that utilized such varied forms as jazz, rock, funk, and African. It was through their association with KRS-ONE, however, that their venture into rap/reggae fusion came to fruition.

Dunbar, who both plays live and programs drums on *Silent Assassin*, says, "Hip-hop music is very raw, very African. It's mostly riddims and drums pushing the message. It seems to hit people very hard, makes them go crazy. It's the same thing in Jamaica. We noticed that whenever they played the dub side of a record at a party in Jamaica, people went into a frenzy, just like they do in New York with some hip-hop records. It's like when James Brown says 'Give the drummer some' and the dancers go wild."[8]

The album features rappers Willie D., Young MC, Queen Latifah, Shah of Brooklyn, and of course, KRS-ONE, throwing down lyrics over some high-tech rhythms generated by Sly & Robbie and their band. Here the distinction between rap and reggae is lost among Robbie's bubbling basslines and Sly's tribal polyrhythms—elements common to both musical genres—but that seems to be the point of the whole record.

"I like everything on the album," says Sly, "but if there's one message that's most important it's 'Party Together.' That song expresses the unity of the reggae and hip-hop community that we're aiming for."[9] Based on the Turtles' 1960s hit "Happy Together," Robbie's bass carries the melody of the original song, while KRS-ONE raps:

> This nonsense of rap being different from reggae, is a big lie
> Black people shouldn't separate themselves in music, no
> reason why.

At the end of the song, they do an all-instrumental dub, with each musician coming in for a solo. Within the grooves of *Silent Assassin*, the possibilities of hip-hop/reggae fusion are thoroughly explored, further defining the close relationship shared by these two musical forms.

For 1987's *Rhythm Killers* (Island), Sly & Robbie used a young rapper named Shinehead, who had one album behind him. On the cover of his *Rough and Rugged* LP (African Love Music, 1986), he poses with a baseball cap worn sideways and his face engulfed by a huge pair of Cazal glasses, striking the figure of a stereotypical B-Boy. Listening to the album, however, reveals the diverse styles of an artist who raps, toasts, sings, scats, and whistles over slow, computer-style dubs, which were becoming standard after the popular "Sleng Teng" riddim.

The man behind the Cazals, Edmund Carl Aiken, was born in Jamaica but moved to the Bronx. He hopped back and forth between the two until 1976, when he finally settled in the Bronx. Growing up under the cross-cultural influences of hip-hop and dancehall, versatile lyrical styles came naturally to Aiken. He started off toasting on July 5, 1982, for a sound system called Downbeat the Ruler, and eventually moved to African Love, which was run by his current manager, Claude Evans.

Shinehead's first album—which included covers of Nat King Cole's "Answer Me" and Michael Jackson's "Lady in my Life" and "Billy Jean"—is considered a classic among dancehall fans. Following his subsequent work with Sly & Robbie, he was signed by Elektra Records and has recorded three albums for them: *Unity* (1988), *The Real Rock* (1990), and *Sidewalk University* (1992), which have installed him into the higher ranks of artists who have blended hip-hop and reggae.

THE ARTICAL
DON SHINEHEAD
ENJOYS
A QUIET MOMENT.

Like KRS-ONE, Shinehead's versatility allows him to tread the fine line between musical styles. On a song like "Hello Y' All," from his first album, he raps New York style over a riddim based on Ed Nangle's "Good Girl," which was originally recorded for Coxsone Dodd's Studio One label around 1968. In his updated version, Shinehead raps:

> Now many have tried to rule the land
> But Studio One is where it all began
> Oh man, it makes me crazy, it makes me smile
> I love the drum and the bass of the rub-a-dub style.
> Got to hear my records got to have a cassette
> If I don't hear no reggae music I'm a total wreck.
> Now the best type of music is in the dancehall
> With the speakers all around about ten feet tall
> The place is packed and the vibes are right
> The deejays are perfect and selection is tight
> The best part of the dance is when you play the dub
> And if the people love the music they say "Forward!"
> You got to take out the bass leave the mids and the treble
> Play it back again and let the young girls bubble.

In this way, he uses a new style (hip-hop) to pay tribute to the origins of the music in the Jamaican dancehall.

Rap is music that constantly feeds off other styles and creates something new and original, but with dancehall it has literally met its match. Says Elias, "To me dancehall beats are hip-hop beats at this point. I see the fusion continuing to happen. I don't think it's a fad. This is just the tip of the iceberg. Reggae will get bigger because it is part of hip-hop." KRS-ONE offers a similar perspective, saying, "Now dancehall, the 1992 dancehall, is like 1992 rap. Dancehall samples old dub basslines and puts a computer to it" in the same way that rap recycled vintage funk from the seventies.

As one of the first rap independents to add reggae to their catalog,

Profile continues to develop the relationship between rap and reggae as it signs more dancehall artists. Frighty and Colonel Mite, Junior Demus, Nardo Ranks, and veteran singer Barrington Levy are just a sample of the Jamaican talent who have sounds out on Profile. In addition, the label continues the tradition of the compilation, introducing top dancehall producers like Steely & Cleevie (*Sound Boy Clash*, 1991) and Mister Doo (*Mister Doo Presents the Doo Experience*, 1991) to a broader audience.

On the hip-hop side, Profile has released *Pure Poverty* (1991), by New Jersey rappers Poor Righteous Teachers, which is strictly raggamuffin toasting over fusion beats. Before that were Special Ed's *Youngest In Charge* (1989), featuring two reggae-influenced cuts, and the seminal *Raggamuffin Hip-Hop* (1989) by Asher D. and Daddy Freddy, the latter of whom has since gone solo as an Elektra recording artist. Some might also have forgotten Run D.M.C.'s second outing, *King of Rock* (1985), which features a collaboration with dancehall favorite Yellowman called "Roots, Rap, Reggae," among the earliest examples of hip-hop/reggae fusion to be recorded.

Ever since Epic signed Shabba Ranks, other majors have followed suit, including Columbia, whose roster includes Supercat, Tiger, Mad Cobra, Tony Rebel, and New York's own roughneck youth, Jamalski; MCA, who signed Barrington Levy; and Mercury, who released 19-year-old sensation Buju Banton's debut *Voice of Jamaica*. If major-label interest in dancehall is sustained and developed, the real reggae explosion is yet to come.

To speak of rap and reggae in the same breath, then, is not so strange when you consider their origins and the increasing amount of crossover that has been going on of late. With one form derived from the other, a constant cross-fertilization has made for a very dynamic relationship. According to Professor Patterson, "It's part of a broader tradition of proletarian culture of vitality. The peasants [in Jamaica] were always tremendously creative." The same can be said for the underclass in America. KRS-ONE, who grew up in the South Bronx and spent four years scraping out an existence on the streets, agrees, saying "When people are under pressure they create art, music, philosophy, and so on, and they do it as a comfort to their own selves."

Like hip-hop, dancehall embodies a whole culture. Columbia artist Cobra explains, "Dancehall is a culture—the life that the ghetto youth live." Expanding on that idea, Supercat adds, "Dancehall is the music about bringing people together, especially ghetto people, who don't know how to have a good time. This is what they use to bring themselves together into one unit. And this is not just entertainment, this is also teaching, 'cause a lot of these youth coming from the ghetto, they sing about many different thing. They sing that they want to have a good life, they sing that life is tough in the ghetto, they sing about school condition, and they sing about girls. And if there is gun also, they can highlight the guns, 'cause that is where some of the bad things go on."

From Kool Herc to KRS-ONE, U.

MAD COBRA BIGS UP THE MASSIVE. Roy to "Rapper's Delight," reggae and rap have traveled far. "Everyone's pretty much doing the same thing," says KRS-ONE, "but they're doing it according to their culture and consciousness."

recommended
listening

1. Various Artists, *U. Roy & Friends "With a Flick of My Musical Wrist . . ."* (Trojan, 1988).
2. King Tubby, *King Tubby's Special 1973–1976* (Trojan, 1989).
3. Various Artists, *Dancehall Stylee: The Best of Reggae Dancehall, Vol. I* (Profile, 1989).
4. Various Artists, *Sleeping Bag's Reggae Dancehall Classics, Vol. 1* (Sleeping Bag, 1987).
5. Various Artists, *Reggae Dance Hall II* (Sleeping Bag, 1988).
6. Boogie Down Productions, *By All Means Necessary* (Jive, 1988).
7. Shinehead, *Rough & Rugged* (African Love, 1986).
8. Sly & Robbie, *Silent Assassin* (Island, 1989).
9. Shabba Ranks, *As Raw as Ever* (Epic, 1991).
10. Supercat, *Don Dada* (Columbia, 1992).
11. Mad Cobra, *Hard to Wet and Easy to Dry* (Columbia, 1992).

ChApTeR 3

Ain't It
Funky

funk n: 3) funky music
funky adj: 2) having an earthy
unsophisticated style and feeling; esp:
having the style and feeling of blues.

Webster's Ninth New Collegiate Dictionary

Betwixt decks there can
hardlie a man catch his
breathe by reason there
ariseth such a funke in
the night that it causes
putrefaction of blood.

W. Capps, 1623
The Oxford English Dictionary
1933 edition

From the oldest known definition of the word—possibly derived from the Flemish for an awful stench—to what is today a term most associated with a genre of music, "funk" has undergone a drastic transition from being practically a four-letter word in polite society to a sound that gets you looser than prune juice on the dance floor. Some might think it's just another example of the African-American cultural penchant for turning language on its head—as in, "bad" meaning good. But a true understanding of funk is elusive, because how can one adequately express in words that which is purely a feeling? Quite simply, he who feels it knows it.

Funk is hearing James Brown's primal scream or the rolling polyrhythms of the "Funky Drummer" while your body uncontrollably does the jerk. It's seeing a 52-year-old George Clinton on stage fronting a 20-piece ensemble of singers and players, his tongue wagging through colored strands of fake hair, stroking you off with a tension-building jam before finally letting the dam burst. Funk is the cascading horn fanfares of Kool & the Gang, the Meters's meandering wah-wah, the elastic basslines of Zapp, flying high hats, electronic hand claps, and tribal congas. Through this potent blend of percussion, syncopation, repetition, and improvisation, the funk flows pure and free like water from an underground spring. You can bottle it, label it, and sell it, but its source still lies deep down below in the soul, from where other sounds of blackness, such as the blues, gospel, and jazz, also emanate.

Funk came screaming out of James Brown's throat in the sixties and landed in the garish seventies, an era ruled by rock and disco. Never as commercially regarded as its cousins, funk is rooted in blackness—"the black, ethnic, housing project, I've been poor all my life, I'm a nigger, black," according to Roger Troutman, the creative force behind '80s funksters Zapp. Though rock and disco originally poured from the same springs of black creativity, they were, of course, soon co-opted by the white mainstream, and became permutations of their original forms. Funk, however, like the blues, remained the unadulterated, renegade sound that adhered to no rules: 200 proof served straight up and with no apology.

The pioneers of rap immediately recognized the supreme rawness of funk, and by spinning the funky sounds that had been bumped off the airwaves by disco, they preserved and simultaneously revitalized the music. "See, that's why hip-hop was so big," explains early rap deejay Jazzy Jay. "Because disco came in and tried to wipe out the funk. How the funk came back on the scene was through hip-hop, through the street, you know? All of them—James Brown, George Clinton, Parliament, all that—that was almost dead. Disco was in, everybody was hustling, and the disco deejays were taking over. Well, what happened, the kids just rebelled. They wanted something that they couldn't hear on the radio and everything. They wanted something else. They were hungry, you know what I'm saying?"

Thus, from within the grooves of countless 45s and LPs released between the late sixties and early eighties comes the foundation of the hip-hop soundtrack. Funky drum breaks, horns, guitars, and basslines provided the building blocks for new tracks when broken down to the strictly rhythmic format of break beats or sampled loops. Without funk there would probably be no hip-hop, and without hip-hop, those old funk sides would probably still be collecting dust.

Observing the crowd at a recent James Brown concert at Radio City Music Hall in New York, one is instantly impressed by its diversity. Blacks, whites, browns, and Asians mingle together in the cavernous mecca of show biz like impressionist brush strokes on a boundless canvas. From young hip-hoppers in baseball caps and baggy jeans to impeccably suited professionals, they're all here, testament to James's universality. For what other artist, living or dead, could command the respect of so many and so many different kinds? Who else generates the same kind of appeal from the grimiest ghettos to the most sparkling suburbs? Certainly, few artists can match the same prolific output, longevity, and sheer charisma as this 64-year-old performer, who has taken a licking but keeps on giving. For these reasons, James Brown has accumulated more titles than a feudal lord: "Mr. Please, Please, Please," "The Ruler of R&B," "Mr. Dynamite," "The Hardest Working Man in Show Business," "Soul Brother Number One," "Mr. Superbad," "Minister of the Brand-New Super Heavy Funk," and as the banner covering the Hammond organ onstage proclaims, "Godfather of Soul."

After a hyperbolic introduction from his MC, the Godfather struts out in a brilliant purple suit set off by gold, Cuban-heeled shoes. His trademark bouffant shimmering under the spotlights, James nods to the crowd in recognition of the deafening ovation, and proceeds to get sweaty with "Living in America" (1986), his most recent hit. Backed by a tuxedoed band, complete with a five-piece horn section, four female singers, and a bevy of Solid Gold style–dancers—not unlike the unrivaled James Brown Revue of the sixties—he grinds through funky staples such as "Sex Machine," "Cold Sweat," "Give It Up or Turn It Loose," and "I Don't Want Nobody to Give Me Nothing." His voice handles those inimitable shrieks with controlled abandon, and while age has forced him to cut down on his famed stage acrobatics, it does not prevent him from pulling off some moves that would make Hammer envious. No, this isn't the Apollo Theater in 1962, where his fabulous, platinum-selling live album was recorded, but the funk is still clearly personified in James Brown.

Born in the backwoods of South Carolina and raised in a Georgia brothel, James started entertaining out of necessity, dancing for dimes on the street as a child. His musical impulses came directly from the black church, where he was influenced by the powerful tradition of gospel. As author Cynthia Rose notes, "Musically, Brown fused rural rhythm and blues (r&b) and its big-band swing with 'sanctified' gospel: the rhapsodic ecstatic religion of the deepest, blackest South. Where Nat 'King' Cole drew the image of the dark man towards traditional sophistication, Brown turned assimilation around. He pulled theatre towards his colour, he used his blackness as a magnet backed with all the force and drama of the charismatic church."[1] Such familiar Brownsian techniques as call and response, vocal improvisation, rhythmic delivery, and the familiar "Ha!" (a rhetorical device for expelling air at the end of a breath before inhaling again) hark back to gospel's traditional interaction between preacher and congregation, and ultimately back to Africa.

If the black church played a role in the genesis of James, funk was also born out of complete dedication to the game (epitomized by such songs as "Givin' Up Food for Funk"). James Brown and his band, the Flames, cut their first wax with "Please, Please, Please" in 1955 on Federal Records, but it was only three years later, in 1958, when they first hit the national r&b charts with "Try Me." Another seven years of tireless working and performing elapsed before "Papa's Got a Brand New Bag" broke the top-ten pop charts in the summer of 1965. Between 1967 and 1969, the James Brown Revue, a revolving cast of about 30, were touring 11 months of the year with some of the finest musicians of the era, including Fred Wesley, Maceo Parker, Alfred "Pee Wee" Ellis, Clyde Stubblefield, John "Jabo" Starks, and "Bootsy" and "Catfish" Collins. The band, better known as the JBs, were also writing and recording constantly while on the road, prodded relentlessly by the maestro himself.

With no formal musical training, James relied on his bandleader to translate the sounds in his head into the rhythmic symphony that erupted onstage and on vinyl. The most potent collaboration occurred with Pee Wee Ellis, who was only 24 when he joined James in 1964. They first cut "Let Yourself Go," which evolved into the hit "There Was a Time," before going on to even greater things with "Cold Sweat" in 1967. The Revue's great innovation came in using all of its power—even the melodic instruments—as interlocking percussion. Anchored by a chugging drum-and-bass groove, they fused a complete rhythmic interplay—the primer for hip-hop—with brash horn blasts, a steady warbling Hammond organ, and whirling slices of guitar. Throw in James's voice, which was thicker and juicier than prime rib slathered with extra gravy, and the visual fireworks of the stage show, and you have the original, uncut funk.

As Mr. Dynamite's explosive success in the late sixties coincided with the Black Power movement, James was certainly not called "Soul Brother Number One" for nothing. If a loose-and-free style characterized his music, his ideology was exemplified in titles such as "Soul Power," "Say It

Loud, I'm Black and I'm Proud," and "Soul Pride," which paralleled such popular expressions of the day as "black is beautiful." Brown brought this slogan to life celebrating his blackness, and also providing his people with a true role model, by exhorting, "Get Up, Get Into It, Get Involved" and "I Don't Want Nobody to Give Me Nothing" ("Open up the door—huh!—I'll get it myself"). He led by example, too, controlling most of his business through his own Fair Deal Productions, a classic example of black enterprise built from the ground up. Even if he did consort with Presidents Johnson and Nixon, and go to Vietnam to entertain the mostly black fighting force, those who called him an Uncle Tom could not possibly have measured his true contributions in promoting black.

Brown's formidable catalog—which includes countless 45s on the King label and his own People label, as well as LPs on Polygram (and he's still releasing albums on Scotti Brothers)—provide a veritable gold mine of funky sounds, which hip-hop pioneers like Kool Herc naturally gravitated toward in the early seventies. Since then it has become virtually impossible to find a hip-hop album that does not embody some part of the Godfather of Soul.

Even before the concept of a twelve-inch single or extended version was embraced by the music industry, Brown usually recorded his songs in two parts, the second part being an all-instrumental jam—the meat of the sound—which featured a breakdown of the various components. From these part twos were culled drum breaks such as "Funky Drummer," an example of the New Orleans beat, which was masterfully demonstrated by Clyde Stubblefield. Few sticksmen today can reproduce Clyde's almost supernatural rhythm, and there has yet to appear someone who can grunt and scream and scat and groove quite like James. Thanks to turntables and samplers, however, their contributions remain fresh and relevant to a whole new generation of listeners who weren't even born during the heyday of funk.

"Free your mind and your ass will follow
For the Kingdom of Heaven is within"
Funkadelic

George Clinton was destined to be funky. After all, he admits to entering this world from an outhouse: "My mother told me she thought she had to go to the bathroom, and I popped out. Her midwife came running, and she had to pull me back up by the cord. I was one turd that wouldn't let go."[2] Touchdown occurred in Kannapolis, North Carolina, on July 22, 1941.

Many, many years later, as legend has it, George was driving down a deserted Toronto highway during the wee hours, with former James Brown bassist William "Bootsy" Collins, when a bright beam of light from the sky struck the car three times before disappearing into the darkness above. From that moment on, the two felt they had been commissioned from a higher order, the "mothership," to let loose the true power of the funk.

Shortly afterward, in 1976, Parliament, one of Clinton's musical entities, released the monumental *Mothership Connection* (Casablanca) LP, which defined a whole funk universe. While James Brown brought funk straight from the roots, Clinton and his crew (which came to encompass JB alumni such as Bootsy, Fred Wesley, and Maceo Parker) took their inspiration from outer space and delivered the most conceptually sophisticated, spiritually relevant, politically conscious, and musically powerful—not to mention wacky and bizarre—album and road show that audiences had ever experienced. In the process, they became to black America what the Beatles or Elvis represented to white America—"Thuh Bomb!"

Parliament was only one part of an amalgam called the Parliafunkadelicment Thang, a zany troupe of roughly 25 musicians and singers who comprised other smaller groups such as Funkadelic, Bootsy's Rubber Band, the Horny Horns, the Brides of Funkenstein, and Parlet. Though personnel drifted among entities, for business purposes each group had their own record deals with competing labels such as Casablanca, Warner Brothers, Atlantic, and Arista. They generally toured, however, under the banner of P-Funk.

Overseeing this thang was George Clinton, saved from the slop by his umbilical cord, frequent sighter of UFOs, but also creative genius, chief songwriter, composer, singer, arranger, and popularly known by his onstage alter ego, Starchild, messenger of Dr. Funkenstein, the self-proclaimed Maggot Overlord (maggots, in P-Funk lingo, were the followers of funk). Clinton and his associates carried the torch of funk through the mid to late seventies—after James Brown's best work was behind him—and no one was quite prepared for what was to follow. Even today, the groove that P-Funk meticulously carved through numerous tours and releases has left a deep and resonating impression on hip-hop.

Clinton grew up in the projects of Newark, New Jersey, influenced by James Brown and the Motown sound, but even more so by the great doo-wop groups like the Dells, the Heartbeats, and the Flamingos. His first musical outing, in fact, the Parliaments, was a doo-wop quintet started in a Plainfield, New Jersey, barbershop in 1956, when Clinton was only fifteen. Other members included Clarence "Fuzzy" Haskins, Calvin Simon, Grady Thomas, and Ray Davis. Though signed to Motown in 1962, the Parliaments made little headway in the industry, and George's only successes during this time came through writing songs for other Motown artists such as the Jackson Five ("I Bet You") and Diana Ross and the Supremes ("I'm Into Something, I Can't Shake It Loose"). After leaving Motown for the more alternative Revilot label, however, the Parliaments found themselves with their own hit "(I Just Wanna) Testify," in 1967.

By then the quintet had their own backing band, made up of some of the younger kids who used to hang around the barbershop, including Eddie Hazel, Billy Nelson, Bernie Worrell, Lucious Tunya Ross, and Tiki Fullwood. Inspired equally by Sly Stone, New Orleans' funky Meters, and Jimi Hendrix's whole psychedelic experience, this outfit became known as Funkadelic. When Revilot folded, taking with them the Parliaments' name in a contractual imbroglio, George took the band to another Detroit label, Westbound, where they released their self-titled debut in 1968. The backup band had suddenly come to the fore, while the original vocalists sang backup. Then, in another confusing twist, the Parliaments' name was given back to George later that year, and he immediately set up Parliament, who released the album *Osmium* for Invictus. Thus, the two groups, while recording for different labels (Funkadelic for Westbound and later Warner Brothers, while Parliament settled at Casablanca), were actually one—the Parliafunkadelicment Thang.

Like any true child of the sixties, P-Funk experimented, expanding lyrical and musical consciousness with such releases as *Free Your Mind and Your Ass Will Follow* (1970), *Maggot Brain* (1971), *America Eats Its Young* (1972), and *Cosmic Slop* (1973) by Funkadelic, and Parliament's *Up for the Down Stroke* (1974), *Chocolate City* (1975), and then the phenomenal *Mothership Connection*. This era of the early seventies proved to be a long, strange trip for P-Funk as they knocked down musical boundaries and worked toward a solid concept and identity, which crystallized with *Mothership Connection*. As P-Funk steamrolled mainstream pop sensibilities, the mission of the mothership became all the more clear—destroy the forces of funklessness and "rescue dance music from the Blahs!"

The "blahs!" was, of course, funkspeak for dreaded disco, a perverse offshoot of the funk that gained momentum around the mid-seventies, initially among the black and Latino gay community. Even down to the derivation of the word, from the French *la discothèque* or "record library," disco embodied a certain chi-chi quality of shallow glamour and cultivated decadence. A song that best defines the disco era was 1975's "Love to Love You Baby" by Donna Summer, at the time an American expatriate living in Germany. Produced by Swiss-Italian Giorgio Moroder, the record was literally one long aural orgasm, with Summer cooing in ecstasy over a synthetic beat. Ironically, she signed with Neil Bogart's Casablanca, the label that made its mark with Kiss; gay, disco ducks the Village People; and, of course, Parliament.

Sitting in a hotel room in D.C., George Clinton ruminates over the topic of disco. The morning after completing the last leg of the 1992 U.S. tour with the P-Funk All Stars, heavy Samsonites hang under his eyes, and his long yellow-and-white extensions resemble a headdress of electrocuted snakes. "Well, disco, you take any disco record by itself, and it was alright, it was good," he says, graciously. "I mean, there was a lot of funky disco records. It was just that when you take one stroke, even in making love, one stroke, you'll bore somebody to death. They'll tell you to phone that shit in, youknowwhatimsayin?

GEORGE CLINTON AND THE P-FUNK ALL STARS FUNK UP THE PROGRAM AT TRAMPS IN NEW YORK.

"Disco was cool, except they tried to narrow it down. They tried to make it a commodity. Music is a vibe, and the minute you try to make it a commodity, where you can build a mold and just pour something in it, and the product comes out, and new and improved every six months, you know, like some phosphate or some shit. It don't work with music." Funk, on the other hand, Clinton describes as being "bluesy," corresponding to Websters' definition of the word. "It was the last of the music that was free, and you did what you wanted and you vibed on it, and it wasn't a commodity."

Such thoughts are reflected in Parliament's *Funkentelechy Vs. the Placebo Syndrome* LP from 1977, which furthered the idea that if you believed in the funk, it would set you free. According to the placebo syndrome, anything the system tried to sell you to keep you happy—from disco to football to lottery tickets—was just a placebo to ensure their control. "The pimping of the pleasure principle" is what George called it. If happiness came in material form, and money was the means of attaining those materials, then you would have to work for the system to acquire the things that made you happy—a powerful concept beneath the quirky cartoon imagery of Pedro Bell's album-cover art. "We tried to terminate that whole concept, the syndrome that fucked with your instincts, that pimped your instincts in order to sell things, you know," says George, scratching a graying beard.

In their heyday, P-Funk took their message to the stage with a spectacular show that featured outlandish $10,000 leather, fur, and rhinestone outfits, a fantastic light show, and props that included a $325,000 metallic mothership that descended to the stage from the ceilings of auditoriums, opening its hatch for George Clinton to step out. Playing to sold-out arenas of predominantly black audiences, Clinton's funk mob rolled through the latter seventies with albums like *One Nation Under a Groove* (1978), *Uncle Jam Wants You* (1979), and *Motor-Booty Affair* (1978). As all good things eventually come to an end, so too did Parliament and Funkadelic (in 1980 and 1981, respectively), for a variety of reasons, both business and personal. George, however, like James, kept on going, and even today sells out venues worldwide with the P-Funk All-Stars, who throw down endless jams in a scorching four-hour set.

"The hip-hop just made our job easier," he says. "I never knew that I would be sampled, 'cause, you know, basically that was illegal for a while. But once it started working, we wasn't gonna get on the radio no other way. And when people started bootlegging, I was glad. All of that was part of keeping the funk, to me, keeping the funk alive." And thanks to all the rappers who made Clinton the most sampled artist next to James, he was able to buy back the rights to much of his music, which was held as collateral for financial debts totaling some $50,000. "Rap is that new, edgy shit," says George, "It's gonna be around and, like I said, the funk is gonna be in it, the jazz is gonna be in it. It's starting all over again. But, you know, we getting ready for communication in outer space. . . ."

———

While the grooves of both King James and Sir George have been plundered mercilessly by younger beat technicians such as Public Enemy, Eric B. & Rakim, N.W.A., Redman, and Digital Underground, there exists a whole realm of more obscure funk that has been utilized equally as well as the foundation for endless hip-hop tracks. Beneath the bedrock—names like Sly & the Family Stone, Kool & the Gang, Earth, Wind and Fire, the Ohio Players, WAR, Curtis Mayfield, Roy Ayers, the Isley Brothers, and the Meters—lies such hidden treasures as the Bar-Kays, Mandrill, the Kay Gees, Rare Earth, the Politicians, the Relations, Dyke & the Blazers, the Jimmy Castor Bunch, Chuck Brown & the Soul Searchers, the 8th Day, BT Express, Con Funk Shun, and the list goes on. Why each of these groups isn't a household name remains a mystery, but through hip-hop, their sounds have gained a second life.

While a whole book could be devoted to examining the contributions of these underground stars, it suffices to say that funk didn't simply stop at James Brown and George Clinton. Representing a true roots movement, funk sprouted from seeds all over the country. While Sly & the Family Stone were making their first stand in San Francisco around 1967, WAR was brewing in Compton, Curtis Mayfield was already pushing product in Chicago, Kool & the Gang in Ohio, the Bar-Kays replaced Booker T. and the MGs as the Stax/Volt house band in Memphis, and the Meters were clocking in in New Orleans. Detroit and Philadelphia were, of course, doing their own things with Motown and Philadelphia International, both of which played big roles in nurturing the funk with early works by Marvin Gaye and the O'Jays. Funk really did create one nation under a groove, but the groove was strictly the domain of black radio and the black record-buying public.

Exemplifying the obscurity in which many of the early funk bands operated—even in their day—are the much underrated Meters, who still pack small venues here and there when they aren't jamming at Tipitina's in New Orleans. Featuring an original lineup of the Neville brothers—Art on keyboards and Cyrille on percussion—Leo Nocentelli on guitar, George Porter playing bass, and sticksman Joseph "Zigaboo" Modeliste, the band were prolific session players during the sixties and seventies, churning out many of their own funky sides as well. Crucial to the Meters' winding, grinding, often unpredictable groove was the city of their birth.

Not only the domain of jazz and blues, the Crescent city encouraged a fermentation of musical styles dating back to its early days. As a major port in the slave trade, European and African cultures collided head-on here. Also a northern outpost of Caribbean culture, New Orleans had its own version of festival, called Mardi Gras—part of the Afro-Christian tradition preserved by the slaves in Trinidad, Jamaica, and Brazil. "Mardi Gras music, I think, is a combination of a lot of African-Cuban musical beats— what the slaves were able to maintain out of being taken away from playing rhythm stuff, yunno?" says George Porter. "They were given instruments because the white community always thought that Africans spoke to each other with drums and rhythms, so they thought they would break the language by, you know, taking away percussive instruments. So we were given horns and stuff like that to play, yunno?"

Playing nonpercussive instruments rhythmically was just one side of the story. The African and Latin influences also manifested themselves in interlocking polyrhythms, which formed a unified groove. These polyrhythms first came from tamborines, cowbells, or congas. When the same patterns were played on the conventional drums, the uniquely "New Orleans beat" was born, popularized by drummers like Clyde Stubblefield of the JBs.

Porter first encountered this style of funky drumming with Smokey Johnson and Hungry Charles Otis. Funk, he says, originates with the drummer. "It's a drum thing, it's a syncopated drum feeling that bass players, very few of them I could say, have learned to play with syncopation or play against it, you know?" says George. "Most of the time when bass players start playing with syncopation, then it gets to be a straight thing again, because everybody's playing in the same place, in the same meter. But the relationship between me and Zig, I was always playing against his rhythm, which made our style of syncopation so unique. It's like he would make a statement and I would answer it."

Originally a seven-piece outfit called Neville Sounds, the Meters emerged from the French Quarter club circuit around 1967. In this competitive realm, musicians had to be well versed in all musical styles, and George fondly remembers starting a gig playing bebop, moving into swing, standards, more funky stuff, "and by the time you get to the end of the night, by the time everybody's drunk and looking for someone to snatch to go home, we singing, yunno, these blues songs—'I'm all alone, baby, by the bar, and I'm looking for someone to go neck with,' kind of stuff. That's the way the gigs used to go in those days."

Making a name for themselves locally, the Meters were soon drafted by producer Allen Toussaint for use in studio sessions for the likes of Lee Dorsey, Betty Harris, and LaBelle. Soon after, in the fall of 1967, they released their own first single, "Sophisticated Sissy," followed by "Sissy Strut," and eventually their self-titled debut on New York's Josie label. Today, these early recordings on Josie and Reprise are incredibly valuable to collectors, though most Meters material has gone the way of CD reissues (on the Rounder label). During the late sixties, the Meters opened for such acts as the Isley Brothers, the Staple Singers, the Spinners, the O'Jays, and practically every other r&b band of note before touring with the Rolling Stones in 1975. Sadly, however, just when it seemed they were getting much deserved national recognition, the band broke up.

The Meters represent funk straight from the bubbling, spicy cauldron of New Orleans, one of the original musical towns. Typical of their creativity and ability to flow with any musical vibe, George relates the story behind "Look-A-Py-Py," a popular Meters jam that proves that funk comes from the strangest places. "We had a '67 Mercury station wagon—no I think it might have been '68—and we were on the road, and I think we were headed to Atlanta from maybe Philadelphia," he says. "And we had a few burned pistons in the wagon, and the wagon made that sound 'Pookacheeah, Pookacheeow,' that's the sound it was making.

"And, ah, I think it was we were waking up, seven, eight o'clock in the morning, and everybody's just starting to wake up in the wagon," he continues, "and I was driving and Leo and Zig were in the backseat of the thing, and Zig started beating on the seat, had a great bass-drum sound on the roof of the wagon. We was pulling a trailer on the back with our equipment in it, and yunno, they started singing 'Bow-chi-bow-chi-bow' next to the 'pookacheeah, pookacheeow,' and we just kept on saying that for 200 miles, yunno? And we were on our way to Atlanta to start recording the next album, and that's what happened. It's all syncopation."

In contrast to the Meters's more rootsy, improvisational funk, Hamilton, Ohio's Zapp focused on heavy repetition, bouncing basslines, and high-tech toys such as the vocoder (or electronic voice box), which hailed the dawn of the electro age, exemplified by such groups as the Dazz Band, the Gap Band, Cameo, and Slave. Zapp's hit "More Bounce to the Ounce," a lolloping bassline set off against a synthesized hand clap to create a hypnotic, thirteen-minute dance groove, perfectly set the tone for this new wave of funk. This big sound provided ripe fodder for rap when EPMD sampled it for their classic "You Gots ta Chill" in 1988.

"Catfish" Collins, brother of Bootsy and former JBs guitarist, discovered Roger and the Human Body, the band that would become Zapp, at a Cincinnati club called Never on a Sunday in 1978. It just so happened to be a Sunday. As Zapp captain Roger Troutman recalls, "I'm tellin' you, man, we performed and we pulled out every stop for Catfish that night, and after that I guess he went back and told Bootsy how good we were. And a couple days later, he [Bootsy] called me and asked if I wanted to come to Detroit and try putting together some tapes and tracks and get a record deal. Of course, I told him I wasn't interested, that I had a lot of other people asking me, like RCA—HELL YEAH!" he shouts. "I was just teasing right there. I said I'll be there in two seconds, man."

The multi-talented Troutman, a musician since the age of six, suddenly found himself in the old Motown studios of United Sound in Detroit, with Bootsy at his side, George Clinton next door, and Johnnie Taylor, the Dramatics, and the Temptations always passing through. Clinton was a particular influence on Troutman, who says, "One profound thing that caused our era was George Clinton, yunno? His avant-garde, his bizarre way of singing, the bizarre way of making records with the ridiculous hand claps, yunno?" He also credits funk's bad boy, Rick James, and the Isley Brothers's "Fight the Power" as prominent influences. Performing live, Troutman covered Barry White and the music of Philadelphia International. "So there I was with all this melting pot of music bubbling in me, and I was excited to make a record, so I don't really know how all my experience yielded 'More Bounce,' a song with no changes, a song with total, complete repetition, and yunno, and electronic voice box and a James Brown guitar track." Other hits, such as "Dance Floor" and "Doo Wa Ditty," came out of these sessions as well.

Through Bootsy, Troutman signed with Warner Brothers and when *ZAPP* was released in 1980, Roger and crew went from being a successful local band whose biggest gigs were an air force tour to a national powerhouse. Troutman credits black radio:

> Now you have to keep in mind, too, that another powerful, powerful entity that kept funk music alive and be what it was was black radio. 'Cause during this time black radio was very strong and very important and it did exist. Some of the black radio stations, some of the black deejays, were just as much stars as the entertainers during this time. 'Cause you can remember, there wasn't like white radio stations that played black, and there wasn't like contemporary urban stations back then. There were hardcore black radio stations where black people advertised, making these stations lucrative and powerful. And I don't know why to this day, but black radio embraced George Clinton, and black radio completely, totally endorsed me like a newborn child and just took my music and blasted it in every project, every hamlet, every black car, yunno, turned me into a household name. . . .
> So black radio helped to seal in the era of funk music.

And then, of course, there were concerts, for which people would often lay down serious money. "I remember being on different shows where every funk group that ever had a hit record, we would all be on one show," Troutman recalls. "And it would be packed and people would be happy. They loved us, and the whole audience would be black and the promoters would be black.

"I guess it was like funk turned out to be whatever the blues was when blues came out—something black people could say, This is ours. It ain't for white people. You can get into it if you want, white people, it doesn't put down white people in any way, it just kinda ignores them 'cause it's strictly for black people," he adds.

At the same time, however, there had always been funky white bands going back to the sixties and early seventies. From Rare Earth, whose cover of Smokey Robinson's "Get Ready" was a popular, early break beat, and the much sampled Steve Miller Band, to the Rolling Stones, Wild Cherry, and the Average White Band, these artists have reached across the barriers of color. Another band to successfully capture the funk was the Tom Tom Club, the alter ego of drummer Chris Frantz and bassist Tina Weymouth of the Talking Heads.

Fronted by the enigmatic David Byrne, the Heads were art school graduates (from the Rhode Island School of Design) who landed right in the thick of the burgeoning alternative music scene at CBGB's in the mid seventies. Though more oriented toward rock, along with contemporaries Patti Smith, Television, and punk's forefathers, the Ramones, the Heads's influences included James Brown, Sly Stone, and Al Green, whose "Take Me to the River" they covered. When Byrne and keyboardist Jerry Harrison decided to pursue solo projects after the release of the Heads's *Remain in Light*, Chris and Tina followed suit.

The Tom Tom Club's debut, recorded at Chris Blackwell's Compass Point Studios in the Bahamas in 1981, garnered unexpected acclaim on the strength of a novelty rap, "Wordy Rappinghood," and the supremely funky "Genius of Love." This slow, loping jam, which paid tribute to such black stars as Bootsy Collins, Hamilton Bohannon, Kurtis Blow, Bob Marley, Sly & Robbie, and of course, James Brown, was in heavy rotation on black radio.

Sitting in the New York offices of their management, the husband and wife team of Chris and Tina discuss the inspiration for "Genius of Love," which was produced by Steven Stanley. "So I had heard this song—it can be told now—called 'More Bounce to the Ounce' that had this great drum part, and pretty slow compared to what all the other tempos were then," says Chris, from behind a pair of demonic Oakley shades. "We weren't into stealing the whole song, but we thought, that's a good groove, we'll start with that. If you listen to both records, though, it's different, it ended up being different, but that song was the inspiration." To that basic rhythm, complete with the requisite hand claps, Adrian Belew added some guitar, and Stanley contributed subtle keyboards. The missing ingredient—some chicken-scratch rhythm guitar licks—was supplied by Bahamian Monte Brown, formerly of funksters the T-Connection. Chris calls this "the icing on the cake," adding, "Then Stevie did this amazing

**CHRIS FRANTZ
AND TINA WEYMOUTH
OF THE
TOM TOM CLUB
CAPTURED LIVE.**

dubwise mix with everything happening. It basically evolved over the period of a week."

A striking blonde-haired, blue-eyed Tina adds, "I think 'Genius of Love' really grew in stature, first by being covered by Grandmaster Flash," who released "It's Nasty," in 1981. Other versions of "Genius," such as "Genius Rap," were done by Profile rappers Dr. Jeckyll and Mr. Hyde, and more recently by X-Clan, who used it as the basis for "In the Ways of the Scales." On sampling, Tina says, "I think it's great when they take something old. I think some of the newest sampling is so freestyle, it's everything, it's what we love. They take it from rock, they take it from soul, they take it from Jamaican and African, they take it from everything. They say this is cool. It's really creative and they really are making something new out of it."

The Tom Tom Club completed the cipher when they brought P-Funk's Bernie Worrell, The Brides of Funkenstein's Lynn Mabry, the Brothers Johnson's Alex Weir, and versatile percussionist Steve Scales on the road with the Talking Heads, making 1983's memorable Stop Making Sense Tour a funky extravaganza. According to Chris and Tina, the additional members helped loosen up the band's live show, and Jerry Harrison, an Aerosmith junkie, never went back to rock.

Funk came from places as bizarre as the Meters's '68 station wagon and traveled worldwide, even to Africa with artists like Fela Ransom Kuti and Manu Dibango. Thanks in part to hip-hop and its counterpart "rare groove" scene in England, which spawned new funk bands like the Brand New Heavies, legends like the Meters, the Ohio Players, WAR, James Brown, and George Clinton and the P-Funk All Stars are getting mileage in 1993. Many are even stepping into the studio with rappers, including James, who recently recorded "Can't Get Any Harder," with rappers Leaders of the New School, and George Clinton, who has collaborated with a whole slew of rappers for his newest release, *Hey, Man, Smell My Finger* (Paisley Park, 1993). Roger Troutman, 41, who still tours with Zapp and notices younger and younger fans who are into "More Bounce," says:

The rappers, sampling, hip-hop, all of that, the whole rap aura, the whole rap scene right now, is doing something for black music that I've never seen happen before in the history of black music. And what they are doing is saying, "Hey, I'm a new star and I'm black." Number two, "Roger Troutman and George Clinton were out ten years ago, and they're great. And they're so great I want to sample their music. I'm proud of them." That's never happened before. They're like saying, Hey, Roger Troutman, you're great and I love what you're doing. . . . If it wasn't for the rappers and sampling, young black people would not be exposed to me and George Clinton, period. There would be no medium for young black people to hear us. Now when "More Bounce" was out and I was on tour, if I would talk to different guys I was on tour with backstage, if I would talk to them about blues or disco, or black stars ten years before us, they would say to me, "Hey man, that's old, that's what my mama listened to," indicating that they were not proud of their past. Well the rappers, yunno, they got respect for it and they're proud of it, and they're doing something about their pride, something positive. That's never happened in black music.

recommended
artists

1. James Brown
2. George Clinton/Parliament/Funkadelic/Bootsy Collins
3. Sly & the Family Stone
4. Curtis Mayfield
5. Kool & the Gang
6. WAR
7. The Meters
8. The Bar-Kays
9. ZAPP
10. Tom Tom Club

ChApTeR 4

Gettin' Paid

The name of the game is beat the lame,
Take a woman and make her live in
shame.

It makes no difference how much she
scream or holler,
'Cause dope is my heaven and my God
the almighty dollar.

I, the Hustler, swear by God
I would kill Pope Paul if pressed too
hard,

I would squash out Bobby and do
Jackie harm
And for one goddamn dollar would break
her arm.

I, the Hustler, kick ass morning, noon,
and night,
I would challenge Cassius and Liston
to a fight.

I would climb in the ring with nothing but
two P-38s
And send either one that moved through
the pearly gates.

I, the Hustler, can make Astaire dance and
Sinatra croon,
And I would make the Supreme Court eat
shit from a spoon.

"The Hustler"
The Life: The Lore and Folk Poetry of
the Black Hustler [1]

Toasting, a uniquely black performance art, represents folk poetry from the underbelly of society. A legacy of the African oral tradition, toasts like "The Hustler" exist independently of author or traceable origins. Most, however, are associated with prisons, where inmates have infinite time to compose, embellish, and pass on an endless compendium of tall tales, street reportage, hard-won wisdom, or boasts. These prison toasts, which tend to depict the criminal lifestyle of the hustler, are the parents of what is popularly known today as "gangsta" rap, which paints vivid scenarios of the violent, often misogynistic culture of the streets. "Gangsta, gangsta," as the world's best-known gangsta rappers N.W.A. proclaim in song, "It's not about a salary, it's all about reality." That reality reflects the day-to-day survival in the ghetto.

Survival demands alternative approaches to making a living. Bereft of opportunities enjoyed by society at large—i.e., jobs, decent schools—the ghetto plays host to a unique underworld culture, historically known as "the Sporting Life," or simply, "the Life." Far from sport, however, hustling—the pursuit of pimps, confidence men, drug dealers, and gangsters—is a means of earning that dollar, or "gettin' paid," by any means necessary. Where many compete for a small piece of the pie only the strongest will survive, and strength of character proves to be the hustler's greatest asset. Striking the figure of one who is cool, streetwise, confident, and resourceful, it is no wonder that he serves as a role model for youths in the ghetto.

The two most common types of hustlers appearing in toasts about "the Life" are the trickster, who lives by his wits, constantly scheming and manipulating others, and the "badman," who rules by force and intimidation. Both victimize others in their ultimate quest to get paid, but on the streets, looking out for self is a necessary rule of the game. While the trickster is as old as Anancy the Spider (of African folk fame), Bre'r Rabbit, and "the Signifying Monkey," a toast hero whose skillful wordplay outwits the mighty Lion, the badman is exemplified in the character of Stacker Lee (known alternately as "Stackalee," "Stackolee," "Stagolee," or "Stagger Lee"), best remembered in Mississippi John Hurt's "Stack O' Lee Blues." As folklorist Bruce Jackson writes, "Stackolee is about an irrational badman who engages in gratuitous violence and joyless sexuality, a man who fires his gun a lot but is almost totally nonverbal. He is the archetypal bully blindly striking out, articulating or discharging his rage on any passing object or person. His sheer strength and big pistol bring him fame."[2] Though more a ruthless outlaw than a hustler, Stacker Lee could well be described as the original gangsta.

The proliferation of such images has made hustling an acceptable, if not downright glamorous, option for making a living in the ghetto. After all, what impressionable kid growing up in such an environment can compare school and a minimum-wage job of flipping burgers against the immediate and grander payoffs of "slangin' rocks" on the corner or "pimping hoes"—and the inherent "juice" or respect that goes with it? Viewing the system as more of a hindrance than a help, many disadvantaged youth feel entirely justified in beating the system. Thus, making ends illegally, or outside the conventional paths, is hardly a dilemma. Rap, in itself, may also be considered a hustle, because whoever thought there would be so much money in rhyming into a microphone?

Rap's fascination with the criminal element is obviously rooted deep within ghetto culture. While outside observers complain that the music glorifies the negativity of the streets, rappers repeatedly claim that they simply are reporting what goes on where they live. Rap may, indeed, reinforce certain ugly stereotypes and celebrate pathological behavior, but can anyone really deny that drugs, prostitution, and violence are all a part of the inner-city experience? This controversy over rap illustrates America's dual nature. In a country where violent crime worsens with the passage of time, the U.S. Constitution and powerful conservative lobbies like the N.R.A. defend the right to bear arms. Also, movies like *The Terminator* that make millions at the box office portraying fictional violence are deemed acceptable, while rap songs based on real situations catch endless flack. At the very least both should be considered equally—as artistic endeavors that ultimately pander to our morbid curiosity for financial gain.

———

The image of the hustler first collided directly with the hip-hop generation in 1973 with the release of an album called *Hustlers Convention*. Recorded under the pseudonym Lightnin' Rod, Jalal Nuriddin, of the highly influential group The Last Poets, tells the tale of a hustler named Sport and his sidekick, Spoon, in 12 prison-style toasts. Combining oral poetry with the funk of Kool & the Gang and Brother Gene Dinwiddie, the album brings to life the infamous hustlers convention at Hamhock's hall in the summer of 1959. Here the two players win $172,000 at the gambling tables and have a few adventures before eventually clashing with the law. At the end Sport, after spending 12 years on death row, renounces his former ways. *Hustlers Convention* was an instant underground classic in the Bronx, inspiring the lyrical stylings of Kool Herc on down. To this day many old-school rappers such as Grandmaster Caz of Cold Crush can recite the entire album by heart.

The early seventies was also the era of "blaxploitation" films on the big screen. So named for their glorification of black criminals and portrayal of blacks as simply pimps, pushers, prostitutes, and gangsters, these rough, low-budget productions achieved cult status in the black community—largely because they were the only films strictly about blacks being made. Beginning with black director Melvin Van Peebles's seminal *Sweet Sweetback's Baadasssss Song* (1971), the cream of the blaxploitation genre includes *Shaft* (1971), *The Mack*, *Dolemite*, *Trouble Man*, *Superfly* (all 1972), and *Black Caesar* (1973). Only one of these films, *Shaft*, starring Richard Roundtree as a black private eye, features a noncriminal protagonist. The blaxploitation films are also known for their excellent soundtracks featuring the music of James Brown (*Black Caesar*), Isaac Hayes (*Shaft*), Curtis Mayfield (*Superfly*), Willie Hutch (*The Mack*), and Marvin Gaye (*Trouble Man*)—all of which have been ravaged for samples by rap producers.

With such prominent influences as these it is no wonder that early Bronx rappers fashioned themselves as modern-day bandits. The Furious Five's Melle Mel and the Cold Crush Brothers are largely acknowledged as the first to come out "hard" when everyone else was rapping about parties, females, or themselves. Though no one in the Bronx was making a living off of rap at the time, "gettin paid" was foremost in their minds, as chants of "make money, money, make money, money, money," became a standard call and response at shows. Ultimately it took Run-D.M.C. with their black leather, sweats, homburgs, and in-your-face attitude, to crystallize the image of toughness into rap chic.

Another factor contributing to the origins of gangsta rap was, of course, the gangs that ruled the streets of the Bronx. According to former Black Spade Afrika Bambaataa, "Mostly everybody in the Bronx in the early seventies belonged to gangs. There was more youth in gangs than was out of gangs. Every street you walked on belonged to some type of gang—black and white." While the South and southeast Bronx served as home turf to such outfits as the Black Spades, the Seven Immortals, the Turbans, and Savage Skulls, the north was the domain mostly of white gangs like the War Pigs, Bronx Aliens, and Ministers Bronx. Well acquainted with the lifestyle of the streets, many kids involved with gangs, such as Bambaataa, played vital roles in the development of hip-hop culture.

Gang activity started to decline around 1973, prompted in part by the growth of hip-hop. "There was a lot of young ladies who got tired of the gangbanging [gang life] and got down on men who wanted to be part of the gangs," says Bam. "Then you had organizations that was speaking to the gangs to try to calm them down, like the Nation of Islam and different youth groups they had on the police force. Then you had the police force cracking down on a lot of gang activity. They also had a group that came from the Vietnam veterans called the Purple Mothers, who was attacking a lot of street gangs and trying to destroy them theirself, 'cause it got so violent and it was, you know, at a big high in New York City." Crews like the Cassanovas, Cheeba crew, and the Nine crew picked up where the gangs left off, and while some of them dedicated themselves to rap, break dancing, and graffiti, others remained stick-up kids.

In light of Los Angeles's serious gang dilemma, people often forget that New York and other eastern cities were and still are plagued by gangs, and that the lifestyle of the streets was first reported about insightfully in rap songs. Boogie Down Productions was a pioneer of the gangsta rap genre with "9mm Goes Bang," a straight crime story from their first album. On the cover of *Criminal Minded*, in fact, DJ Scott La Rock and KRS-ONE set a precedent, posing proudly with guns, bullet belts, and grenades, reflecting the environment of urban warfare in which they lived.

Other rappers also successfully distilled the gangster attitude on wax. Once a member of north Philly's Parkside Killers gang, Schooly D. burst upon the scene in 1986 with a self-released album that featured graffiti style cover art by the rapper himself. At a time when crack ruled the streets, turning many inner-city teens into big-time businessmen on par with Black Caesar, Schooly D. rapped about the style (Filas, Gucci, gold chains) and hardened attitude that defined a new breed of hoodlum caught up in a mad quest for the material wealth of the eighties, as well as in a fight for survival against those who would challenge his drug turf.

Rap continued to reflect "the Life" on releases such as 1987's *Back to the Old School* (Sleeping Bag/Fresh) on which Just Ice calls himself the "original gangster of hip-hop," no idle boast considering that he appeared on an early episode of *America's Most Wanted* as a murder suspect in Washington, D.C. Though not overtly portraying gangsters, Queens DJ Eric Barrier and his MC, Rakim Allah (William Griffin), from Wyandanch, Long Island, came with rough lyrics and rugged beats on their 1987 debut, *Paid In Full* (4th & Broadway). While Rakim reflected on his former life as a stick-up kid on the title track, Eric B.'s homeboy from Queens, Kool G. Rap (Nathaniel Wilson), speaks unabashedly of homicide as if he had a license to kill. On *Road to the Riches* (Cold Chillin'/Warner, 1989), his debut LP with DJ Polo, and *Wanted: Dead or Alive* (Cold Chillin', 1990), the follow-up, he takes out more enemies than 007.

A true underground talent, G. Rap spins action scenarios better than the most compelling crime novelist. On his 1993 release, *Live and Let Die*, he takes on the Mafia, the police, and all other competition—leaving behind a trail of bodies—in songs that have cinematic clarity. Discussing the reality of his lyrics, a lisping G. Rap says, "Well, a lot of the things are based on personal experiences and shit. And, um, I'm not trying to say I lived all that shit out—I'd be dead or in jail. Nobody talkin' all that shit on they

KOOL G. RAP (right) AND HIS DEEJAY, POLO.

record, nobody did half of that shit they talkin' about, you know what I'm saying? You make shit like this 'cause that's what go on around you. I ain't doin' it, but I know people that kill mufuckas, you know what I'm sayin'?" While admitting that he hasn't personally lived all the experiences related in his raps, G. Rap agrees that gangsterism is far from fiction. Strange cases always surface, too, in which real life actually does imitate art.

Take, for instance, the story of Ricky Walters, an eccentric, London-born Bronxite better known to rap audiences as Slick Rick. Though he fit the part of a gangster—with his flamboyant dress and the $60,000 worth of gold chains he lugged around his neck—his 1988 debut, *The Great Adventures of Slick Rick* (Def Jam/CBS) sold 1.2 million copies, making

Rick a certified rap star. He evokes the image of pimp/gangster on such hits as "Treat Her Like a Prostitute" and "Children's Story," an eerie, bedtime tale about a hapless villain who gets caught by the cops. In the song he raps: "He raced up the block doing 83 / Crashed into a tree near university / Escaped alive though the car was battered / Rat-a-tat-tatted and all the cops scattered / Ran out of bullets and he still got static / Grabbed a pregnant lady and pulled out the automatic / . . . Sirens sounded and he seemed astounded / Before long the little boy got surrounded."

On July 3, 1990, two years after that song's release, Rick, accompanied by his girlfriend (who was six months pregnant), was driving a rented Dodge Shadow by the corner of East 241 Street and White Plains Road in the Bronx when he spotted his cousin Mark Plummer, who allegedly had threatened him days earlier. Choosing from an arsenal of guns stashed in the car—including two Tec-9s, two .25-caliber automatic pistols, one .38, and one shotgun—he fired six rounds from the .38 at his cousin and fled. Two police cars pursued him immediately as he weaved through traffic at 80 miles per hour. The chase ended when he slammed his car into a tree near Allerton Avenue, injuring both him and his girlfriend. Rick was tried, convicted of attempted murder, and sent upstate to the Woodburne Correctional Facility in South Fallsburg, New York. His girlfriend had the baby, as remembered on the track "It's a Boy" from *The Ruler's Back* (Def Jam/Sony, 1991), one of two albums written and recorded before his incarceration. In the spirit of the regretful hustler Sport, from *Hustlers Convention*, Rick's album also included the apologetic, "I Shouldn't Have Done It."

Still, Rick acted in such a manner simply because he was following the harsh code of the streets: Stand up for yourself or be victimized. His cousin, who allegedly had been extorting money from him, had also threatened Rick and his mother. Thus the rapper felt he had to act. As he revealed in an interview with *The Source* magazine, "They [the New York Police Department] told me to get a restraining order, but that wouldn't do nothing. If I had left it up to a restraining order, I would be dead

today."[3] Behind bars Rick has had plenty of time to reflect on the conse-
quences of his actions, and his experiences there will no doubt provide the
the fodder for future rap songs.

To Live and Die in L.A.

> TOPEKA, Kan., Feb. 27 (AP)—Often perceived as a pastoral land
> immune to urban ills, Kansas has a growing problem: street gangs.
> The Kansas Bureau of Investigation's most recent figures show
> 3,100 gang members around the state, most of them youths from
> 11 to 21 years old who are engaged in drug dealing, gun smug-
> gling, theft and even murder.
> The gang activity is not limited to cities like Kansas City, To-
> peka, and Wichita.
> "We're starting to see gangs in smaller communities," said Scott
> Teeselink, a special agent with the bureau. "They follow the path
> of least resistance: When the heat's on from police in bigger cities
> around the country, the gangs reach out to other communities. It's
> a sad situation."
>
> *New York Times*, February 28, 1993

Long known for the frequency and ferocity of its gang violence between
rival Crip and Blood "sets," Los Angeles, it seems, has started a trend.
USC gang expert Malcolm W. Klein reported that the number of cities
with known gang activity increased from 23 in 1961 to 187 today.
Compton, California rapper DJ Quik noted these recent events in song,
observing that Oakland, St. Louis, San Antonio, and Denver are all "Jus'
Lyke Compton" with respect to gangs. Ice Cube's "Summer Vacation"
also deals with exporting gang violence to smaller locales. With other
parts of the country picking up L.A.'s bad habits, and the plague of
violence spreading, these copycat Crips and Bloods hint at the larger
inequities and lack of opportunities that contribute to the lifestyle known
as "gangbanging."

Rappers take a lot of heat for glorifying this lifestyle, but for many, banging is as normal as a corner office on the eleventh floor and softball in the park on weekends. It all goes back to the City of Angels, which Ice-T, among the first street reporters, dubbed "home of the body bag." As the territorial stomping grounds of some 1,000 gangs claiming a membership of 150,000, according to a May 1992 report issued by the Los Angeles district attorney's office, L.A. is also naturally acknowledged as the gangsta rap capital.

Though the gangs of L.A. have a long history—with the Mexican gangs of East L.A. dating back to the twenties and the predominantly black gangs of South Central originating around the fifties—the situation has grown progressively worse in recent years. According to the same district attorney report, gang-related homicides in L.A. county alone increased more than 200 percent between 1984 and 1991. The Los Angeles County Sheriff's Department reported 800 gang-related deaths for their district in 1992, compared to 771 the previous year. The Justice Department's reaction has been to allocate a $500 million gang budget, mostly toward enforcement: No wonder the L.A. P.D. resembles a small army, complete with the Vietnam-style aerial support of helicopters. Behind this surge in gangs and crime lurks a mass-marketing nightmare known as crack.

The expensive white powder that was the fashionable high during the late seventies and the eighties first came to L.A. in its new form as early as 1979. Developed in South America and the Caribbean, where freebasing (smoking) a coca paste was preferred to snorting the powdered form, crack answered consumer demands for a cheap and easy form of free base. Made simply by cooking cocaine hydrochloride with warm water and baking soda and letting it harden, crack became the illegal drug trade's answer to McDonald's. The first reports of the "rock houses" from which dealers operated came from South Central's community paper, the *Los Angeles Sentinel*, in 1983. On November 25, 1984, the *Los Angeles Times* jumped on the story with an article entitled SOUTH CENTRAL COCAINE SALES EXPLODE INTO $25 "ROCKS." By 1986, crack was a household word and available in practically every major U.S. city.[4]

A TATTOOED
TONE-LŌC MAKES
NO BONES ABOUT
HIS GANG
INVOLVEMENT.

Though studies have never conclusively linked the crack trade with the escalation of gang violence, many gangbangers-cum-rappers, are of a different opinion. Tone-Lōc (Anthony Smith), who would never be mistaken for a gangsta from such popular hits as "Wild Thing" and "Funky Cold Medina" (which catapulted him to fame in 1990), shows off a tattooed bicep that bears the insignia of his Westside Tribe Crip set. From his comfortable home in West L.A., Lōc, 27, says, "It [gangbanging] wasn't as strong then as it is now," in a gravelly voice. "When we was doin' the shit, we just drink and fight, and whatever. It wasn't too much of no gun activity, you know what I'm saying? We ain't have the money for a high-powered rifle, plus the rocks and shit came out, they started slangin' [selling]. That's when these L.A. gangs really came up, like the mid eighties and shit, and that's when they started making all that money, and that's when the shit got out of control. 'Cause with the money they had power, and with the power they got a lot of respect.

"One thing about Los Angeles is the money that's out here," he continues. "There's so much money here, and people here, we exposed to a lot of shit at a young age, where I suppose somebody growing up in the South or somewhere, yunno, don't see that. They don't see the cars and the kind of badass houses that we have out here. These kids want that shit, you know what I'm saying? And they don't want to go to school for it. They don't want it that way, 'cause that's not how they's peoples is gettin' it, you know what I'm saying? So as long as you have the drug thing it [gangs] will never die."

"Sen Dog" Reyes, 25, of Cypress Hill, corroborates this opinion, saying, "That whole gang shit, like for me is different because I come from the days, yunno, when people would catch you and beat your ass real good. And there was guns and you heard about so-and-so getting shot—maybe not killed—yunno, but all of a sudden like, yunno, it's funny. It seems like when this whole crack thing came on, people really started getting smoked, yunno? That was like in '85, '86—crack shit hit big out in L.A. and a lot of niggas started getting smoked, yunno? And that's just part of the deterioration of the gangs, yunno, the drug element that comes in." His partner, B-Real (Louis Freeze), who banged with the 89th Street Family Bloods and once took a bullet in the back, adds, "The messed up thing about it is that there's no other way to make money for them, you know what I'm saying? They can't go try to get a job 'cause people are gonna look at them and say, 'Get the fuck outta here,' yunno?"

> Well I'm the dopeman, yeah boy, wear corduroy
> Money up to here but I'm unemployed
> You keep smoking that rock and my pockets get bigger,
> Yo, got that 5-0 double up nigger!

> "Dopeman"
> N.W.A.

Before 1988, Compton, a city of 90,454 in Los Angeles county, was just another lower income enclave of little significance to anyone besides, maybe, those who lived there. Maybe is the operative term, because the city's feuding gang sets showed no respect for human life there. Compounding existing territorial warfare, the crack trade fueled a frenzy of bloodletting on the streets. When the Pacific sun set on seemingly placid neighborhoods of single-family dwellings, drive-by shootings and automatic gunfire became the norm. The body count mounted, but no one seemed to care. It took a rap group known as N.W.A. (Niggers With Attitude) to put Compton on the map and bring this grim situation to the attention of the whole nation. With their release of *Straight Outta Compton* (Ruthless Records, 1988), an underground album that went on to sell over two million copies, N.W.A. established the genre known as gangsta rap.

Started in 1985, Ruthless Records was the brainchild of group-member Eric "Eazy-E" Wright, a very shrewd and tight-lipped businessman who released his solo album *Eazy-Duz-It* simultaneously with the N.W.A. debut. At the Woodland Hills offices of Ruthless, Eazy-E evokes the image of a latter-day Capone, sitting behind his huge desk, surrounded by black Lucite walls and facing a plush black couch, a big-screen Mitsubishi TV, and a deafening sound system. Engulfed in the modern gangster garb of an oversize Pendelton shirt, black jeans, a baseball cap, and Timberland boots, he peruses an article about himself in a fanzine, his loaded .25 resting beside him on the desk. "Dope Man," one of N.W.A.'s first two singles "was about me because that's what I was at the time," says Eazy, not even looking up from his reading. Long rumored to have started the company on drug profits, he will only say, "I don't know how Ruthless was formed. I think I probably did a little jackin' [stealing] for that money, I don't know. Or either I have a money tree in the backyard. We'll never know anyway. Nobody can go back and find out how this money was made." The volatile history of N.W.A. is a little easier to trace.

The West Coast rap scene started simmering around 1985–86, when basement studios were bumping with beats and you could cut a twelve-inch single for about $200. Taking a copy of the record over to the once mighty KDAY, the nation's only 24-hour rap station (before it changed formats in March 1991), and making some noise with it, often led to orders of up to 35,000–40,000 by the next day. Following this route, such popular jams as "Egypt, Egypt" by Egyptian Lover, "Rumors" by the Timex Social Club, "In the House" by the LA Dream Team, and "Juice" and "Surgery" by the World Class Wrecking Cru initially made their mark.

Jerry Heller, a longtime music industry player, keenly observed this new scene. Though traditionally rock had been his realm since he started managing groups in 1965, he was intrigued by rap's potential as a commercially viable art form. A business acquaintance, Alonso Williams, who managed the World Class Wrecking Cru (whose members included Dr. Dre and DJ Yella of N.W.A.) and the Stereo Crew (which featured Ice Cube), introduced Heller to Eazy-E, whom Heller works for today. In his office across from Eazy's, a white-haired Heller says, "So when I met Eric, I had a meeting with him over at Macola [Records], he played me "Boyz 'N' the Hood." I thought that was probably one of the most important songs that I had heard in rap in a long time, and I devoted my total attention to that from then on.

"In the beginning," he continues, "Eazy was the conceptualizer of Ruthless Records, so he would think of concepts. It was then my job to bring that into reality however that had to be done. So whatever deals that had to be made, he'd just tell me what he needed, and I would work out

ERIC "EAZY-E" WRIGHT READS THE PAPER AS HIS MANAGER, JERRY HELLER, DISCUSSES THE FINER POINTS OF THE MUSIC BUSINESS.

those kinds of deals for him. But before he met me, the original financing for all this stuff was his own personal."

One of Heller's first deals involved securing open time at Audio Achievements, a 24-track studio in Torrance, California, where N.W.A.

(and subsequently all other Ruthless acts) recorded all of its material. With everyone producing tracks at various home studios, the best demos were chosen by group members—including Eazy, Dr. Dre, DJ Yella, Ice Cube, and Arabian Prince—and allotted time at AA. After much experimentation, Dr. Dre (André Young) emerged as the musical muscle in the group, and he and DJ Yella produced the classic *Straight Outta Compton*, which took about six or seven weeks to do, according to Dre. "What we were doin' back then was just making records to make some fast money—to stay off the street, yunno," he says. "And we'd just go into the studio, and do shit we wanted to hear, and hopefully the homies would want to buy it. And shit just blew up, yunno. We wasn't trying to. We had no plans of none of the shit that happened, yunno, we just trying to make money."

Without the help of outside promotion, and relying strictly on a network of record pools, college stations, and clubs, this local favorite found a huge audience as far away as Houston, Dallas, New Orleans, Atlanta, and Miami. "We didn't do anything," says Heller. "And, yunno, it was just a great situation 'cause for once, the hip, music-loving part of the music business—the music part of the music business—suddenly had some kind of effect, rather than just the business part of the music business." They eventually inked a distribution deal with Brian Turner's Priority Records in L.A. and received orders in the hundreds of thousands—without the support of FM radio or MTV (due to the record's explicit lyrics). "So it was unbelievable," says Heller. "We were on a roll, yunno, what can I tell you? It was phenomenal to be involved with."

On the inner sleeve of the album, N.W.A. thanks "all the gangsters, dope dealers, criminals, thieves, vandals, villains, thugs, hoodlums, killers, hustlers, baseheads, hypes, winos, bums, arsonists, police, maniacs & badass kids for listening to our shit." Ironically, they also owe a lot of their popularity to a very different segment of the population. To have shipped as much product as they did, Heller notes, "obviously inner-city kids aren't buying the volume of rap records that sell. So when you're talking about those kinds of albums, Public Enemy, N.W.A., those have captured middle-class, white America, yunno, as far as the kids go." This phenomenon was corroborated firmly when N.W.A.'s June 1991 follow-up, *NIG-GAZ4LIFE*, debuted at number two on the *Billboard* pop chart with neither a single or a video. Under a new charting system called Soundscan, in which sales figures were compiled by computer using bar codes, the favored pool of retailers were department stores and suburban Sam Goody–type operations that carried only highly sellable product. The system did not incorporate sales at "alternative" urban outlets such as Tower and the numerous mom-and-pop shops in the ghetto. Rap had hit the suburbs with a vengeance.

N.W.A. also transcended the traditional regional biases persistent in rap—especially the snobbery of New York's hip-hop community, which rarely embraces rap from outside the area. Screaming from systems all through the east, this new, angry sound could only be described as turbulent, raw, jarring, and as black as tar. Some of the stuff that Eazy, Dre,

Yella, Ice Cube, and MC Ren say, in fact, makes Stagger Lee look like *Cheers's* Norm Peterson:

> Straight outta Compton, another crazy ass nigga
> More punks I smoke, yo, my rep gets bigger.
> I'm a bad muthafucka and you know this,
> But the pussy ass niggas won't show this.
> But I don't give a fuck I'ma make my snatch
> If not from the records then from jackin' a crowd
> Its like burglary, the definition is jackin'
> And when I'm legally armed it's called packin'
> Shoot a muthfucka in a minute
> I find a good piece of pussy and go up in it.
>
> "Straight Outta Compton"
> N.W.A.

At the time, Hollywood's treatment of gangs in the movie *Colors* paled in comparison—though subsequent black-made films, such as *Boyz N the Hood* and *Menace II Society*, have set the record straight. True pioneers of gangsta rap, N.W.A. provided an accurate and explicit status report straight from the streets of L.A. to your speakers.

Like any rock group worth its electric guitars, N.W.A. caused mass hysteria in most of the population over 30. As heartless, AK-47-wielding black males rallying under the cry of "fuck the police" (for which they were censured by the F.B.I.), they represented white America's worst nightmare—except, of course, for the rebellious youths who ate it up. The critics asked why there was so much negativity, violence, and profanity. For N.W.A., the answer was simple: This is our reality, unadulterated and without apology.

"I firmly believe that N.W.A. are audio documentarians," says Heller, deflecting notions that the group glorifies the gang lifestyle. "They tell a story that happens where they grew up, and is still happening where they grew up and live, that needs to be told. And they tell it in the first person, even though much of it is from a third-person perspective. It just happens to work better musically in the first person." Obviously well equipped to handle the standard criticisms, he adds, "When you say that they're chauvinists, all I can say to you is, well, if ghetto life is chauvinistic, then that's realism. It's not chauvinism, it's what happens there. That's a way of life and they're talking about it. They're telling you what it's like there. And all these people like Tipper Gore who are talking shit about this music, then these people should spend their time dealing with the problems of the inner cities—that's what they should be focusing on. Not the people who are telling everyone what it's like there."

Though Jerry Heller understands N.W.A. better than any other 50-something Jewish guy would, he is also at the center of a controversy that has torn the group apart. First, Ice Cube left, embarking on a highly successful solo career because he felt he wasn't receiving his fair share of record royalties. Then Dre dropped out for similar reasons, accusing Heller of manipulating his longtime "homie" Eazy-E against him. Heller dismisses both claims as being unsubstantiated and motivated by racism and anti-Semitism.

Dre, it seems, was involved in a little manipulation of his own, allegedly sending representatives wielding baseball bats to coerce Eazy into releasing him from his contract with Ruthless so he could start his own Death Row label. The matter gets quite complicated, with Eazy filing a $13.5 million racketeering suit against Dre and Sony Music, the label that released Dre's immensely successful first single, "Deep Cover," from the movie of the same name. Meanwhile, Interscope Records paid Ruthless a huge undisclosed sum (Heller produces three checks from Interscope made payable to Ruthless totaling almost one million dollars) for the rights to release Dre's debut album, *The Chronic*, which quickly sold double platinum. Although the individual members of N.W.A. are pursuing solo projects, and a serious rift has developed between Eazy and Dre, Heller thinks that the world has not seen the last of "the world's most dangerous group."

While N.W.A. will always be a name synonymous with gangsta rap, they were not the first or, by any means, the last to tell it like it is in their town. A former gangbanger and hustler himself, Ice-T first tapped his criminal experiences for "6 N the Morning" from his debut *Rhyme Pays* (Sire), released in 1987. After that he realized, "I can talk this crime stuff till the wheels fall off," and he has on four consecutive gold albums. But in the aftermath of N.W.A.'s success, the very mention of Compton suddenly held such powerful cachet in the music industry that major labels began signing any voice from the 'hood. Rappers like DJ Quik, whose first single was "Born and Raised in Compton," and Compton's Most Wanted proved themselves to have the talent and authenticity to outlast the imitators.

MC Eiht of CMW is quick to point out, in fact, that while "N.W.A. opened the door for gangsta rap, we don't like to say they paved the way and they are originators because they are not. Because it was a lot of brothers from Compton who were rapping about they 'hoods and other enemy sets before N.W.A., you know what I'm saying? They opened the door for major labels to experience gangsta rap, but they didn't originate gangsta rap. It goes way before that. It goes back to gangbanging, OG [original gangsta] homies sitting up writing about they 'hood going to shoot other enemy 'hoods. I made raps about my 'hood before N.W.A. came out, you know what I'm saying?"

While Quik, who was "down" with a Blood set called the True Top Pirus, is mistaken for a gangsta rapper simply due to his address, his music stays away from topics usually associated with the genre. CMW, on the other hand, are much underrated when it comes to speaking on the life of a "G" (gangsta), describing run-ins with the police (or "one-times"), jacking (a holdup), and drive-by killings with chilling realism. Eiht, who grew up in West Compton, and attended Domingus High, started banging with a Crip set when he was only 13. "I got involved because, yunno, you just grow up into it," he says. "You 12, 13, you growing up and you see the dudes hanging in the streets and they cordially invite you to hang on the corner with them and drink a 40, play some dice, or what have you, go

DJ MIKE T AND MC EIHT OF COMPTON'S MOST WANTED.

up to one of they little parties. Next thing you know, you down there with 'em all the time. And that's how I got took into it." Eiht describes this gradual process of "claiming a set," which provides the only support network in the ghetto, and requires killing to eventually prove that one is truly "down for the 'hood," in "The Hood Took Me Under": "Pop, pop, pop goes the sucker / If he's from another 'hood I got's ta shoot the Motherfucker / Geeeah, I'm in it to win it and can't quit / Fool, and ready to die for the shit."

Sen Dog and B-Real of Cypress Hill, however, feel that banging is not inevitable for youths growing up in a gang-infested neighborhood. Sen, who sought out the gangs and chose to be a part of it, says, "You don't have to grow up in that city and automatically be in a gang, yunno? There's plenty of kids that live on gang streets who are good athletes and students and all that shit, and the gang shit don't fade 'em. It's all about who's weak-minded and who's not." A strong parental influence is also a crucial factor.

According to B-Real, the gang makes up for a bad family life at home. "Sometimes a gang is more your family than a real family is, and that's what a lot of people don't understand. Why do you want to be in a gang? Well because my homeboy loves me more than my fuckin' mother or father does, you know what I'm saying? And that's that. When you're getting love from your homeboy more than you are your own family, there's something wrong there, yunno?" Though he admits to having a mother who cared, he adds, "I felt a certain security with my homeboys knowing, O.K., I'm here and they're watching my back, you know what I'm saying? Not that I didn't love my mother, it's just for some reason, that security that I had with my brothers right then." In an environment made up of the predator and the prey, one offers an easy target without the strength and support that a gang provides. "People don't realize that this is what we go through, yunno? This is what people go through. Not 'cause they want to, but because sometimes they have to or they need to."

Another thing that many people don't realize is the true nature of the gang conflict. "It's not over a word 'Crip,' 'Blood,' and it's not over a color," explains Eiht, who no longer bangs. "It's over territorial rights. It's over—

like say you were a kid and you hung with the boys from your block. And another set of boys come to your neighborhood and write all over the walls and put up they gang, and then they jump one of your friends. See that's how it all starts, it's over territory, and it's controlled 'cause the neighborhoods are controlled by dope and money and gangs. And nobody wants an outsider to come into they neighborhood taking over they spots, and they territory. That's why there are gangs." It is a case of the Biblical law of "an eye for an eye" gone out of control. Eiht adds, "Just like America has wars with other countries, it's like gangs, we have wars over territory, over territorial rights. If you stayed in your 'hood and we stayed in our 'hood there would be no killins. But if you come over to our 'hood and shoot up, we gonna come right back over there and shoot up."

Like any dispute worldwide—the Northern Ireland situation, Bosnia, Sri Lanka—the root cause of L.A.'s gang rivalry has long been obscured by the irrevocable debt of blood paid by both sides. Though the L.A. rebellion brought about some kind of consensus in the form of a truce (that remains effective in Watts, where it was started), deep-seeded

SPEAKING BLUNTLY: THE AUTHOR WITH B-REAL AND SEN DOG OF CYPRESS HILL.

grudges are often difficult to overcome. For Quik, whose music took him away from the perils of the streets, there are many dead homies to account for as well as a certain level of caution whenever he rolls through the danger zone. "Bloods and Crips ain't never truly be together," he says. "And I don't know why mufuckas thought that truce shit was gonna last. I was like, man, you mufuckas is crazy. Too many niggas done lost they lives. Too many niggas done lost a gang of people. . . . It's too much involved." Ice-T sums up these views in the soundtrack to *Colors* when he says, "The gangs in L.A. will never die. Just multiply." Thankfully, however, there is another side to the coin.

Once Upon a Time in the Projects

Coming from a New York frame of mind, everything seems so much more vibrant in L.A. Pastel green, pink, and blue storefronts, the requisite bronzed beauties with golden hair, luxuriant lawns and palm trees, and Mexican men hawking bags of inviting oranges and bananas at stoplights all contribute to the Lifesavers landscape. More suburban in feel with its low skyline, few pedestrians, and abundance of elbow room, one can seemingly drive for hours across the sprawling flatness.

Cruising south down Imperial Boulevard on an untypically overcast day, my photographer and I are headed toward Watts to get a firsthand look at the place where the gang truce is supposedly holding firm these many months after the L.A. rebellion. We are at a loss for what to expect—our only prior notions of Watts supplied by the popular seventies sit-com *Sanford and Son*. With its few stores, vacant lots, and graffiti-covered walls, the area obviously reeks of poverty, but it's mild in comparison to Brownsville, Brooklyn or the South Bronx. Taking a left onto Compton Avenue, we drive into a settlement of low-rise, concrete buildings—not in the best repair, but painted pastel blue to conform to L.A. style codes. These are the housing projects of Nickerson Gardens, stomping ground of a Blood set called the Bounty Hunters.

It's on in the projects from the day that you're born
Where the fact that you're black ain't a plus but a thorn
We, we're poverty-stricken so I started slangin' dope
I'm a criminal at large with a short horoscope
So don't fuck wit my bizness if you wanna keep yo' dome
'Cause I'll cut you into pieces and send the body home
Watt's life ain't a life it's a game
Where most brothers have numbers for a name
But the only life I know is the land that I roam
And with no place else to go we had to call it home.

"OFTB"
OFTB

Waiting for us in front of the projects' recreation complex—an otherwise grim structure animated by a huge mural that commemorates those killed in gang wars—are several members of the set as well as a bunch of curious, younger kids. The senior guys—Busstop, OMB, and Flipside—comprise a rap group called OFTB (Operation from the Bottom) who have just released their debut *Straight Up Watts* (1993) on New York's Big Beat label. Also present are Rick Rock, Smurfy B, and Speedy of Juvenile Committee, and Brian G. and Tone T.K.O., OFTB's producers. When it starts raining I ask them if it's O.K. to get my blue jacket, which I had left diplomatically in the rental car because of its color. Even though everyone wears some form of red, they assure me that it's alright. After all, the truce is on.

Orienting me to the surroundings, Busstop says, "Watts is the hardcore ass muthfuckas. Poverty city. Not a residential city, this is a poverty city. The difference between this and Compton, Compton is a residential district. This is poverty right here, homeboy. We ain't got no courthouse, no mayor, no city hall—we ain't got shit. We just out here. That's the difference from us and Compton." Boldly expressing the regional rivalries, he adds, "But yet Compton, you see these videos, other people, they see these mufuckas on these videos dressing like this, rapping, saying this and that, and they all fake-ass niggas. Set Compton up to be this gladiator dome or something. While Watts all the time, that's where they get their ideas."

Walking around the grounds, I almost feel like I've been transported to another time and place: The word "reservation" comes to mind immediately. The construction of Nickerson Gardens was begun in 1952 and finished in 1957, "and they still standin'," says Busstop. "Earthquake can't put a crack in the wall. It's still standin', solid ground. And the brothers just get harder by the years." In the vicinity is Hacienda Village (Bloods), separated from the Jordan Downs (Crips) and Imperial Courts (Crips) projects by train tracks.

I ask them why the truce started in Watts. OMB replies, "Well, before the rioting had jumped off, it was like, mufuckas was like starting to fade away from that shit 'cause a lot of niggas who was really deep off into it, they was in jail. Then a lot of other mufuckas who was on the street was about making money. So they was willing to talk to this man over here and this man over here, meeting and shit, before the Rodney King shit even jumped off. But it was still a little antimosity [sic] towards, man, what choo doin' bringin' that nigga over here, and now he from across the tracks. You go over there and it would be the same shit. And then when the riot kicked off, mufuckas was lootin' and shit together and getting along, so mufuckas just kept it going."

Of the local businesses, only a couple of hamburger stands are black-owned. The three liquor stores and one grocery store in the vicinity, all Korean-owned, were casualties of the riots. "Basically, it wan't nuthin' but a big ole party to me," says OMB, of those last days of April 1992. "Mufuckas was just stilin' [stealin'], drinkin', havin' parties everyday, just gettin' to know each other again." Busstop adds, "The authorities ain't got no control over what the brothers want to do. If the brothers want to move, we can move. Brothers is just chillin', you know what I'm sayin'. If anything's gonna happen, it's gonna happen. They can't stop nuthin' from happenin'. They can send all the police officers they want, but if it's gonna happen, it's gonna happen."

As the downpour continues we take refuge on someone's porch. I ask them why these newfound notions of unity have been so difficult to realize. Smurfy B, in his laconic drawl, answers, "Every different gang is trying to compete with this gang to be number one."

"It ain't about colors," Busstop chimes in. "That's just an ID that they gave us. Brothers is fighting over keeping they 'hood. You know what I'm saying, your territory, that's what all this shit is about."

"If a muthafucka do something to your brother or your homeboy, that you been growing up with forever, you gotta go back and handle that. So I mean, shit, that's how shit starts. If you kill him, then you gonna have his

A MURAL COMMEMORATING THE HISTORIC GANG TRUCE BETWEEN CRIPS AND BLOODS ADORNS A PROJECT WALL AT NICKERSON GARDENS IN WATTS.

OFTB, JUVENILE COMMITTEE, AND THEIR CREW AT THE NICKERSON GARDENS HOUSING PROJECTS IN WATTS.

homeboys mad. They gonna go back and kill one other nigga, and all his homeboys gonna be mad. But, I mean, it's kill or be killed when you see a muthafucka on sight," adds OMB, echoing the words of Eiht.

"We not livin' down here, we survivin'," continues Busstop. "It's not a way of life, it's survival. That's all it is, man. You gotta make sure that you and your loved ones is O.K. That's all it is."

The easiest way to survive down here is the drug game. "When a nigga sell drugs around here," explains OMB, "he ain't selling for no big thing, 'cause his family is starving, he's starving, so he gotta make some kind of move to get what he gotta get, and I mean dope is the most popular and quickest way he can get money. If you didn't have no way out, you would do the same muthafuckin' thing."

Almost on cue, a neighborhood dope dealer saunters by displaying a Ziploc bag full of rocks and a smirk on his face. Everyone laughs at the timely show-and-tell, treating the guy as if he were as normal a fixture as the Good Humor man. The dealer also flashes his weapon, but I don't see it. Everyone shouts, "Yo, show 'em what choo got, show 'em what choo got." Ten feet away, but still looking over at us, he whips out a nine-millimeter handgun and fires absently to his side. "BOOM!" My photographer and I instinctively flinch, while everybody else breaks out into laughter. I wonder where that bullet landed or if it struck someone. My escorts tell me that to start up in business selling *lleyo* (cocaine), all one needs is a $100 sack such as the one the dealer had. People will come from as far away as Las Vegas to buy it, they say.

As we trudge ten deep through a soggy field in the center of the projects, I can't help but feel slightly nervous in my blue jacket as I gaze around the complex. The bodies of dead groundhogs are scattered everywhere—target practice, I'm told. "But don't worry," says someone, because the Bounty Hunters get respect. As the subject turns to respect, Smurfy B says, "Some niggas might smoke big weed to be respected. Niggas come up to him and respect him—'let me hit that joint.' Some niggas might have a big gun to be respected. They gonna go up to him, 'Watch my back homeboy.' Some other niggas might be respected 'cause he can squab [fight] real good, and most niggas gonna be behind him, just so they don't fuck with him. And it's respect with the hoes, just like he said, respect with the hoes. He come around with fifteen hoes behind his back and niggas want to be with him 'cause he got hoes. Respect comes from all type of ways."

"You know what respect is? Power. Whenever you got respect, you got power. Power brings money," says Busstop. "It's survival, man, survival of the fittest."

Pimpology 101

In the parasitic world of hustling there are many ways to earn money and respect. If prostitution is considered the world's oldest profession, pimping, with all its glamour and prestige, is right there behind it. While robbing, stealing, and dope-dealing are the pursuit of the "badman," all the pimp has to do is look good, dress well, drive a fine car, and have the golden tongue of a trickster in order to manipulate women into his service. As Bruce Jackson writes, the pimp "makes his money by trickery: he tricks his whores; his whores 'turn tricks' and call their customers 'tricks.' Most of the customers and some of the whores are white. And all the money comes rolling into his pocket. At once he fills a sparkling range of roles or options: he turns away women Whitey comes uptown to buy; he slaps senseless any of his women who hold out for money; he is paid absolute respect by those women and has little to do in return except be himself; and in his family it is the women who have to feel guilty and inadequate if they don't bring home what he considers enough money."[5] It is no surprise that the pimp is a ghetto superhero providing inspiration to many rappers.

> Who's the mack? Is it some brother in a big hat
> Thinking he can get any bitch with a good rap?
>
> "Who's the Mack"
> Ice Cube

In the ghetto, where reputation among one's peers and the opposite sex is especially important, the pimp has elevated sexual gamesmanship to a high art. Not only can he attract women, but they are also pliable under his influence. In short, he is a champion in the battle of the sexes. While today's r&b might deal with some poor guy who's had his heart broken by the woman he loves, rap doesn't readily lend itself to such drippiness. Rappers favor the opposite approach, and the "bitch" and "hoe" lyrics that have caused endless controversy are the result of this macho posturing. Needless to say, rappers have grandmothers, mothers, sisters, girlfriends, and wives, too, and they do not universally consider every female a "bitch" or a "hoe." In a macho culture, the pimp simply represents every brokenhearted young man's revenge. Many rappers portray themselves as this colorful character as a means of getting respect. But for rapper Too Short (Todd Shaw), it's all in day's work:

And when hoes go to jail, pimps make bail
Take 'em to the stroll and let the pussy sell
'Cause to a trick they're just a quick nut
But to a grandmother, they're like big sluts
And if you're Short Dog they look like bank roll
If I ever go broke I just break hoes
'Cause hoes were made to be broken
It happens everyday in Oakland
I need a bitch, that's one thing I know
Put my money where my mouth is and break them hoes
To a foe, they like to run in pairs
Hit small towns and sell pussy everywhere
I ain't givin' no bitches no kinda slack
'Cause Oakland, California's, where they made the Mack.

"Hoes"
Too Short

Though it might disappoint a few fans to know, Todd Shaw says he's nothing like Too Short and has never "pimped a hoe." He has been dedicated to the rap game, however, since moving from L.A. to Oakland in 1980. As a sophomore at Freemont High School around this time, he first heard "Rapper's Delight," Spoonie Gee, and Kurtis Blow, which inspired him to start writing his own rhymes. "It was more of a bragging thing, saying what you did, really, extremely basic rhymes, you know what I mean?" says Short. "And it was just more or less mimicking what they were doing, and yunno, you rap about how live the party is or how you rock the mike, the basic subjects." By the time Grandmaster Flash's "The Message" came out in 1982, he had hooked up with partner Freddie B. and they started rapping more about reality. The city of Oakland inspired their rhymes.

Across the bay from San Francisco, Oakland is a tough, working-class town of 372,242, and most definitely a chocolate city. As well as being the birthplace of the Black Panthers, Oakland also served as the B-movie backdrop for *The Mack*, a popular blaxploitation film about pimps and hustlers released in 1973. *The Mack* provides an honest celluloid document about getting by in the streets, and its main character, Goldie (played by Max Julien), serves as a metaphor for the self-knowing, business-minded, risk-taking man who ends up on top. In one scene, where the Mack returns to the ghetto to disburse some cash rewards to all the good kids who are attending school, one boy says, "I want to be just like you, Goldie."

Obviously a lot of other people wanted to be like the Mack, too. "When I moved up here," says Short, "I noticed that a lot of people looked like pimps, yunno, they were dressing like pimps, acting like pimps, talking like pimps, wanting to be pimps. A lot of them were pimps, a lot of them weren't, but it was a pimp thing." Things have changed somewhat today. Short adds, "As a glamorous thing I don't think it's all that anymore—on the reality tip. But as a nostalgic type thing, yunno, to me the best music came from the seventies and yunno, just everything. That's when people did what they wanted to do, yunno?"

"I wouldn't say I was trying to keep it alive," he continues. "I would just say that the raps I do are street raps, and I don't know what anybody else is really thinking about, but when I do it, I more or less try to do street rap in street language, according to the street game, yunno what I mean? And a lot of things that you would apply when you're pimping, if you apply to other things then you'd get decent results."

Short's immensely successful career, in fact, almost parallels the story of *The Mack* himself. He rose from the streets on the strength of his product—Short's were CDs and cassettes. He started off doing routines with his partner, which he recorded on 30-minute tapes and sold for the price of a nickel bag (five dollars) at the local marijuana spots. "We weren't really trying to make ourselves famous," says Short. "We were just trying to make a little money—that's what it was all about, just a cool little hustle, yunno. And at different times I would like sell weed, but I never really took that on as a profession, like, here, I'm gonna be a drug dealer. But the tape thing was a hustle we could get into. And you didn't have to hustle everyday.

You could go out and just make $50 in one day and that would last a few days, and go out three, four days later and make $50 more, yunno."

These simple pause-button tapes, with such raunchy titles as "Fucking a Basehead Bitch," required neither explicit-lyrics stickering nor promotion, and spread quickly through the underground. Coupled with Short's performances at house parties and high school dances, he made a name for himself locally. His big break came in 1984, when a promoter asked him to open up for UTFO, who had a huge hit with "Roxanne Roxanne." Short recalls, "I did about three or four songs, and what tripped everybody out was, here I was standing there, I never had a record out, I never gave a concert, and here was 7,500 people singing with me word for word."

From there, Short hooked up with a big-time cocaine dealer, who set him up in a state-of-the-art studio, rented him a Cadillac, and gave him $2,000 cash for two more underground releases that came out in 1985 and 1986. Though they did very well locally, Short saw no other compensation or royalties. "One thing he did give me over those two years," he says. "Everything we did in selling records and making them, I was involved in all of that. I saw where he went to press records, I saw and I met the people where he went to master the records. Where he went to take them to the distributor, who was the distributor, you know what I mean? That's how I worked my business." He is referring to Dangerous Music, today a production company and studio which has helped develop other Bay-area talent such as Ant Banks, Pooh Man, and Spice 1. About seven months after starting this company with partner Randy Austin, Short was picked up by Jive Records, in February of 1988.

Speaking as Todd Shaw he calls Too Short "a marketing vehicle" as well as a character created by a writer. He writes about what he thinks his audience will enjoy and, sales wise, he is right on the money. "I look at the pen and paper," he explains, "and ask what's a Too Short subject? Getting my dick sucked in a Cadillac? Oh, I'll write about that." The freaky tales he spins on wax blend a street reality with his own experiences and, of course, a little bit of exaggeration. "In real life," he says, "I don't really come off as obnoxious as I do on tape but, I mean, if you figure at times in my life when I've not been committed to any one woman and I play the field, you gotta figure that every time I had sex with someone and never called 'em again, is that Too Short? I don't know, yunno. It's a fine line right? But when I got that sex I didn't say, 'Bitch gimme some head.' " But, as any good writer, he also knows his subject well and has spent plenty of time with pimps and prostitutes. Of these experiences he says, "It's cool, it's cool, it's very entertaining, yunno? If you hung out with pimps, you'd always be entertained." Despite the blatant chauvinism in his work, Short also enjoys tremendous popularity and respect as an entertainer—especially among the ladies.

Aside from Too Short and L.A.'s Above the Law, who deal with pimping on a literal level, there are also those who play the role—and quite convincingly. St. Louis rapper Sylk Smoov appropriated the cover design of the *Superfly* soundtrack (a popular blaxploitation film) to evoke the pimp/gigolo image. On the song "Klientele" he raps, " 'Cause I'm a pimp, in other words I keep the upper hand / And all the ladies be sweatin' me, even with they man / To make it simple see I got klientele / And the other brothers get it from the 'cane they sell." Respect for him comes from his reputation as a ladies' man, and his ability to handle women without being "played" by them. Mr. Scarface, a member of the notorious Geto Boys, takes it to the next logical step by bragging that his sexual prowess keeps the ladies under his control. On the XXX-rated song "The Pimp," from his solo album *Mr. Scarface*, he explicitly describes his methods of "sending bitches home with a limp / 'Cause I'm the muthafuckin' Pimp."

Big Daddy Kane, on the other hand, doesn't even call himself a pimp, but gives new meaning to the word. Always pictured on his album covers surrounded by scantily-clad females who are catering to him and loving it, Kane also has posed with Madonna and model Naomi Campbell in Madonna's book *Sex*. In "Pimping Ain't Easy," he knows the ladies know, "I'm tall dark and handsome and all that junk / Even white girls be sayin, 'oh Kane's a hunk' / Puerto Rican girls be callin' me Papi / Some try to copy, but they look sloppy." Kane's pimp persona is that of a smooth, suave, and debonair stud.

Ultimately, however, the one specific quality that pimps and rappers share is their way with words. Anyone can play the role—as long as they have the talk to back it up. As Positive K raps on the cut "Nightshift": "So let me work my manuever, there's none smoother, so yunno that I'm a soother / And ah, when I start to shoot the gift, the next day, I got you working on the night shift."

While most women justifiably take offense at being objectified, manipulated, or called a "bitch" or "hoe" in a rap song, Def Jam recording artist Boss (Lichelle Laws), a female gangsta rapper, explains, "I don't have no problem with it at all. Most bitches do act fucked up, and most bitches are hoes." As she points out, these labels apply to specific types of women and not all females in general. Of the artists spouting this bold and blatant chauvinism, she says, "They just doing what they want to do, just like I'm doing what I want to do, so I have no problems with that at all." While the male-dominated rap scene is undeniably sexist, it is simply a reflection of the culture of the streets. The entrance of more strong female figures such as Boss is bound to have a more balanced effect on peoples' perceptions of the art form.

As a result of rap's influence on the youth, controversial elements such as violence, cursing, and sexism receive the most attention. But Boss says, "Whoever said that rappers have to always teach people something or set an example, you know what I'm saying? It's entertainment. You don't hear people telling Luther Vandross to sing about AIDS or some shit like that, you know what I'm saying? They need to go figure out AIDS, some cure for that shit, instead of trying to figure out why rappers curse, yunno? They be worrying about the wrong shit. To me it's entertainment." After all, comedians—especially black comics such as Redd Foxx, Richard Pryor, and Eddie Murphy—have gotten away with a lot of gutter humor that has been popular among white as well as black audiences. When rappers have aspired to this same degree of rawness suddenly the same people are not laughing anymore. This inconsistency no doubt hinges on a generational gap, as well as the fact that society still has problems with black youth communicating with each other. Whether rappers remain grounded in reality or stray into fiction, their art is simply a mode of expression and just another means of gettin' paid the old-fashioned way—by the wits.

recommended
listening

1. Lightnin' Rod, *Hustlers Convention* (Douglas, 1973).
2. Boogie Down Productions, *Criminal Minded* (B-Boy, 1987).
3. Schooly D, *Saturday Night* (Schooly D. Records, 1986).
4. Kool G. Rap & DJ Polo, *Live and Let Die* (Warner/Cold Chillin', 1992).
5. N.W.A., *Straight Outta Compton* (Ruthless, 1988).
6. Cypress Hill, *Cypress Hill* (Ruffhouse/Columbia, 1991).
7. Compton's Most Wanted, *Straight Checkn' 'Em* (Epic, 1991).
8. Ice-T, *Original Gangster* (Sire/Warner Brothers, 1991).
9. Too Short, *Shorty the Pimp* (Jive/RCA, 1992).
10. Above the Law, *Livin' Like Hustlers* (Ruthless/Epic, 1990).
11. Boss, *Born Gangsterz* (DJ West, 1993).

ChApTeR 5

The Final Call

Rebirth
of a Nation

This is what we're saying:
If the Black Man must
create, create a new music
brother. No more blues—
Black Man don't SING
BLUES NO MORE!! Listen to
what we're saying: No!
Black Man don't play jazz
no more. Not jazz—not
that stuff that comes from
our slave day. If you are a
free man, then speak to
the free idiom. Make your
poetry that speaks to the
new. Make your art and
drama that of the new.
Then you are creating a
new thing that the world
must come up to. Then
you're the original man
again.

The Honorable Louis Farrakhan,
from a speech in Brooklyn, New York
January 1971

I don't claim to be a preacher
Not paid to be a teacher
But I'm grown
I try to be a leader to the bone . . .
Then I sing a song
About what the Hell is goin' wrong
You never know
If you only trust the TV and the radio
These days
you can't see who's in cahoots
'Cause now the KKK
wears three-piece suits.

"Rebirth"
Public Enemy

Behind the glorious multiculturalism, the noble democracy, and the comfortable standard of living that America projects to the world there hides a shadow nation. As gruesome as Germany's concentration camps during World War II, places like the South Bronx, Bedford Stuyvesant, Brownsville, Compton, Watts, Cabrini Green, East St. Louis, East Oakland, and Liberty City represent factories of destruction and discontent throughout the country. Here the poor, predominantly black masses grapple with the same problems they have faced since being brought to "the land of the free" some 438 years ago. Though it might have taken a civil war and a presidential decree to physically free the captives from their shackles and chains, freedom is a relative term considering the mental and spiritual slavery enforced by welfare, drugs, and a substandard educational system, all of which maintain the cycle of poverty. From Bensonhurst to Simi Valley, we are also constantly reminded of racism.

Progress, it seems, is also a relative term. During the sixties the civil rights movement sought to bring an alienated people into the fold of mainstream society, working through the system to secure such important legislation as the Civil Rights Act of 1964, the Voting Rights Act of 1965, and the Fair Housing Act of 1968. Even before such corrective efforts, the Supreme Court had ruled that separate-but-equal school systems for black and white were unconstitutional in the landmark *Brown* v. *Board of Education* case of 1954. Integration and such equalizers as affirmative action became the hallmarks of governmental policy aimed at redressing the damages of the past. However simple these solutions, they did at least set the wheels of change in motion.

Unfortunately, any advances made during this era slowly unraveled during the Republican eighties, when the new official policy became one of neglect. In contrast to President Lyndon Johnson's War on Poverty, for instance, the focus shifted to a largely ineffectual War on Drugs, which diverted more funds to law enforcement as precious social programs fell by the wayside. As a direct result of the government's apathy, America's urban crisis grows more dismal by the days. Today, while the inner-city public school system stands in shambles, there are more black males in prison than in college, and violence and poverty are pushing an all time high in black communities—not to mention the double whammy of crack and AIDS. These conditions are best summed up by rappers WC & the MAAD Circle, who observe, "Ain't a Damn Thing Changed."

With very little to grasp onto from the civil rights movement besides Martin Luther King, Jr.'s, fleeting dream, a new brand of black activism is building in the nineties, its voice manifest in rap music. Galvanized by the radical politics of the sixties—the Black Power movement, the Black Panthers, and Malcolm X—as well as the musical lead of performers such as James Brown ("Say It Loud, I'm Black and I'm Proud"), rappers are realizing their potential as leaders and communicators within their communities. But as troubled times call for tough tactics, their rhetoric usually reflects rage, vented against a system that has kept blacks and other minorities down. While this militant approach might be the cause of much hysteria in white America, for a people with their back against the wall it is a last, desperate solution.

Revolution might be a scary word to some, but America, herself, was born out of a revolution, which brought about change and created the foundation for a new society. In this respect, rap, too, is a revolution. Through its continuous dialogue, African Americans come to terms with their true identity, teach and build, and take their destiny into their own hands. Rap represents a renaissance of black culture—the rebirth of a nation.

"The Day the Niggas Took Over"

The last three days of April 1992 mark a watershed event in American history that will be discussed and debated from this time on. Alternately described as "the L.A. riots" by the media, and "the rebellion" by those involved and their sympathizers, this momentary plunge into anarchy has already been immortalized in rap, through the songs of such West Coast rappers as Dr. Dre, Kam, Da Lench Mob, and Ice Cube. The rebellion amounts to the beginning of a civil war that should not be defined simply in terms of black versus white. Mexicans played a prominent role in the orgy of burning and looting, while armed Korean store owners seized their constitutional right to defend their business with bullets. In the spirit of classic revolution, this was a clash between the haves and the have-nots. For many rappers, such as PE, who had said (in 1989) "Burn, Hollywood, burn I smell a riot goin' on / first they're guilty now they're gone," it was a prophecy fulfilled.

A spontaneous, mass uprising of people triggered by what they perceived as injustice, the rebellion may also be seen as a human rights protest and an exercise of street justice. Despite the fact that many capitalized on the opportunity to help themselves to materials and goods they did not have the money to buy, the verdict in the Rodney King trial provided the impetus to hit the streets and openly vent rage. No one who has repeatedly seen the video of Rodney King's beating at the hands of L.A.'s finest can deny that there is something very wrong with the whole picture: four armed men in uniforms against a single unarmed man on the ground. Fifty-six blows in 82 seconds. Not guilty. This decision followed another incident in which a Korean grocery-store owner got probation for shooting a black girl, LaTasha Harlins, in the back of the head after she allegedly stole a carton of orange juice. In all segments of the black community, these events suggested and confirmed that black life did not have too much value in America. All those angry, young black voices were suddenly vindicated.

> Just one more punk attack
> On a black and now the shit is on
>
> "Watts Riots"
> Kam

Raised in Compton and currently residing in Watts, Kam had not even been born in 1965, when the Watts Riots erupted, but these lines, written in April 1989, served as a chilling harbinger of the L.A. rebellion. Distilling the feelings of so many in his community, he explains, "We not living no American Dream, you know what I'm saying? We in a nightmare. Like I said, this is hell for us. Anything else would be an improvement, you know what I'm saying, we can't get no lower, we can't get no farther back. We at the bottom of the barrel, or whatever you want to call it, so we ain't have nothing to lose. We ready to die, we really ready to kill, and so we do whatever it takes to get justice."

While recording an album for an independent label in 1989, Kam met Ice Cube, who was in the next studio mixing his solo debut *AmeriKKKa's Most Wanted* (Priority, 1990) after leaving N.W.A. They became friends, and Kam eventually signed with Street Knowledge Productions, Cube's label and management company. Kam's album, *Neva Again* (East-West/ Atlantic) was released in April 1993, one year after the rebellion. Of this title, he says, "The generation that we living in right now, it's a fact that we living in the last days. . . . All the shit that the people took in the sixties, all of the injustices, the atrocities, the oppression, the brutality—we ain't taking it, we ain't born for that. We born to bring justice—I'm talking about this generation, the ones they claim cannot be rehabilitated, the permanent underclass—that's our soldiers. Those are the ones who are going to bring justice to the planet.

"Never again will we be silent either," adds the boyish 22-year-old who speaks with such authority. "Rap is supposed to be a tool of true media. We don't speak the best English, but we tellin' the truth and we speakin' from our heart." While network news choppers circled above burning South Central, observing the "rioters" scurrying around below like ants and speculating on what was happening, many rappers were at ground zero. Kam provides a crucial perspective on the rebellion in his song "Peace Treaty":

> Lookin' at the aftermath of the riot
> I could still smell ashes from all the clashes
> But quiet as kept, it wasn't just the blacks
> Everybody lootin' and had each other's backs

> We came to an understandin' demandin' justice, bust this,
> We all had a hand in the cookie jar and took it far enough to
> make a statement: Daryl Gates,
> That's where all the hate went.

The song commemorates the historic gang truce forged between Crips
and Bloods from Watts, who first hung up their colors to mobilize against
a common enemy, the Los Angeles Police Department, epitomized by
now former commissioner Daryl Gates.

Though Kam describes those first few days of the truce as a "party,"
he adds,

> Once the novelty wears out, it's time to go to work, you know what
> I'm saying? It's time to do for self. And we already put the weapons
> down against each other, it's time to do something constructive, yunno,
> it's time to establish a future for ourselves. 'Cause the gangs did it on
> their own, no Jesse Jacksons came here. It was a strong Nation of Islam
> influence, you know what I'm saying. So I guess it finally sunk in. They
> was ready for change, ready to stop killing each other, and all you saw
> was hugging and crying, so it was real, it was genuine. Definitely the
> most historic event in the history of black America, you know what I'm
> saying? And it got no coverage. That's why we did "Peace Treaty."

The rebellion also figures prominently on Da Lench Mob's *Guerrillas in
Tha Mist* (East-West/Atlantic, 1992), a title that plays off a movie starring
Sigourney Weaver. The Mob's radical stance is reinforced in such titles as
"Buck Tha Devil," "Lost in the System," and "Freedom Got an A.K."
Lench Mob members T-Bone, J-Dee, and Shorty recall religiously watch-
ing the first trial for the four police officers accused of beating Rodney
King, which was broadcast in L.A. every morning starting at 9:00 A.M.
"One of them pigs that was on trial in the Rodney King case," says a bald-
headed Shorty, "I think it was Officer Powell, he said beating Rodney

King was better than the prior call they had responded to, which was a family disturbance. And he said the family was so buck wild it was something like *Gorillas in the Mist*."

Their play on words—transforming "gorillas" to "guerrillas"—also extends to the name of the group. Appropriating "lynch mob," the term for vigilante groups in the South who hung blacks accused of any wrongdoing, J-Dee says, "We takin' they bitch asses, the oppressor, the system, and we hangin' them upside down. When we do our music, we gonna let other motherfuckers know, other brothers and sisters know, that hey, the best way to beat this mufucka is to break him financially." The "mob," according to T-Bone, means, "Gettin' all our homies together, gettin' 'em

J-DEE, SHORTY, AND T-BONE OF DA LENCH MOB.

out of the negativity and gettin' them into something positive. Like coming out on the road, seein' places, learning to work the drum, and experience a lot of different things, you know, so they can say 'I'd rather do this shit than sell dope.' "

Ice Cube, who gave both Kam and Da Lench Mob the chance to escape the streets and pursue music, is the pulse behind Street Knowledge, a thriving black business located in South Central. Known for point-blank rhymes about life in the 'hood, as well as for movie roles in *Boyz N the Hood* and *Trespass* in which he has played characters close to his street persona, Cube has evolved from a hard-core gangster to a prophet of rage. Speaking strictly in the idiom of the street, however, his message is often regarded as racist. In the song "Black Korea," from 1991's platinum-selling *Death Certificate* (Priority), for example, he voices black frustration at not owning any community businesses. In a bizarre foreshadowing of events to come, he tells the Korean merchants so prevalent in the ghetto, "We'll burn your store right down to a crisp."

At a press conference following the release of *Death Certificate*, Cube also advocated a book published by the Nation of Islam called *The Secret Relationship Between Blacks and Jews, Vol. 1*, which blames the whole slave trade on European Jews who allegedly financed it, among other claims. When confronted with charges of racism and anti-Semitism, Cube, interviewed on the "Rebel Voices" radio show, spouts the party line: "I ain't got time for this bullshit, know what I'm saying. I ain't got time to be fuckin' anti-Semitic, anti-this, anti-that, anti-Korean. I ain't got time for that shit. I'm too busy bein' pro-black, you know what I'm saying?" Obviously a thick line exists between the media's interpretation of his music and ideology and his own perceptions of it.

Not one to avoid controversy and criticism, however, Cube comes out harder than ever on 1993's *The Predator*. In addition to paying homage to the riots ("We Had to Tear This Motherfucker Up") he details the media's assault on him ("When Will They Shoot?") and tells of police harassment ("Who Got the Camera"). He directly addresses charges that he is racist, sexist, and an instigator of violence in a series of inserts between songs.

Borrowing PE's technique of using actual media snippets over a beat, Cube seems to revel in the criticism, and in one case, answers a reporter's questions with "Fuck 'Em," showing that he really doesn't care how the press perceives him as long as he is able to reach his community.

ICE CUBE
SIZES UP THE
APOLLO'S AUDIENCE
BETWEEN SONGS.

In an opportunity to speak his mind directly to the white community, Cube, on the "Rebel Voices" radio show, says:

We've cried out, we've marched, we've picketed, we've protest, we've wrote letters, we've voted. We've wanted to do nothing but fit into a culture that, ah, forced itself on us. We didn't want nothin' but to fit into a society that was forced on us, a religion that was forced on us, and we said, O.K., even though you've stripped us of everything that we've known, and you givin' us your way of living, your civilization, you know what I'm saying, we adapted all that and you still diss us, you still don't give a fuck about us, you still lie to us, and all that. And my philosophy is, we through talkin', we through doin' all a the above, yunno? It's definitely on. And if you think that just because three days after April 29th [1992] shit was calm and cool—not for a minute. We still got shit on our mind. We know that the power is not with singin' but with swingin, you know what I'm saying? And we sick of it, man, we tired. We damn near at the point of no return.

Prophets of Rage

If rap reveals the struggles within the black community today, addressing problems in the frankest possible manner, rappers are simply this genera-tion's equivalent of The Last Poets, an incendiary group of philosophers who emerged from the turbulence of 1968. The Poets were more than just socially conscious bards grooving on the vibes of the sixties and giving the finger to the establishment while promoting peace and love. Their mis-sion, in fact, was quite the opposite. With compositions such as "Die, Nigga," "Niggas are Scared of Revolution," and "When the Revolution Comes," they spoke directly to the black man—grasping him by the shoulders, shaking him up, and spraying spit into his face with frothy declarations of militancy and self-accountability. Accompanied by African drums, jazz, or sometimes simple, repetitive chants, the Poets elevated art to a state of warfare, and with such finesse:

When the moment hatches in time's womb, there will be no more art talk. The only sound you will hear will be the sound of the spear pivoted in the punctured marrow of the bone of the villain, and the native son dancing like crazy to the retrieved rhythms of memory fading into desire.

"This poem had such a deep impact on me," says David Nelson, an original member of The Last Poets, reciting the words from "The Birth of Memory" by South African poet K. William Kokafili. "What it said to me was that the art will be in the warfare and the warfare will be in the art. And so I wrote a poem called 'The Last Poets,' and in that poem I said, 'We are a new breed of men—black warriors, the last poets of the world—and we will re-create this world in honor of our fathers, whose unwept tears, even now, well up inside us turning into spear points,' and I went on from there. So basically, we could take our anguish and suffering and put it into our words and our art, and by doing so it would become our warfare." Influenced by Martin Luther King, Jr. (though they did not really acknowledge him at the time), and Malcolm X, their central hero, Nelson describes the Poets as a "nonviolent liberation army" whose weapons were words and ideas.

Nelson met Harlem actor and poet Gylan Kain at a poetry reading only two weeks prior to Malcolm X's birthday celebration of May 19, 1968. After the two were invited to read for this occasion, Kain tossed around the idea of starting a group based on poetry. "Another influence was Amiri Baraka [formerly Leroi Jones] because Baraka was performing with a group called the Spirithouse Movers," says Nelson, from his home in North Carolina. "I had heard Baraka say at one of his performances, we need groups of poets who are as proficient and as profound at what they do as the Temptations are in what they do."

On a sunny May 19, in Harlem's Mount Morris Park (also known as Marcus Garvey Park) on 120th St. and Fifth Avenue, Kain and Nelson were joined by Nelson's friend Chuck Davis (Abiodun Oyewole), who also had been moved to write some poetry for the occasion. "And I had an idea," says Nelson, "I gave him a chant that I had heard in a video of the student takeovers at Howard University. 'Are you ready nigger, you got to be ready. Are you ready nigger, you got to be ready.' I said, 'Hey, let's take this chant, I've got a poem called 'Are You Ready,' we'll go up singing this chant—the three of us—and I'll jump into my poem, and then you jump in spontaneously with something that's a response to what I'm doing, and we'll just flow on through." Nelson also enlisted the aid of a drummer and horn players to provide some musical accompaniment.

"O.K., so we go up on stage," he continues. "The musicians go up and set up, and we start chanting. Then I did my poem, and, you know, they did a little ad-lib 'are you ready, are you ready,' and then the next person jumped in, did their poem, then the next person, and we just did a rondo, with each of us just kinda throwing in little statements completely unrehearsed. When it was over there was an artist, a folksinger sitting out in the audience, and he said, 'Shew! Man, that was great.

ABIODUN AND UMAR BIN HASSAN OF THE LAST POETS PERFORM AT THE NUYORICAN POETS CAFE IN NEW YORK'S EAST VILLAGE.

You guys really did it. How long you been working on it?' I said, 'Nah, bro, it just happened spontaneously.' "

Soon after performing their next gig, at New York University, they took on the name inspired by Nelson's composition and started a workshop/cultural center on 125th St. called the East Wind. Felipe Luciano, a former member of the activist street gang the Young Lords, participated here before joining the group. Next came Jalal Nuriddin (a.k.a. Alafia Pudim), whose own influential *Hustlers Convention* was yet to come, and then Umar Bin Hassan, who followed the group back from a performance in Ohio (the same performance that supposedly inspired Gil Scott-Heron on to a long and prolific career in jazz poetry). The last member to join was Suliaman El-Hadi. Though liberation and unity were their ultimate goals, seven individual minds attempting to fuse a collective black consciousness were destined to clash, and an ideological rift split the Poets into two separate entities—both of whom performed under the same name.

"What had happened is, some dissension had arose—and that's one of the significant things to be learned from The Last Poets, and I hope The Last Poets themselves in their maturity can learn it," explains Nelson. "Black men are affected by this society into having difficulty putting together the unity that would allow them to be totally successful. And so we ran into some snags and ended up split into two camps, into two groups, and each group recorded." With Abiodun in jail, Nelson, Kain, and Luciano formed one group, releasing *Right On* (Juggernaut Records), also the title of a 1969 documentary on the Poets. Nuriddin, Bin Hassan, and El-Hadi (later joined by Abiodun), meanwhile, released a well-received self-titled album on Douglas Records in 1969.

With such titles as "Run, Nigger," "Niggers Are Scared of Revolution," and "Wake Up, Niggers," this latter album predates rap's casual use of a once derogatory term. Though sometimes used affectionately within the black community, Nelson explains, "Most of us who were thinking about it finally came to the conclusion that we didn't need the term 'nigger,' so there was a strong effort to eliminate the term." Influenced by Kain's "Niggers Are Very Untogether People," Nelson penned the classic

"Die, Nigger," which appeared on the *Right On* LP. This song, incidentally, figures prominently in the title of H. Rap Brown's pro-black text, *Die, Nigger, Die*.

"So 'Die, Nigger' was the cap. Ain't much can be said about the nigger after 'Die, Nigger.' The nigger needs to die so that black folks can take over," he says paraphrasing that composition's well-known punchline. Much to his ire, however, N.W.A. sampled several lines of this poem for the title track to the platinum-selling *NIGGAZ4LIFE*. Nelson, who did not appreciate N.W.A.'s gratuitous use of the word "nigger" or their message, wrote his own response to the group, which begins: "It's about nigger and Niger, the difference between a mule and a tiger / It's about Niger and nigger and the difference is getting bigger / 'Cause the mule works hard in the heat of the day, foolishly giving his work away / The tiger waits in the cool of the night, waiting for his prey to come into sight."

The militant side of the Poets saw light in such compositions as "When the Revolution Comes" (*The Last Poets*, Douglas, 1969), in hindsight also a harbinger of L.A., which says: "When the revolution comes / Some of us will probably catch it on TV / With chicken hanging from our mouths / You'll know it's revolution / Because there won't be any commercials." Though the Poets's apocalyptic visions of change were not realized fully, Nelson says, "I believe we did see a revolution, and it was essentially— even though people would argue against it—a cultural revolution, and it produced hip-hop."

Despite the commercial nature of the art form and the fact that "there's a lot of people in the music industry now who are two-dollar whores" simply out for the money, Nelson credits hip-hop with a "media hijacking" that was first successfully pulled off by the Poets themselves. He also admits to feeling like a "proud papa" after hearing Public Enemy's mouthpiece, Chuck D., speak at the University of North Carolina. "Once you talk about hip-hop and Public Enemy," says Nelson, "it's going beyond hip-hop. I mean Public Enemy is a part of black liberation much more so. I really appreciated the idea that that was Chuck D.'s own phraseology—'media hijacking'—that he wasn't even interested in being a performer. I think that's one of the most significant developments: That thinking young black men, and some black women now, but particularly the black men who needed it so badly, have been able, because of this incursion into the media, to launch an assault on business. And I think it'll have some fallout."

Culturally, the Poets represent the crucial connection to an African past. "And we were very much aware of the need to make that connection," says Nelson. "You see, we were built upon those who had gone before us very strongly. We were very much aware of the Garvey movement, the Africa movement. We were very much aware in terms of what was going on with the Nation [of Islam] and Malcolm. We were very much aware of African history and the history of our people and the music—we consciously integrated black music into our performance." In much the same manner, through groups like A Tribe Called Quest or Digable Planets, who have sampled the Poets's music, or rap militants like PE and Paris, who have carried on the revolutionary rhetoric, the Poets have left an indelible impression on hip-hop culture.

Communication and awareness link The Last Poets with today's rap activists. "We went into this thing to hijack the media so we can communicate to our people," Nelson says. "We came to a door that was closed, and we put our shoulder to the door and it flew open. And a lot of people have come in."

Too Black, Too Strong

On location in Brooklyn for the filming of the "Fight the Power" video, Chuck D., sporting his usual jeans, sweats, and baseball cap, is swarmed by crowds carrying various banners. Some bear the images of noteworthy blacks such as Harriet Tubman, Nat Turner, and Malcolm X, while others are emblazoned with state names—apparently an allusion to 1963's civil rights March on Washington. Though clips of this famed nonviolent march are used to introduce the video, Chuck shatters any comparison when he shouts into a megaphone: "We ain't goin' out like that '63 nonsense." Director Spike Lee's camera pans across a field of black fists pumping in the air, as the song kicks in:

> As the rhythm designed to bounce
> What counts is that the rhymes
> Designed to fill your mind
> Now that you've realized the pride's arrived
> We got to pump the stuff to make us tough
> From the heart
> It's a start, a work of art
> To revolutionize make a change nothing's strange
> People, people we are the same
> No we're not the same
> 'Cause we don't know the game
> What we need is awareness, we can't get careless
> You say, what is this?
> My beloved let's get down to business
> Mental self-defensive fitness
> Yo, bum rush the show
> You gotta go for what you know
> Make everybody see, in order to fight the powers that be.

The battle-ready SIW's or Security of the First World, PE's protection, who appear in concert toting fake Uzis, march in synchronized steps. Clad in all-black combat fatigues, they perform stylized martial arts routines led by a scowling Professor Griff. Even Flavor Flav, who usually plays jester to Chuck's dead seriousness, looks scary, flashing a row of gold teeth and holding the huge clock that hangs around his neck right up to the camera as if counting down to Armageddon. As the crowd marches forward, a white policeman, a comic gesture of authority in this movement of the masses, is swept along for the ride. You can almost smell the smoke from the war clouds floating in the air.

Musically and lyrically, no other group in rap music today has better expressed black rage and alienation, mobilizing their community toward action and awareness, than Public Enemy. With a lyrical volley of knowledge to the head, drummed in by a chaotic barrage of beats, they stand at the forefront of rap activism as well as of commercial success and appeal. PE was the first rap group to snatch the gangster's Uzi and point it toward the white power structure. They assaulted previous rap stereotypes of the gold-chain-wearing shit-talker with a politically motivated, punk rock attitude, which also manifested itself in using pure noise as music. Chuck, who coined rap as the "black CNN," was the first rapper to mention minister Louis Farrakhan, controversial leader of the Nation of Islam, in song. But unlike the ex-con/ghetto image of their militant uncles The Last Poets, Public Enemy hails from suburban Long Island.

THE HARD RHYMER, CHUCK D., FLASHES A RARE SMILE.

Around 1982 Chuck (Carlton Ridenhour) was a graphic arts major at Adelphi University who MCed and made flyers for a crew of mobile deejays from Long Island called Spectrum City, which was run by Hank Shocklee. Meanwhile, fellow Adelphian "Mr. Bill" Stephney sent rap out across the Bronx, Brooklyn, and Suffolk County from his radio show on WBAU. When the two forces collided, they provided a platform for Chuck to develop lyrically—at live gigs as well as on the air—while Shocklee created dense radio mixes that inspired the musical mayhem of PE. Unlike the spontaneous birth of the Poets, Chuck, Hank, and Bill sat down and formulated the group's concept, a combination of Run-D.M.C. and political rockers The Clash. The name came from one of Chuck's original demos, called "Public Enemy #1."

The first sign of PE's ground-breaking, revolutionary-rap format came on their 1987 debut, *Yo! Bum Rush the Show* (Def Jam), which featured a closed caption at the bottom that read "The Government's Responsible." Such sloganeering continued on other releases, extending to song titles as well as with "Don't Believe the Hype," referring to the media's negative portrayal of the group; "911 Is a Joke"; and "Shut 'Em Down," a message to companies who profit off the black community without investing back into it.

Chuck really proved that he was "loud and proud, kickin' live, the next poet supreme," on PE's first huge single, "Rebel Without a Pause," whose sirens screamed relentlessly through the long, hot summer of 1988. Featured on 1989's *It Takes a Nation of Millions to Hold Us Back* (Def Jam/Columbia), this track shared space with the rabble-rousing "Louder than a Bomb," "Black Steel in the Hour of Chaos," and the pure adrenalin of "Bring the Noise" (from the soundtrack of *Less Than Zero*), which described perfectly what PE was doing. The complex layers of sound supplied by the Bomb Squad, which included Chuck, Hank Shocklee and his brother Keith, and Eric "Vietnam" Sadler, created the ideal cacophony to back Chuck's hard rhyming and pushed hip-hop production values through the roof. As musical chance takers and rule breakers, the Bomb Squad has everything to do with descriptions of rap music today as a sonic collage.

But as PE began to blow up, greater media attention uncovered controversial views that suddenly made the group a target—just like the figure caught between the cross hairs of a rifle sight in their logo (which Chuck, incidentally, designed). In a May 9, 1989, interview with *Washington Times* reporter David Mills, Professor Griff (Richard Griffin), PE's "minister of information" and a member of Louis Farrakhan's Nation of Islam, said that Jews are responsible for "the majority of wickedness that goes on across the globe,"[1] among other anti-Semitic remarks. The full extent of his statements surfaced in a lengthy May 22 *Washington Times* article and three weeks later in the *Village Voice*, creating a controversy that almost tore the group apart bringing more negative press to rap.

In 1990, however, PE came back fiercer than ever with *Fear of a Black Planet* (Def Jam/Columbia). "I got so much trouble on my mind," says Chuck, reflecting on the situation in "Welcome to the Terrordome." He speaks further on his feelings of alienation: "Crucifixion ain't no fiction / So-called chosen frozen / apology made to whoever pleases / Now they got me like Jesus." Incorporating snippets of news and re-creating media broadcasts about the group, PE played off the controversy and criticism, portraying themselves as victims of the real enemy, the system of white world supremacy. The album's liner notes defines black power as "a collective means of self-defense against the world-wide conspiracy to destroy the black race. It's a movement that only puts fear in those that have a vested interest in the conspiracy, or think that it's something other than what it actually is." In an open letter dated June 19, 1989—PE's official response to the Griff incident—Chuck further clarifies this definition of black power, saying, "It does not mean anti-white, it means anti-a-system that has been designed by the European elite for the wrong purpose of benefitting off of people of color or at Black people's expense." Chuck's response to the conspiracy was "Fight the Power," a revolutionary anthem that provided the soundtrack for race rioting in Spike Lee's *Do the Right Thing*. That song also set the tone for the next album, *Apocalypse 91 . . . The Enemy Strikes Black* (Def Jam/Columbia, 1991).

As outspoken and influential as any black leader today, Chuck, who goes on lecture as well as concert tours, realizes that he is but a catalyst for change. Interviewed in the *Village Voice*, he said, "Public Enemy's just one fucking thing. I'm only one person. And I'm saying to each and every black person, you look in your family—it might not be your immediate family—you're gonna find either murder, drugs, alcohol abuse, and disease, or jail, somebody getting jailed. I'm saying you can run but you can't hide. Which means that everybody gotta be able to at least work forward or try to remedy the situation."[2] He thus advocates change in the Islamic tradition of each one teach one.

Rap activism has proven to be so fertile a grassroots movement because people—especially the large majority of blacks who are locked out of the power structure—have little faith in politicians. "Politicians are not even close to holding our best interests at heart," says Oakland-based rapper Paris, who cites Louis Farrakhan and writers as being the black leaders of today. "Let me add rappers to that, too, because nobody reads—let alone black people—just nobody generally reads," he says. "And if you don't read, and you listen to what is given to you by the media, yunno, the majority of what's given to you by the media is false truths. So then you have the universal medium of music that directly affects people one way, be it negative or positive. But I've seen the positive firsthand, 'cause PE was responsible, for the most part, for my turnaround, yunno, so I know the power of positive music, and that's why that's what I do."

Shortly before receiving a degree in economics from the University of California at Davis in 1990, Paris released *The Devil Made Me Do It* (Tommy Boy), an album that put Black Panther politics to a beat. The Panthers, of course, were a black militant cell started by Huey P. Newton and Bobby Seale in the late sixties who openly brandished firearms, patrolling their Oakland community to deter police harassment of young blacks, and called for a separate black nation in their "Ten Point Program," also a song on Paris's debut. The Panthers "were about defending yourself, doing for yourself, and looking out for your own community," says Paris, who still finds relevancy in their radical approach.

Thus, the most striking imagery on his 1993 release, *Sleeping With the Enemy* (Scarface), is that of insurrection. "Coffee, Donuts & Death," released following the media storm created by Ice-T's "Cop Killer," described a revenge killing of police officers in retaliation for the rape of Oakland resident Nina Gelfant by one of Oakland's finest. Paris raps: "Black folk can't be nonviolent now / I'd rather just lay ya down, spray ya down / Till justice come around / Cuz without it there'll be no peace." If that wasn't controversial enough, he went even further in "Bush Killa," which he describes as "an angry, fictional response to real-life drama and murderous intent on behalf of the government." The inflammatory remarks made on both songs sparked another censorship battle that forced Paris to release the record on his own Scarface label after the Time Warner–backed Tommy Boy refused to distribute it.

As with similar controversies involving rap lyrics, the focus rested solely on Paris as the aggressor—not the social and political climate that fostered such militancy. Though an infant during the Black Power movement of the sixties, Paris has observed the further disintegration of the black condition since then due to crack and AIDS, problems which statistics show disproportionately affect the black community. "Then you have the constant, constant negative bombardment in the media, yunno, and stereotyped images. And less of a concentration on our history in the school system. And, yunno, more of just a social relations process that fosters a kind of inferiority complex in most black people," he adds. "And it's just like all these negative things are bubbling up."

Far from being the complacent critic, however, Paris offers solutions to these problems as well. While integration represents the liberal ideal in a Eurocentric society, he believes that this also means assimilation. "The alternative," he says, "is real education, and taking education and revamping it. And, of course, making it affordable for everyone—including higher education. And make it a requirement to know everybody's history and everybody's culture. It's a requirement to learn American history, which is the history of brutality, yunno, oftentimes which I don't fit into, other than the fact that I was once a slave. So it's very important that everybody learn, you know, what they were, where they come from, what they can be. 'Cause you can never know what you can be unless you know how great you were."

While Paris and Public Enemy represent hip-hop's overtly political left-wing, renouncing the system that has kept blacks oppressed, other rap renegades have used varied approaches to pull themselves up into positions of power. On wax, KRS-ONE advises, "Black drug dealer, you have to wise up / organize your business so that we can rise up / If you're gonna sell crack then don't be a fool / organize your business and open up a school." America, after all, respects money, and capitalism the entrepreneur, and the rap world is full of former gangsters who have parlayed illegal profits into a recording career and other avenues of legitimate business. Today, a recording contract itself involves significant compensation, and a successful record can provide the means to build and invest in the future. The truly intelligent rapper is also a businessman, and as a result of his climb up the ladder, people listen when he speaks.

A case in point is Ice-T. As a gangster turned businessman/voice of the community he could almost be compared to another black leader who went from Detroit Red, small-time Harlem hustler, to revered role model and cultural icon Malcolm X. One of hip-hop's elder statesmen, Ice-T (Tracy Marrow) is also concerned with the liberation of his people. Named 1992's solo artist of the year by *The Source*, he has four gold records to his credit. In addition, he has all the material trappings—a fleet of cars and boats, a house in the Hollywood hills—of one who has made it. Heading a musical organization known as the Rhyme Syndicate—a label/production house/management company whose name alludes to his outlaw persona—his stance on both his albums and lecture tours is revolutionary.

Strolling up to the podium at New York University's Eisner & Lubin Auditorium to meet a wall of applause, Ice-T looks every bit the "original gangster" that his various movie roles and album cover shots suggest, wearing a leather coat, gold link, and New York Yankees cap—with briefcase in hand. A former gangbanger, pimp, and admitted felon from involvements in insurance fraud, credit card fraud, and armed robbery, his crime stories find basis in actual experiences. "Crime," he says, "is very glamorous. I made far more money as a criminal than I do now," a dubious claim considering the amount of legal product—CDs and cassettes—

**ICE-T LOOKS
INTO THE FUTURE.**

he has sold in his career. On a more responsible note, he adds, "The reason you get into crime is the lack of hope."

Throughout this lecture/open forum Ice-T skillfully deflects criticisms of his music. "I am not sexist, I am sexual. I deal with sex point-blank," says the rapper who gave us "Girls Let's Get Buck Naked and Fuck." Of the controversy surrounding "Cop Killer," a song with his heavy-metal band, Body Count, that was eventually pulled from the shelves by his former label, Warner Brothers, he says, "God knows I didn't think 'Cop Killer' was a controversial record. I thought everybody hated the police. I don't know nobody who like the police—all of my friends hate the police." He also calls it a "protest record" as well as a "revenge fantasy" of those who have suffered harassment or brutality at the hands of the police. While these answers might gloss over the issues at stake, his real message to this crowd of mostly white college students, who comprise a large share of his audience, seems to focus on education. "Go to school, gain capital, infiltrate the system, and take it over," he urges this upcoming generation, whom he envisions as being young, urban, capitalist guerrillas.

By the end of two hours he has thoroughly charmed the collegiate audience, disposing of one or two would-be hecklers in his usual blunt manner. Ice-T is black and strong, and though he does not consider himself an activist, in closing he observes, "I'm the first generation of talking nigger. Thirty years ago I was on the back of the bus. Now I'm at NYU."

Mecca & the Soul Brother

On the streets of South Central, Los Angeles, you might see clean-cut, nicely suited men in crisp white shirts and bow ties selling bean pies. In New York they are usually more casual—in flowing white robes and *kufi* skull caps, sitting behind fold-up tables that display everything from incense and body oils to literature. Sometimes they greet you with an "*Assalaam alaikum*," Arabic for "Peace be with you." Besides that, their whole way of life is largely shrouded in mystery.

These are the Black Muslims, whose estimated ranks in the U.S. range from between 500,000 and 1.5 million. This steadily growing group of zealots has modified classical Islam to speak specifically to the condition of blacks in America. Yet, far from representing a unified front, they are subdivided into as many as 18 different sects—the most well known being the World Community of Al-Islam, the Nation of Islam, and the Five Percent Nation. Predating formal notions of black power and the civil rights movement, Islam played a key role in black liberation, educating the minds of its adherents to the evils perpetrated against the black man and disciplining their spirit for the struggle ahead. The Nation of Islam, especially, achieved a degree of notoriety through the influence of Malcolm X, a political and cultural firebrand whose life was eventually claimed by his own when he separated himself from the fold of spiritual leader Elijah Muhammad. But today, Malcolm X's legacy, as well as the Louis Farrakhan–led Nation of Islam, remain vital symbols of black empowerment whose teachings many rappers (even those who aren't Muslim) apply in their lives as well as their music.

"The most important thing that's taught in the Nation of Islam," says Kam, a gangbanger turned Muslim,

is knowledge of self—and not through American eyes or American history. We are the fathers and mothers of civilization, of creation, so in other words, we have a far greater potential for greatness than we know, than we are ever taught in American schools. So it's a school of knowledge, self-knowledge of the American so-called Negro, you know what I'm saying, and it teaches a very strict discipline. Basically it's just truth. I mean it brings you a peace of mind, a contentment, a confidence in yourself. Once you have that foundation, and you know who you are and what your contributions have been to humanity, then you ready to go on a mission, you know what I'm saying. You want to be as great as your ancestors.

While some equate the separatist Nation and its splinter group the Five Percenters with the same degree of racism espoused by the Nazis or the Ku Klux Klan, Kam adds,

It's not about white this or white that. Black people can be bigger devils, you know what I'm saying. It's not about the skin color, it's about the mentality behind the skin color. Black people never made race an issue, ever in history. We never grabbed white people and subjected them to 438 years of slavery, suffering, and death. We never did this, you know what I'm saying? We victims, you know, don't treat us like we the predator and not the prey, we the victims of all of this. So we just expressing ourselves. We learning about what happened to us—yunno, this is part of the self-knowledge I'm talking about—learning what happened to us, learning what's going on now, and that prepares us for the future.

The convoluted history of the Black Muslims begins with two organizations: Marcus Garvey's United Negro Improvement Association, founded in Jamaica in 1914, and Timothy Drew's Moorish Science Temple, begun in Newark, New Jersey in 1913. While Garvey promoted the idea of a glorious past and an African identity for all blacks, exemplified in the slogan "Africa for Africans, at home and abroad," the Noble Drew Ali, as Timothy Drew came to be called, taught his disenfranchised followers that they were originally "Asiatics" whose true religion was Islam.

Both men had a profound influence on Wallace D. Fard (or W. Fard Muhammad), a door-to-door salesman in Detroit who claimed to have been born in the Muslim holy city of Mecca. While presenting himself as an almost Christlike figure, he believed that Christianity held no answers for the black man. He also described an inherently evil white "devil." Beginning at house meetings with a small group of followers, Fard had recruited some 8,000 followers by 1933. One of his most devoted disciples, an unemployed auto worker named Elijah Poole, also became his first minister, Elijah Muhammad. After a series of confrontations with the police, Fard disappeared mysteriously, and Elijah Muhammad ascended to the leadership of a growing organization. He taught his followers that Fard was, in fact, God (Allah) in the flesh, automatically setting himself up as the messenger of Allah.

Elijah Muhammad instituted such strict moral codes as prayer five times a day and abstaining from gambling, smoking, drinking, drugs, sports, and eating pork. He also advocated economic self-sufficiency within his community and an Islamic education. All of these measures served to create a very disciplined and independent Black Muslim nation who had seemingly little to do with the American nation—the "uncivilized wilderness"—in which they lived. Even among this very committed group, however, there was dissent.

The renegade Clarence 13X challenged some of the moral codes, eventually leaving the Nation to start his own sect, known as the Five Percenters. After experiencing the diversity of classical Islam, Malcolm X also challenged Muhammad's notions of separatism and was assassinated by members of the Nation. Then, when Elijah Muhammad passed, his son Warith Deen Muhammad steered the group back toward a more orthodox form of Islam and renamed them the World Community of Al-Islam. Minister Louis Farrakhan, who had been bypassed for leadership of the Nation, at first assented, but then returned to the teachings of Elijah Muhammad and became the leader of the contemporary Nation of Islam.

As with any powerful black fringe group, the Muslims engender terror in mainstream society, in sharp contrast to the meaning of "Muslim" as a "peaceful being." But, as always, the media's penchant for the negative does not tell the whole story, and misunderstanding may explain part of the fear. Considered the "scariest" of the lot, the Five Percenter's philosophy is one readily embraced by rappers such as Brand Nubian and the Poor Righteous Teachers.

"The Black man's God, it ain't no mystery," claim Sadat X and Lord Jamar of New Rochelle's Brand Nubian, echoing the philosophy of Clarence 13X on their second release *In God We Trust* (Elektra, 1993). About half the album, in fact, is devoted to hard-core Islamic instruction. They even address outsiders perceptions of their sect in "The Godz . . . [Must Be Crazy]." In "Meaning of the 5%," a speech by Farrakhan set to a beat, 85 percent of the world's population is defined as the uncivilized masses; 10 percent as the rich slave owners, bloodsuckers of the poor; and the remaining 5 percent as the poor, righteous teachers, whose mission it is to spread awareness.

As committed Five Percenters, Profile recording artists Poor Righteous Teachers—Father Shaheed, Culture Freedom, and Wise Intelligent—are typically forthright about expressing their philosophy. A dreadlocked Culture explains, "Yunno, a god is a god, when he practices the ways and actions of a god. A devil is a devil because he practice the ways and actions of a devil."

"Nothing is real unless it is shown and proved," says Wise. "That's another thing the Five Percent believe—is that nothing is real unless it's made manifest. We don't believe in a lot of mystery that, if you can't see it, if you can't smell it, see it, or hear it, then it don't exist."

Culture adds, "See that's the misunderstanding the Nation of Islam people had, 'cause the Nation of Islam don't believe that Allah is a spook," or spirit, as they teach in church. "They teach that Allah is not a spook, yunno, because that's, to be exact, the fourteenth degree, you know what I'm saying," referring to a set of codes the Muslims follow.

"It's like this: If you want to see God. We all know that God's way is good. God is love. So if you want to see God, go out and do something positive, and then you see the power of good," says Wise taking the ball again. "Say, for instance, you want to be a hardcore raggamuffin type kid. If you practice that and that's what you go out and portray, that's what you gonna reflect. You gonna reflect that type of individual. So if you want to see God, you gotta get with the program, man." Though young in appearance, Wise, Culture, and Shaheed have obviously studied their lessons and are able to flip through more aspects of the Judeo-Christian tradition than a Baptist minister.

All three former churchgoers, who grew up in the projects of Trenton, New Jersey, were attracted to the Five Percent Nation for a specific reason. "It offers you an upright life and opportunity and a chance to deal with our specific situation in North America, you know what I'm sayin?" says Culture. "For black people, man, you just gotta grab hold of something that's positive, because it's so many things out there that's negative that's coming at you from all different angles. You need something, you know what I mean? That's just the bottom line."

These sentiments are shared by Daddy-O, formerly of the group Stetsasonic, himself a Muslim. "Islam to me is a way of life. As a religion, I think it's the most practical religion for the black man in America. And the only reason I say that is because we as black men in America are known to get into so much trouble and mischief that it would make your head spin on any given day," he says. "And if a man is praying five times a day, if he has to observe, once a year, the fast of Ramadan, which we are doing right now, which you fast from sunup to sundown, you don't intake any stimulants [coffee, tobacco], you don't do any sexual things. Yunno, then that humbles the soul, it humbles the spirit." But far from being a humble philosophy, Islam instills a righteous pride in its adherents, who regard themselves as the original man.

Africa for Africans

My forefather was a king
He wore fat gold chains and fat ruby rings
Nobody believes this to be true
Maybe it's because my eyes ain't blue . . .
All you read about is slavery
Never 'bout the black man's bravery

"Acknowledge Your History"
The Jungle Brothers

Islam is not the only strand of black nationalism that finds inspiration in history. Vindicating the black man through his glorious past in Africa—where the oldest human remains have been found, as well as some of the oldest and most complex civilizations (Egypt and Ethiopia) —has also been the pursuit of countless scholars, authors, poets, and, today, rappers. Taking their cue from Jamaican activist Marcus Garvey— who went so far as to start the Black Star shipping line to physically transport blacks back to the motherland and inspired the African consciousness of Rastafarianism—some rappers embrace Africa as a spiritual sanctuary.

The Jungle Brothers were probably the first to express their Africanness overtly when they debuted with *Straight Out the Jungle* (Warlock, 1988). They expanded on this motif with 1989's *Done By the Forces of Nature* (Warner Brothers), which presented them as hip-hop's first Afrocentric hippies, wearing dashikis and beads, growing dreadlocks, not eating meat, and even incorporating African rhythms and chants into their music. As leaders of a rap collective known as the Native Tongues which included De La Soul, A Tribe Called Quest, Queen Latifah, and Monie Love, the JBs spoke of "a group of people, a tribe of people / Joined together for one cause / Sellin' you and tellin' you / Get up and go for yours." The tribe, according to their thinking, promotes a level of consciousness: rap's equivalent to Bob Marley urging "Africans Unite."

Also in 1989, a Brooklyn-based crew called X-Clan invoked the mysticism of Egypt in their *To The East Blackwards* LP (4th & Broadway). Comprised of Paradise, Brother J, and Professor X (Lumumba Carson), son of activist Sonny Carson, the group was at the center of a black youth organization called Blackwatch, which also included rappers Queen Mother Rage, Isis, and YZ. Striking, impressive figures with their nose rings, ankhs, carved wooden canes, and black leather crowns, X-Clan proved themselves as far more than entertainers with a very visible presence in the community. When they weren't promoting a knowledge of the ancients—set, of course, to a funky beat—they participated in workshops and marches, such as the one to protest the killing of black youth Yusef Hawkins at the hands of a white mob in Bensonhurst, Brooklyn, in 1989.

Then, of course, there is KRS-ONE, a rapper with a very unique philosophy when it comes to the uplift of the African. On the cover of *By All Means Necessary* (Jive, 1988), KRS re-creates the familiar photograph of Malcolm X peering out a window cautiously with a shotgun in hand, instead brandishing an Uzi, de rigueur artillery of the nineties street soldier. Repudiating the gangsta image of his first album with such songs as "Stop the Violence" and "World Peace," from his second and third albums, his career, in fact, has seen him go from *Criminal Minded* to pro-black to humanist.

Symbolizing rap's efforts to educate and entertain, 1990's *Edutainment* captures the many faces of KRS-ONE. First he criticizes blacks who are not true to themselves in "House Niggas" and "Ya Strugglin' " (which features Kwame Toure, formerly Stokeley Carmichael, of the All African People's Revolutionary party). Speaking of Egyptology and ancient history in "Blackman's in Effect," he then delves into Zen Buddhism with "Love's Gonna Get Ya (Material Love)," a song that warns against being materialistic. KRS, who has always advanced the notion that rap is a tool of revolution, says on the liner notes of *Edutainment*: "The true revolution will unite humanity. Not Black or white or Asian or Indian, all races. . . . Forward ever, backwards never, prepare for whatever, and always stay clever, in any endeavour intelligence is better, and be on guard for false prophets in leather." For remarks like these he has been criticized by the "blacker" factions of rap, such as X-Clan, who feel his humanist views do not specifically address the plight of the black man. KRS counters these claims on a song called "Build and Destroy," from 1992's *Sex and Violence* (Jive), in which he says, "Africa is the whole of humanity / which makes the African a humanist challenge me." Despite the kind of liberalism that he displays, it is doubtful that KRS will ever have his ghetto pass revoked.

Primarily a medium of entertainment, rap also conveys the more serious voices of the black community. These voices are concerned with forging an identity, encouraging unity, and above all, liberating the race from its long history of oppression. Though the approaches are varied and styles unique, rap is a potent form of dialogue that speaks bluntly about the problems faced by the black community—and on possible ways to solve them. Socially, rather than politically, driven, the message of rap inspires consciousness in a whole new generation of youth in whose hands the future lies.

recommended
listening

1. Kam, *Neva Again* (East-West, 1993).

2. Da Lench Mob, *Guerrillas in tha Mist* (East-West, 1993).

3. Ice Cube, *Predator* (Priority, 1992).

4. The Last Poets, *The Last Poets* (Douglas, 1969).

5. Public Enemy, *Fear of a Black Planet* (Def Jam, 1990).

6. Paris, *The Devil Made Me Do It* (Tommy Boy, 1991).

7. Brand Nubian, *In God We Trust* (Elektra, 1993).

8. Poor Righteous Teachers, *Holy Intellect* (Profile, 1990).

9. Jungle Brothers, *Done By the Forces of Nature* (Warner Brothers, 1988).

10. X-Clan, *To the East Blackwards* (4th & Broadway, 1989).

11. Boogie Down Productions, *Edutainment* (Jive, 1990).

business contemporaries have des
suit tags branded into their breastb
Russell promotes street music and n
no apologies. The staccato, cras
drums, the gritty, uncompromised v
about life in Kochtown, and the d
playing of melody that mark the mus
Blow, Whodini, Run-D.M.C., LL Ko
and the other acts he manages are
lifeblood. He loves all this loud, ob
ious aural graffiti. As far as I can t
and I've known Russell about six y
worth of headaches, triumphs, and
night phone calls—he never intends t
anything else but make street reco
chain smoke, talk fast

House
of Jam

In the highly competitive business of music, Def Jam is not the biggest, richest, or most powerful recording label, but its name engenders the same kind of respect as, say, Chanel's in the world of fragrances or Jordan in the land of hoops. A major player in the evolution of hip-hop, Def Jam is well on its way to becoming one of those legendary institutions in music itself—just like Motown, Stax/Volt, and Blue Note. Almost every record they have released—from a modest roster of 22 artists that includes such heavyweights as L.L. Cool J., Public Enemy, and Onyx—has sold gold (at least half a million copies), prompting the media to dub label owner Russell Simmons the "mogul of rap." Simmons's former partner, Rick Rubin, who has since gone into business for himself, was also once called the "king of rap" for his hit-making production skills and knack at finding and developing street-level talent that kids wanted to hear.

Today, Def Jam's parent company, Rush Communications, overseen by Simmons, is a multimedia conglomerate involved in television, film, radio, music publishing, artist management, and even a new line of clothing. Rush's expansion into the mainstream of American culture, in fact, mirrors the explosion of rap and hip-hop culture, whose commercial success Russell and associates had everything to do with. Back when many in the industry downplayed rap's significance, dismissing it as a fad, Simmons's love for the art form, commitment to presenting as undiluted as possible a version of black culture, and plain tenacity—coupled with the considerable talent and appeal of his artists—helped launch a massive assault on pop music and culture that came straight from the streets. The story of Def Jam illustrates rap's rise from the underground to its current position of power and prominence. From the boardrooms to the suburbs, it is also just as much a tale of the rest of America stooping down to street level to see what all the noise is about—and getting hooked.

A short car ride from the slums of the South Bronx are the comfortable, single-family dwellings of Queens, often considered the most affluent and suburban of New York's boroughs. But Russell Simmons's neighborhood of Hollis, in the far reaches of Queens, was an area in transition while he was growing up. He saw Hollis go from being predominantly white when his family first moved there in 1964 to all black by the time he was in high school. Thus, from an early age Russell learned to walk the line between the middle-class mentality of his parents, both college-educated professionals, and the mercenary activity of the streets, where you were either "down" or a "sucker."

After school he was indoctrinated into street life by hanging out on the corner and, in a brief stint as a member of the Seven Immortals, a citywide streetgang. He also loved going to see the blaxploitation films that played regularly at the Loews theater on Jamaica Avenue. Like the big-time hustlers on screen, all black kids had to have their hustle too, and Russell's was selling reefer. Down the block from his parent's house, at 205th Street park, Russell began this first business venture, working most nights from seven in the evening to one in the morning, sometimes coming home with $400 for his toils. Perhaps it was more than just coincidence that Russell rhymes with hustle.

One of the ruling influences of his youth was music, and Russell would never miss an opportunity to go and see such groups as the Delfonics, the Dramatics, the Temptations, and the Moments perform their popular love ballads. He was also intrigued by the beat on certain records— sometimes just several bars of a particular song that he would keep rewinding on his eight-track cassette. Russell's recognition of these funky, rhythmic snippets from songs by the Pointer Sisters, Bill Withers, Al Green, and the Chi-Lites occurred independently of the burgeoning hip-hop scene in the Bronx.

Upon graduating from high school in 1975, Russell entered City College of New York (in Harlem) as a sociology major. As one who liked to observe and interact with people, he figured this would be the easiest major to handle, but he spent more time soaking up Harlem nightlife than at school. Disco was all the rage, but one night in 1977 at the Charles Gallery, a club on 125th Street, near the Apollo Theater, he got his first taste of something new. Bronx Community College student and radio deejay Eddie Cheeba was delighting the crowd with a barrage of rhyming slang: "It's Cheeba, Cheeba, chee-chee-chee-Cheeba / Up my back and around my neck, Ooh ah! Got the girl in check / Come on, come on, you do the jerk / Let me see your body work / Slam dunk, feel the funk, come on, come on, shake your rump."[1] Meanwhile, his deejay Easy Gee was cutting up the first eight bars of Parliament's "Flashlight" on two turntables. Russell, like everyone in attendance, was completely bowled over, and as the coursing blood tingled in his veins he realized something that the hip uptown crowd already knew: A rapper is the life of the party. In the fall of 1977, with his crew at CCNY, he decided to throw a party of his own.

Due to stiff competition in Manhattan among already well-established party promoters, Russell staged his inaugural fete at a Queens club called the Renaissance. Putting up $500 for the space, and an additional $300 on promotion—flyers, stickers, and posters distributed citywide—"Rush, The Force in College Parties," as his flyers touted, was in business. "Rush" was the nickname he had earned for the frenetic pace at which he ran his life. All he needed now was a rapper, and a young Harlemite named Kurtis Walker, a communications major and one of Russell's best friends, was the man for the job. Though unknown at the time, Kurtis "Blow," as he had been dubbed by Russell, went onstage that night and thoroughly charmed the overflow crowd of 800. The next month they staged an event in Times Square's Hotel Diplomat. One successful party after another made Rush a force to be reckoned with and, soon, his gigs featured such popular Bronx acts as Lovebug Starski, Grandmaster Flash and the Furious Five, and Grand Wizard Theodore.

Kurtis Blow's star was also on the rise, and by early 1978 he needed a deejay of his own for all the gigs he was performing. Russell's younger brother Joey, 13 at the time, had been practicing on the turntables and had become quite adept at cutting up such hits as Chic's "Good Times," as well as writing rhymes himself. Russell put him on as "Kurtis Blow's Disco Son—DJ Run," but at Run's first gig at the Diplomat he was rapping

**RETURN OF
THE KINGS—
RUN-D.M.C.**

onstage with Blow as Grandmaster Flash manned the turntables. With the success of "Rapper's Delight" in 1979, Russell was ready to take Kurtis, whom he was managing, to the next phase. He hooked up with *Billboard* reporters Robert "Rocky" Ford and J. B. Moore, who wrote and financed Kurtis's first single, "Christmas Rappin'," which was also the first rap single to be distributed by a major label (Mercury). This successful record was followed by the even bigger hit "The Breaks" in 1980.

Meanwhile, young Joe (nicknamed "Run" because he used to run his mouth so much) had been bugging his brother to let him make a record as well. After soloing on a track called "Street Kid," which went nowhere, he decided that his next attempt would include his partner from the neighborhood, D. (Darryl McDaniels), who also rapped. At the time, a slick, disco, backing track laid by a live band was the dominant sound of rap records on Joe and Sylvia Robinson's dominant Sugar Hill label, which had signed most of the major rap talent. Russell, however, wanted to make records that reflected the raw, break-beat sound of rap in the clubs and parks. When he realized that his brother had the talent to step up to this challenge, he finally took him seriously and set about making a real rap record with him.

Enlisting the aid of Larry Smith, the bass player on Kurtis Blow's hits and Russell's collaborator on "Action" by the band Orange Krush and "The Bubble Bunch," a rap by Jimmy Spicer, they made a sparse drum-machine track for a song called "It's Like That," which Joe and D. had written. On the B side was "Sucker MCs," which was equally sparse and equally hard. The small, independent Profile Records, which had had success with "Genius Rap" by Dr. Jeckyll & Mr. Hyde, decided to release it in 1983 after none of the majors would. A month later they were selling 20,000 copies a week. Joe and D., two 17-year-olds from Queens known on the record as Run-D.M.C. were suddenly on the map.

Run-D.M.C. revitalized the whole rap scene at the time, as well as setting trends for all rappers who came after them. Their attitude, like their beats, was hard. Their dress, unlike the extravagant leather, sequin, and feather outfits of most rap acts at the time, reflected a street aesthetic to which the average B-Boy on the corner could relate. Run and D.'s career was carefully guided by Russell through his Rush Management.

Thirty-year-old Rick Rubin was but a young lad of 20 studying film at NYU when Run-D.M.C. made their explosive entrance onto the rap scene. Though loyal to the white, adolescent noise of AC/DC, Ted Nugent, and Aerosmith, his tastes were much broader than your average teen from Lido Beach, Long Island. "Probably one of the things that got me into hip-hop when I was in high school," says Rick, "was all the white kids pretty much liked rock 'n' roll that was already dead, and black kids were into hip-hop and their tastes would change really quickly, yunno? A new record would come out and the record that came out last week didn't really matter anymore. And that wasn't the case at all with the white kids who liked rock 'n' roll. They all liked Led Zeppelin and the Doors, and all that stuff that they still like today." When Rick came to the city in 1981 he started checking out rap shows. His thirst for progressive, alternative sounds fueled an interest in the burgeoning hardcore punk scene, too.

Rick's musical eclecticism was further defined by his longtime love of James Brown and the blues. "There's funk in, like—I'm not gonna say there's funk in everything—but there's a lot of funk in a lot of places that you wouldn't expect to find it," he explains from the living room of his comfortable Hollywood abode overlooking Sunset Strip. "That's kinda what the hip-hop deejays were about, yunno, playing the funky breaks off rock records, or off anything, and, yunno, that was one of the things that really attracted me and made me want to make records, was going out to Negril, and hearing what was going on musically, and then hearing these records coming out on Sugar Hill and Enjoy. Even though I liked the records on Enjoy, they weren't musically what the scene was all about. They were disco records, really."

Negril, on Second Avenue in Manhattan, was the first downtown club to feature such pioneering Bronx deejays as Jazzy Jay, Afrika Islam, D. ST., and Grand Wizard Theodore. As a regular there, Rick eventually met and befriended Jazzy Jay, who schooled him about all the important break records to have and invited him to some of the real outdoor "jams" in the Bronx as well as to uptown rap clubs like the Disco Fever and Broadway International. Jay even set him up with a custom sound system for his MG convertible, long before such booming systems even existed. "I remember going to all the audio places on Long Island, and saying, 'OK, I want twelve-inch woofers in the back of my car,' " recalls Rick, in his typically deep and soft tone of voice. "They were like, 'Can't do that, it doesn't exist, yunno, those don't go in cars'. And I said, 'No, I've seen them, I've heard them, and that's what I want.' And they said, 'It can't be done.' So, yunno, Jazzy said, 'You gotta know where to go.' He said, 'Go to J&R Music World, downtown, yunno, the Wall Street district, buy the stuff, come to my house, and I'll install it.' And he did. I remember him cutting these twelve-inch holes in the back of my car. It was only a two-seat car, so I had these two twelve-inch speakers aimed at the back of the seats. In that time it was just completely ridiculous."

What seemed even stranger was a white, Jewish kid from suburban Long Island as an insider in the black underground movement of hip-hop. "I think I was kind of a novelty," says Rubin, clad in his just-got-up outfit of bright red pajamas and brown moccasins, his long hair and beard giving him the appearance of having slept for 20 years. "They appreciated the fact that I was such a fan and knew so much about the music." Knowing about the music only fueled his desire to make it, and to make it as real as possible—not like the watered down disco sound of most of the rap records out there at the time. "That's what I wanted to do, was make records, and again, not for any reason other than I liked 'em and wanted to hear them. Yunno, I never thought I was going to be doing this now and I never thought I was going to make any money doing this at all." With "Sucker MCs" in mind, Rick approached Jay with the idea of cutting a record and starting a label, and in 1984 they went into PowerPlay studios in Queens.

"PowerPlay now, they got the 48-track digital, boom, all full-blown. We was in PowerPlay when it was a dungeon. I'm talking about a nightmare. A nightmare," recalls Jazzy Jay from his Bronx studio. The condition of the studio, however, did not affect the quality of the track they produced, called, "It's Yours." Originally, Rick had wanted Special K of the Treacherous Three to record the rap, but as K was contractually tied to Sugar Hill, he suggested using his brother T LA Rock instead. Jay, who thinks the song had a "dismal" beat, says, "What happened to liven the beat up was the scratches and the amount of bass that they put on that shit. 'Cause that's what separated it from every record at that time. When you put 'It's Yours' on, it drowned out every other record."

To ensure that the sound was kosher for the street, Jay and Rick would make a tape of the song during the session, run outside to Jay's car, and test the sound. "If it sounded good in my car he liked it," says Jay. "If it didn't sound good in my car, he'd go back upstairs and give that engineer hell. 'Yep, I want more bass,' you know what I'm saying? So he pressed up the records, he paid [$300] for studio time, Special K wrote the lyrics, T LA Rock executed the lyrics, I did all the scratching, and when it was done I was like, cool." The record was eventually picked up by Arthur Baker's Streetwise/Partytime label, though it also bore the imprint of Def Jam, a name Rick had been toying with. Released in October, it took until the following summer before the record kicked in, selling 90,000 copies, and making it a local hit. What Rick didn't make in financial returns—he maintains that Baker cheated him out of profits for the record—he made up for in juice. With the success of "It's Yours," Rick Rubin, a fringe player, was suddenly catapulted into the center of the scene.

"Russell, in a lot of ways, was the fucking scene," says Bill Adler, a freelance writer who joined Simmons's outfit as a publicity person in the summer of 1984. "Russell created the scene. Russell was a party giver, a party promoter, and a record promoter and artist manager. He was one of those guys who had tremendous social mobility. I know he was throwing parties pretty early on, and when it wasn't his party, he was still out. He's one of those guys who's gone out every night of his life since he was 15 years old." Russell's own father even wrote a poem about him that went: "Eat, sleep, don't shovel no snow / Get up, get dressed, go disco." Says Adler, "Nightlife was his life, O.K.? So he and Rick were gonna meet."

And they did, at a party at the trendy downtown club Danceteria, where a short-lived TV show called *Graffiti Rock* was filming the performances of Run-D.M.C. and the Treacherous Three. In fact, Jazzy Jay, with whom Rick had originally talked about starting a label, introduced them. While Rick was a big fan of Run-D.M.C. and Russell's other work, he says, "Russell loved 'It's Yours' and he couldn't believe before he met me that I was white and that I had made that record. So we started hanging out, and he started taking me up to the Disco Fever and Harlem World, and I used to hang out in his office, and we just became friends."

While Russell was building Rush Management, which by this time included such artists as Run-D.M.C., Kurtis Blow, Whodini, Dr. Jeckyll (who was André Harrell, also a vice president at Rush before starting his own successful Uptown label) & Mr. Hyde, Jimmy Spicer, Spyder D., Sparky D., and singer Allyson Williams, Rick also kept busy with three zany, white teens who called themselves the Beastie Boys, a hardcore punk band who had been dabbling more and more in rap. They had already released the rap-influenced single "Cookie Puss" on the independent Ratcage label, and met Rubin while looking for a deejay so they could perform the song at live gigs. "So a friend of ours knew of this guy who had a bubble machine—yunno, the Lawrence Welk–type of thing—and he deejayed," says Beastie Mike D. (as in Diamond). "So we figured, alright, we gotta give him the job. He's got the bubble machine, he's got the equipment, and he can deejay O.K., cool." When not fulfilling his role as DJ Double R, Rick took the Beasties into the studio and produced "Beastie Crew," "Party's Gettin' Rough," and "Rock Hard." This last song featured a grinding guitar lick from "Back in Black" by AC/DC, one of Rick's favorite bands.

Meanwhile, after the success of "It's Yours," which bore the imprint and address of Def Jam Records—then located in Rick's dorm room in NYU's

Weinstein Hall—he started receiving demo tapes over the transom. Ad-rock (Adam Horovitz) of the Beastie Boys first heard "I Need a Beat" an a cappella rhyme by a young kid from St. Albans, Queens, who called himself Ladies Love Cool James, and he brought it to Rick's attention immediately. After speaking on the phone with the 15-year-old rapper, whose real name was James Todd Smith, Rick says, "He came over, we met at the dorm, I worked on the beats, and then we went in and recorded that at Chung King," a studio in Chinatown (previously called Secret Society, but renamed by Rubin because the owner's name was John King). "And when it was done I played it for Russell, and he said, 'This is really good, maybe we should put it out on Profile,' 'cause that's who he was putting his records out through. I said, 'Maybe we should do this our-selves. Let's start this label and do it.' And he said he didn't want to 'cause he was waiting to make a deal with a major label. And I said, 'I'll make the records, I'll run the business, and you'll just be my partner.' He said 'O.K.' "

With each partner contributing $2,500, Def Jam took its first steps and was formally introduced to the industry with a small blurb, written by Bill Adler, that appeared in *Billboard* in the fall of 1984. In November, the label's first twelve-inch single "I Need a Beat" (DJ001) hit the streets, selling over 100,000 copies and propelling L.L. to stardom at an age when most teens are getting their first part-time jobs. "L.L.'s a genius," states Adler, who first met him when he came to sign with Rush Man-agement. "Not to take anything away from anybody else, but if there's anything like a natural-born genius it's L. He was just this little 15-year-old kid who had a troubled home life, who, I think, lived in his own head quite a bit, who was not doing well in school—he might have dropped out of school at the age of 15, alright—who had set his sights on a career as a rapper. So he was following it fiendishly, buying all the twelve-inches that were coming out. He had all the skills. He was ridiculous.

"I remember times when they would have these battles in this little two-room office," says Adler, referring to the first headquarters of Rush at 1133 Broadway, at West 26th Street. "And Joe [Run] and L. started cracking on each other. They started out with these two-line rhymes, and pretty soon one guy would say a line and the other guy would crack back and rhyme his insult to the other guy's line. Fast, furious, hilarious, and they were buggin'. They were following each other from room to room, out in the hallway, back into the office, cracking on each other, high speed. And it was just, no quarter given, but, yunno, tremendous admiration in it."

Close on the heels of L.L.'s success, Def Jam released the Rick Rubin–produced Beastie Boy tracks in December, followed by a spate of other singles, including a Jazzy Jay scratch record called "Def Jam" (with an inebriated Russell stopping by the studio to add some vocals) and music by Jimmy Spicer and the Hollis Crew. Things were also happening for all of Russell's other artists: the Brooklyn trio Whodini released hits like "Friends," "Freaks," and "Five Minutes of Funk"; Kurtis Blow was still a force to contend with; and Run-D.M.C. emerged from the studio with the *King of Rock* LP (Profile, 1985), which further defined their musical niche as a group who melded rap and rock. Meanwhile, the Fresh Fest, the first major rap concert tour, was getting ready to rock the nation, and Russell secured a deal to supply all of the talent. In New York itself, Adler says, "the scene was just crackling," adding that "the coolest thing was that there was a kind of family feeling for a while there."

Mike D. agrees, adding, "The beginning of Def Jam was very exciting in a way, because I always remember hanging out at Rick's dorm, yunno, with all these records sitting out there, and just in terms of the downtown clubs, yunno, that was actually a really exciting time because, yunno, it was like the music was totally new 'cause Rick and Russell were, yunno, all of a sudden putting out records that other labels would probably be afraid to release because they were too extreme"—though not by today's standards.

Def Jam, at this point, was also very much a mom-and-pop operation. "It was run from the dorm room, and I made the records, I made the deals with all the companies to press the records and the jackets, to make the labels," says Rick. "I designed everything, all the artwork, and dealt with all of the distributors around the country, and it really was like the record business in the fifties. It was great." Rick's friend George Drakoulias, who was studying music business at NYU, also joined the operation, going around to all the one-stops to deliver records and pick up cash. He also dealt with the distributors over the phone, taking orders and shipping out product. "Russell's main function at the time," according to Rick, "was promotion. The reason I wanted him to be my partner was he was really tied in more to the rap community and the radio stations around the country, and he really was good at that, and that was what he did. To this day he's one of the best rap promoters."

From another perspective, Mike D. says, "The main thing with Russell was, here was this guy who was our manager, and he'd be out drunk every night till five in the morning. Like, he was worse than us, yunno. I'm not saying that in a bad way—that's what was cool about it. This guy would be out drinking, like, 12 screwdrivers and going to three clubs every night." But clubbing was Russell's unique manner of conducting business. It was in the clubs that he heard which songs got a response, checked out the latest styles, and really stayed in touch with rap's consumer market.

"The key thing is that Rick and Russ, you know, had this consciousness that they would not be confined to the ghetto," explains Adler. "You know, they already had a pretty good idea of what the music was, what the potential for the music was, who the audience was. They also had a pretty good idea about the wheels that needed to be turned, O.K., they had a good idea about the mechanics of the record business, certainly Russell did, and what they didn't know they invented, and what they invented they believed in." Though they had been turned down for a distribution deal by nearly every major label, by 1985 Def Jam could no longer be ignored. Seven twelve-inch releases had sold over 250,000 copies. Al Teller, then head of Columbia Records (now chairman of MCA), approached Russell and Rick in the summer of 1985, and began negotiations. By October, they had signed a deal said to be worth at least a million dollars.

"The deal that they cut with Columbia was unprecedented, at least with regards to creative control," says Adler. "Rick and Russell went into the studio, made the records they wanted, turned over the finished tape to

Columbia, and said, 'no, you have nothing to say about this. This is the record, this is the artwork, this is the logo.' " Def Jam basically furnished artists to Columbia, who pressed up their records and distributed them. The first single released under this new relationship was "She's On It" by the Beastie Boys, followed by L.L. Cool J.'s *Radio* LP, which easily went gold. Rick Rubin, who produced both of these albums, also had his hand in Run-D.M.C.'s *Raising Hell* (Profile, 1986), which was the first rap album to go platinum (with sales in excess of one million copies). When the Beastie Boys finally released their debut album *License to Ill* in the fall of 1986, they broke the bank, selling an incredible four million copies.

Rick remembers attending a dinner at the house of a big record company executive following the success of the Beastie Boys. "First his wife made a comment about, yunno, why did these groups incite all these violence at these shows," says Rick. "I said, 'They don't incite it, it's crazy, they don't incite anything. They try to incite people liking their music, is all they incite.' " After the exec apologized for his wife's ignorant comments, "Ten minutes later he said to me, 'So why do you think all these people are buying these records. I mean, after all, it's not music,' " says Rick with a laugh. "And he's trying to be nice to me, and that's really what they thought. It was so foreign. It's just, you don't understand at all, so the fact that we knew what was going on in this genre made us really valuable to them. They would fuck it up because they didn't know. They didn't know what was good because to them it was barely music. All they knew was people were buying it, and they wanted to be in that business from the sales side, not from the artistic side."

The relationship between Def Jam and Columbia, according to Adler, "was tremendously fruitful because Columbia was, at the time, the biggest and strongest record company in the world. It was Columbia's muscles behind Rick and Russell's creative talent. Tremendous synergy, and then it went booooom!"

———

Rap's move into the boardrooms of big business had been foreseen in a front-page *Wall Street Journal* article on December 4, 1984. Long before Russell's baseball-cap-and-jeans, perpetually-attached-to-a-cellular-phone image graced the pages of *Time, Rolling Stone, Vanity Fair*, and *GQ*, the *Journal*'s Meg Cox called the then 26-year-old the "Mogul of Rap." In May of 1985 the meteoric rise of Def Jam, Run-D.M.C., Russell, and Rick received the Hollywood treatment in the movie *Krush Groove*, by director Michael Schultz. Previously, Russell had turned down involvement in such purely commercial endeavors as *Rappin'* (1985) produced by Israeli filmmaker Menahem Golan and Harry Belafonte's *Beat Street* (1984), both of which he perceived as corny efforts to make a fast buck off of the music and culture he had worked so long and hard to promote. Though *Krush Groove* can hardly be considered a serious film, it was moderately successful at the box office, mainly due to amazing musical performances by Run-D.M.C., L.L. Cool J., and the Beastie Boys, among others. Basically, it provided a 90-minute plug for Def Jam.

Rush Management was also given a needed administrative boost with the addition of Lyor Cohen, a former financial analyst and L.A. club promoter, who literally showed up on Russell's doorstep in February 1985. A couple of years earlier he had dealt with Russell when he booked Run-D.M.C. at shows at his Mix Club in Hollywood. Shrewd, savvy, and highly intelligent, albeit "goofy" in manner, this Israeli's drive and character showed in the way he quickly became vice president of operations and, finally, Russell's equal partner in Rush Management. Early on, Lyor secured the first rap endorsement deal with a major company, for Run-D.M.C. to promote Adidas's products—not too difficult considering that the group's hit song "My Adidas" was a heartfelt tribute to their favorite footwear. He arranged for Adidas P.R. director Angelo Anastasio to attend a Run-D.M.C. concert at Madison Square Garden in which nearly the whole sold-out house took off their Adidas and held them high in the air when the group performed that song.

Def Jam, too, acquired a valuable asset in the person of Bill Stephney, an Adelphi University graduate and former rap deejay who started the rap

("Beat Box") section of the alternative *College Music Journal*. After meeting him at 1984's New Music Seminar, Rick Rubin invited Stephney to join the company, but he was initially hesitant, saying, "I can't work for you guys, you're unorganized." Careful prodding by Rick finally got the best of him, and he started off in promotions at the end of 1985. He brought a group called Original Concept (which included the current host of *Yo! MTV Raps*, Andre "Dr. Dre" Brown) to the label and introduced Rick to a rapper then known as Chucky D., with whom he had worked as part of Long Island's Spectrum City mobile deejay crew.

After having released one lackluster single, "Lies" b/w "Check Out the Radio" with Spectrum City on the independent Vanguard label, Chucky D. faded from the rap scene. Rick, however, was very excited about the demo of "Public Enemy #1" and repeatedly called to persuade Chuck to make a record. The 26-year-old former rapper, who was working as a messenger for a photographic service in Long Island to support his wife and child, said no. A persistent Rubin would not give up, calling him every night for about six months, but to no avail. Finally, as Stephney recalls, "Rick was saying to me, 'If we don't sign Chucky D., you're fired,' and this is the way Rick would be. So wait, hold it, we're successful on L.L., the Beasties are doing well, you're gonna fire me? So I didn't tell Chuck or Hank [Shocklee, Spectrum's producer], at least I don't think so, that Rick is threatening to fire me if you don't sign. But that's when I said, 'Well, rather than be Spectrum City again,' 'cause I understood why Chuck didn't want to be Spectrum City—he didn't want to go to Vinylmania and see another single with his name on it in the 99-cents bin. The idea was to come up with a concept that we could work well with the press and also just the times, politically."

"Back when I was at *CMJ*, around the time of Run hitting," he continues, "I always had at least the desire that the most incredible group to me would be one that meshed the level of politics of The Clash—'cause I was heavily into The Clash and *Sandinista* and 'Rock the Casbah,' the whole nine—and, yunno, Run-D.M.C. was probably my favorite music group of all time. The group that would combine these two things would probably do very well." Hank and Chuck helped to develop this concept further, and the only thing left was coming up with a name. "One day I came back to the studio—510 South Franklin Street in Hempstead, where Spectrum was—and I looked on the board and Chuck had written on the board 'Public Enemy' from that original tape, 'Public Enemy #1.' And I thought that would be fantastic."

Assembling the production team that would be known as the Bomb Squad—including Chuck, Hank and his brother Keith, and Eric Sadler—Stephney got the green light from executive producer Rick Rubin to go into Chung King and INS studios, where the album *Yo! Bum Rush the Show* was assembled for about $17,000. Though selling only about 150,000 copies upon its initial release in 1987, the album launched the career of one of the most influential groups in rap. A sign of the divergent paths that the two label heads were taking, Rick threw his full weight behind the project, while Russell, who was concentrating on building up a roster of r&b artists such as Oran "Juice" Jones, called it "black punk rock."

Despite the overabundance of success at the label, there were also some chinks in the armor. "We were all too young," says Stephney. "When I started at Def Jam I was 23 years old, Rick was 22, Russell was 28, nobody knew anything about business, yunno, George Drakoulias was 22 years old. There were battles sometimes between Def Jam and Rush Productions, which was run for Russell by Lyor Cohen, who still runs Rush, and there were battles between Rick and Lyor. It was a lot of success, but with success came a lot of responsibility, and you had these young people who weren't ready to be responsible yet."

One of the major setbacks suffered by the label was the loss of the Beastie Boys. In the fall of 1987, after touring constantly and selling four million records, the group expected to receive their royalty checks. "So October hit, time to get paid, no check," says Mike D. "So finally we called, and they said, 'We're not paying you till you go back in the studio and make a new record.' So, we sold all these records, we're gonna make another record, but we sold these records, yunno, you gotta pay. That's just the way it works. Well, we're not paying you, we think the group's breaking up, that's it." He adds, "Russell is a lot of fun to hang out with and a brilliant marketing guy, but when it comes to scruples, there's not that many that he has, yunno? So we finally said, 'fuck it, we're breaking out.' " In the spring of 1988 the Beastie Boys were picked up by Capitol, who released the critically acclaimed *Paul's Boutique* (1989) and *Check Your Head* (1992).

Since Rick was producing a lot of Def Jam releases, he received a producer's royalty that Russell did not. Also, on November 4, 1986, the *Village Voice* ran a lengthy article on Rick proclaiming him "The King of Rap." But by around 1987, he was growing weary of the rap scene. "By the time that Public Enemy record came out," says Rick, "you could listen to most shows on BLS and KISS [New York's popular black radio stations], and everything that was coming out sounded like another version of what we had done, and nobody was pushing the limit anymore. Nobody was trying to do new things with it and that was the thing that always kept it exciting for me."

Despite his own prominent role in expanding rap's commercial viability, Rick also laments the fact that it had indeed become a business. "At the time that I started it was still kind of a pure thing, that people weren't doing it thinking they were going to get anything out of it, they were doing it out of love for it. And I think that changed to people thinking they could get something from it. And when that happened the art kind of went away, and it became commerce, and people trying to put records together to sell. And that's really what ruined it for me. The excitement had gone from the music, and it seemed just a way people could think they could cash in."

Russell welcomed the commercial success, for it was the breakthrough he had been working toward for years. Rick, on the other hand, disillusioned by the greening of rap, drifted back toward his more alternative roots, signing the metal band Slayer and comedian Andrew Dice Clay. As Def Jam, then responsible for roughly 70 percent of sales in Columbia's black music division, renegotiated its deal with its major label sponsor, the two partners' conflicting visions collided. When given the opportunity to work on the *Less Than Zero* soundtrack in 1988, Rick shipped out to California—and never returned. He started his own Def American label (now simply American Records) as the lengthy divorce proceedings commenced. Subsequently, in 1990, Russell finalized a deal with the Sony-owned Columbia that made him equal partners with that industry giant.

By the time Carmen Ashhurst-Watson started at Rush, assisting Bill Adler with Run-D.M.C.'s 1988 summer tour, Rick Rubin was already waxing his surfboard. After the summer, Russell kept her on as his own assistant, working out of his Greenwich Village apartment. "When I started working for him," she says, "I saw that while he was only talking about Rush and Def Jam, he actually had a bunch of companies, or there were a lot of different activities and they were crossing over." In addition to the inherent conflict of interest posed by Russell managing the same acts whose records he released, there were undeveloped properties to contend with, as well as a disorganized, corporate structure. Aware of the potential problems in this disarray, she said, "There's a lot going on, we need to backtrack, and you need a parent company so that you're protected both personally and corporately, so your money doesn't get caught up in these things—especially when sampling was becoming so major. So we started Russell Rush Associates, and basically Russell and his activities came under there.

"My primary element was media and culture from the African-American experience and trying to make African-American culture and images significant to black people," says the Boston University graduate, who has extensive experience in television in addition to working with such foundations as Oxfam. Though 37 and of a generation who typically viewed rap as noise, Ashhurst-Watson quickly discovered rap's potential as a powerful musical medium that transcended the frivolity of most popular music. "To me, Russell, although he did not have the same kind of political agenda that I was talking about directly, what he was trying to do fit exactly with what I was trying to do. I mean, he was not going to put out any Tarzan image, and he was really talking about letting black people speak for themselves, and yunno, he wasn't even comfortable with the Cosby image—yunno, he liked it, he thought they were O.K., but he didn't think that was real black America. So I really felt comfortable about helping him build the company."

In 1990, Russell Rush Associates was renamed Rush Communications, Inc., the second largest black-owned entertainment company (next to Black Entertainment Television), whose interests had been clearly delineated into film and television, music publishing, artist management, and, of course, the record label, which had launched it all. After a brief stint as president of the label, Ashhurst-Watson ascended to the top post at Rush and began handling the day-to-day operations, freeing up chairman Russell to pursue his creative vision of selling hip-hop culture to the mainstream. The comparisons to another successful black entrepreneur, Berry Gordy, were obvious, but while Gordy's Motown sold a whitened version of black musical talent to the mainstream, Russell had pulled off the unthinkable: making the mainstream crossover to hip-hop.

"I feel personally very lucky, and I guess we as a company are very lucky, and frankly vindicated, because Def Jam's success has historically been grounded in the validity and the credibility of the artist," says David Harleston, 35, the current president of Def Jam and its counterpart RAL (Rush Associated Labels, an entity to which other subsidiary labels, run by an artist or producer with a proven track record, are signed). "We have never signed an artist who's fakin' it. We don't believe in that. We don't believe in the concept of a one-hit wonder. Why we feel lucky is because over the last five or six years, the entry of rap into more mainstream America or the crossing over of our kind of hip-hop into the pop world has really been more about the pop world coming to us, and less about us going to them." This policy even applies to the manner in which new artists such as Onyx and Boss are brought to the label: While the A&R

department receives about ten unsolicited demo tapes a day, only those acts with some kind of buzz or proven track record are signed.

The Harvard and Yale Law–educated Harleston helped negotiate the legal aspects of the Sony/Columbia joint venture in 1990 before being lured into the Def Jam fold by Ashhurst-Watson and Russell. As vice president of business affairs, he was also instrumental in creating a corporate structure that transformed the company into a legitimate business institution. "Having come from another corporate context, yunno, there were certain things I thought could be imported into this place without destroying its critical character, which is an intimate, street, valid, legitimate, credible kind of place where, frankly, young black kids who have important things to say get to say them," he explains from behind a desk cluttered with paperwork. "So that was the real, not dilemma, but issue, for me, and that was maintaining or creating that critical balance between a company that functions like a company, that fulfills its responsibilities to the outside world and its employees, while at the same time preserving that character that was specifically Def Jam."

This character can be found in the person of Russell himself, who's never worn a suit, never keeps an appointment book, prefers working out of his bedroom rather than an office, and casually flings more expletives than a drill sergeant. Walking through the corridors of the combined Def Jam/Rush Management offices in lower Manhattan, one also senses it in the youthful exuberance of the staff, many of whom are in their twenties. In contrast to what one might expect, there are several white faces here, and women seem to outnumber the men.

As one of the company's elders, Harleston jokes, "Carmen and I evolved into a wonderful unit, if you will, over time, and began putting the house in order. I think—and I don't mean to speak for her—but I think she found in me, kind of, as she would jokingly say, at last another adult, and another person who could back her on the structural stuff that she was trying to put into place." Unlike the chaos of the early days, Def Jam's various departments—artists and repertoire, publicity, marketing and promotion, art, and artist development—have brought the company up to par organizationally with its partner, Columbia, who splits profits equally with Def Jam while supplying them with $3 million a year for operating costs.

Harleston characterizes the initial relationship between Def Jam and Columbia as "fractious" due to a misunderstanding of each other's roles. "When I came on board here," he says, "it was more of a them against us sort of thing. What my mission really was, was to make them understand who we are and help us understand, yunno, who they are, what they do, why they have some of the kind of bureaucratic procedures that we just don't understand down here because they're not necessary in a much smaller outfit." Certainly, at Columbia there is a rigid hierarchy and various levels of approval for each decision made. At Def Jam, Harleston says, the ideas come from many different places, and that is encouraged.

"So over the course of the last couple years," he continues, "we've really had this wonderful marriage of kind of understanding and respect, and acknowledgment that—this sounds corny, but it's true—that when we're talking to each other—I'm talking about Columbia and Def Jam—when we're not being defensive and recognizing that, gee, yunno, maybe, this person does have a good idea about this. And Columbia is realizing, gee, maybe we really don't know the first thing about promoting street products and ought to be giving discretion and leeway for Def Jam to do that sort of stuff, which is sort of what happens now. We have tremendous results." Def Jam/RAL accounted for roughly 60 percent of Rush Communications' $34 million in revenue in 1991. Also, according to Wes Johnson, senior vice president of marketing and promotion, every Def Jam single released in 1993 occupied the number one spot on the *Billboard* rap charts.

In addition to Def Jam and Rush Management, which guides the careers of most of the biggest acts in rap, Russell's golden touch has extended to other efforts to diversify his portfolio. The highly successful (and outrageous) *Def Comedy Jam* evolved out of Rush's *New Music Report* video show, which was syndicated by Guber Peters Television. A longtime patron of uptown comedy clubs, Russell discovered that the show's comedic skits were almost as popular as the videos themselves. When Guber Peters sold out to Columbia, he set about trying to find another format in which to combine hip-hop and street humor. With associate Stan Lathan, a director of such TV shows as *Roc* and *Frank's Place*, Russell approached Hollywood megaproducers Bernie Brillstein and Brad Grey (managers of Dan Ackroyd, Dennis Miller, and Dana Carvey and producers of both *Ghostbusters* films as well as *Wayne's World*) to develop *Def Comedy Jam*, which they sold to HBO. The first episode aired in the winter of 1992, and following impressive ratings, SLBG's (Simmons, Lathan, Brillstein, and Grey) contract was renewed for 22 shows. Then, in April of 1992 they pushed it one step further with the Def Comedy Jam live tour. Phat fashions, a line of "classic," hip-hop–inspired clothing sold out of the Phat Farm store in Soho, is Russell's latest expansion into a new area, though one still based in hip-hop.

Evaluating Def Jam's role in the explosion of hip-hop culture, Harleston says, "Well, I would say that if not for us, it probably would not have happened. I mean, that sounds so arrogant, so obnoxious," he concedes, "but hip-hop has exploded because Russell Simmons made hip-hop explode. Hip-hop exploded because when all he was doing was managing Run-D.M.C., before Def Jam, he was in program directors' faces saying, you cannot ignore this, you cannot ignore this—because he was relentless. And why? Because it's in his heart and soul. Because he was relentless, avenues of radio, whatever, paid attention. He was able to deliver to kids something they really wanted. And he was able to make the middle people deliver it. So I really believe that the explosion—and I'm calling the explosion like years ago—is because of him."

But without the right talent behind him, his efforts would have been in vain. Prime Minister Pete Nice (Pete Nash) who, along with former partner MC Serch, was signed to Def Jam in 1988 as the label's second white rap act 3rd Bass says, "I think a lot has changed in rap. I mean, a lot of other labels have caught up—now you have Priority, Tommy Boy, all these other labels, doing virtually the same thing, yunno. I think Def Jam kind of set an example for other people to follow. We owe a lot to the company, as they owe to the groups, because if it wasn't for the groups, they wouldn't have nothing."

Bill Adler, a longtime friend of Russell's and author of several books on hip-hop, including *Tougher Than Leather: The Story of Run-D.M.C.* best sums up his former boss's contributions when he says, "Russell's genius was to say that there was such a thing as hip-hop culture. It was more than music, it was a whole lifestyle, and it was creative and unique on its own. You could throw away the showbiz—it stood up on its own." In a business where success is fleeting and longevity rare, Russell Simmons has stood the test of time. On the strength of hip-hop, a culture of vitality and change, his vision continues to unfold.

recommended
listening

1. Run-D.M.C., *Run-D.M.C.* (Profile, 1984).
2. "It's Yours," T LA Rock (Def Jam/Streetwise, 1985).
3. L.L. Cool J., *Radio* (Def Jam, 1985).
4. Beastie Boys, *License to Ill* (Def Jam, 1986).
5. Run-D.M.C., *Raising Hell* (Profile, 1986).
6. Public Enemy, *Yo! Bum Rush the Show* (Def Jam, 1987).
7. Slick Rick, *The Great Adventures of Slick Rick* (Def Jam/Columbia, 1988).
8. 3rd Bass, *The Cactus Album* (Def Jam/Columbia, 1989).
9. Nikki D., *Daddy's Little Girl* (Def Jam/Columbia, 1990).
10. Nice & Smooth, *Ain't a Damned Thing Changed* (RAL/Columbia, 1991).
11. Onyx, *Bacdafucup* (RAL, 1993).

ChApTeR 7

Straight from the Boondocks

Two hooded figures pace a small stage waiting for the digital audiotape to kick in. Their heads hang low, like boxers', concealing looks of stone-faced seriousness. Black fists clench microphones, and new Timberland boots shine under the track lights.

Suddenly, a keyboard phrase rips through the giant JBL speakers like a jet passing overhead. As the sound segues into a creeping, bass-heavy beat, Dray, the shorter of the duo, says, "The funk is in the house . . . Peace to my niggers, and all a that . . . We comin' straight from the sewer," punctuated by the "yeahs" of his partner, Skoob. With precise timing, they start trading scatlike rhymes over the beat as they move around one another onstage. Pointing up and around at imagined hordes, the two observe their movements on the wall-size mirrors they face. This time it's just for practice.

Six heads bob in approval as they are treated to a sneak preview of Das EFX, a rap group whose name stands for Dray and Skoob Effects. It's mid-February outside but womblike within the dark rehearsal space of SIR studios on West 25th Street in Manhattan. Here the novices work on their stage act in preparation for their first New York performance on March 6. Soon after that the video for their single, "They Want EFX," will appear on MTV, with the release of their debut album *Dead Serious* (East-West/Atlantic, 1992) following in April. So begins another career in rap music.

But unlike other new acts, Das EFX has the advantage of guidance from proven professionals. Their mentors are EPMD (Erick and Parrish Making Dollars), who had stepped into the scene in 1988. Since then, Erick Sermon, 22, and Parrish Smith, 24, have built a small rap empire on the strength of three gold albums and a very serious approach to music that is reflected in their album titles: *Strictly Business* (Fresh, 1988), *Unfinished Business* (Fresh, 1989), and *Business As Usual* (Def Jam, 1991). Like most rappers, EPMD roll with a "posse" of supporters, or a close circle of friends, including K-Solo (Kevin Madison), Redman (Reggie Noble), and Tom J. (Jiminez), who also are involved in making music. Collectively known as the Hit Squad, this formidable group of rappers is poised to make a significant impact in the world of beats. As the newest members of this crew, Das EFX have all the clout of a trust-fund child in the Ivy League.

When the song ends, Parrish, who has been directing the movements on stage, scrutinizing every step, says, "Yo, Dray, when you start losing energy, your crowd is gonna start losing energy. You guys gotta be in shape for that. And remember to tell 'em the name of the group and the name of the album." A strapping six-footer in a dark blue sweatsuit, Parrish seems an unlikely choreographer, but he has stepped on many stages in his career and knows how to move a crowd. As his protégés take a break, he cues up a tape of EPMD's latest material and adds some lyrical relish on the microphone.

Underlying a slow, staggered beat, the bass shakes the entire room and is complemented by Parrish's smooth, deep delivery. He stalks the stage like a panther, using his free hand to emphasize his words. Dray and Skoob note the laid-back strut and the ease of his delivery, which has earned him the nicknames "Microphone Doctor" and "Slow Flower." Their road manager, Anthony "Blitz" Botter, along with Das EFX producers Chris Charity and Derek Lynch, nod their heads to the pounding groove. As laughter interrupts the flow of words from his mouth, Parrish prompts the young rappers to pick up where he left off. Then the mike lands in the hands of Tom J., a clean-shaven, white youth bundled in a hooded sweat-shirt, Giants cap, and chunky, down parka. He is part of a duo called Knucklehedz, who are working on an album with the help of Erick and Parrish. Lounging on the black couch with Chris and Derek, he takes his feet slowly and throws some freestyle rhymes over the music as the others encourage him on. Everyone is impressed, and they give him a pound when he finishes. Then it's back to business.

Dray discards his hooded sweatshirt, revealing a thick clump of dread-locks and a red, gold, and green tie-dyed shirt. Skoob, too, strips down to a T-shirt, but keeps his dreads tucked in a black, wool tam. Both are engulfed in faded, baggy blue jeans hanging down around hip level, with beepers clipped to their front pockets. As their backing track, with its catchy guitar loop from James Brown's "Black Caesar," booms over the sound system again, the two start moving with renewed vigor. Skoob mimics the mechanical movements of a robot, while Dray, thrashing his head about, raps:

> Bum stiggety, bum stiggety bum, hun,
> I got that old rump-pa-pum-pum
> But I could fe-fi-your fo diddly fum, here I come
> So Peter Piper, I'm hyper than Pinnochio's nose
> Cause I'm a supercalafragalistic tic tac pro
> I gave her oopsie, daisy, now you got the crazy,
> Drayz with the Books, skoogly goo where's the gravy
> So one, two, unbuckle my, um, shoe
> Yabba do, hibbedy hoo, crack a brew
> Trick or treat, smell my feet, let me drippety drop a hit
> So Books get on your mark, and spark that old ill shi . . .

**THE DREAD-HEADED
DUO OF DAS EFX.**

They successfully maneuver around each other despite a jumble of microphone cords, and when the two-song set ends Parrish says, "You niggas is ready for the Apollo." Then he takes them aside to discuss some finer points.

Das EFX's association with the Hit Squad began on January 31, 1991, a date Dray calls, "The most memorable night of our lives." The young rappers, then roommates in their junior year at Virginia State University, entered a rap contest in Richmond that Erick and Parrish were judging. Dray (Andre Weston), 21, from Teaneck, New Jersey, and Skoob (Will Hines), 21, from Brooklyn, had heard about the contest on the radio while working on a math assignment. "We just heard the commercial about the talent show, and we heard it once that day," recalls Dray. "We just happened to be listening to the radio." Hearing of EPMD's involvement, they just dropped their pencils and looked at each other in amazement. "We be like, a rap show, what's up man?"

Erick and Parrish, on a promotional tour for Def Jam, were seeking to develop new talent. "So we got up to the club," recalls Parrish, "and there was a lot of rappers out there, and when they get up there, some of them feel like they all amped, but they could be doin' a whole lot better." Das EFX, however, "caught Erick and I attention. What they had was put together, and their lyrics was decent, and they ripped stuff, but the club was so hectic and there were so many knuckleheads in there that, ah, you know, we let this other guy win." After the show, however, EPMD approached Dray and Skoob, offering them a chance to record instead of the $100 first prize. Parrish remembers thinking, "Yo, these guys could be diesel with some work," and he said he would give them a call when he returned to his home in Long Island.

An excited Skoob passed the news on to his friend Derek Lynch in Brooklyn. While students at Bishop Ford Central Catholic High School in Park Slope, they had dabbled in making music using a simple drum machine and two turntables. "We were like, doin' songs," explains Derek, "rap songs, right out of the crib, for fun. Like on the weekends." Hearing of EPMD's apparent interest, Derek was leery. "I was like, nah, stop lying. I couldn't believe it. When he first told me I was like, aw, this is like another one of those things where EPMD would never call back again."

An employee at Abraham & Strauss department store at the time, Derek, 21, desperately wanted to pursue music. At an earlier stint at Kingsborough College, he had met fellow Brooklynite Chris Charity, 20, an electronics major, and in December 1988, Derek, Skoob, and Chris stepped into a studio for the first time. With Skoob playing keyboards and Derek on the turntables, Chris produced a house song called "Acid Prism." They made more jams during sporadic studio sessions when the money permitted, but when Das EFX began, both Derek and Chris were still working full-time.

"I always thought like, oh, whatever, we'll see what's up with that," says Derek, "and then, like, as it went on, it was like, oh, yo, Parrish called and he was, like, 'Bring me five songs' and all this, and that's when we got serious."

Investing $2,300 in an Ensoniq EPS II keyboard sampler, they started working on tracks at Chris's closet-size, home studio in Brooklyn's Crown Heights. Dray and Skoob would drive up from Virginia on weekends to pick up new beats and return a week later with lyrics. Then they pooled their funds for studio time, and within a month had recorded five songs. Das EFX had originally captured EPMD's attention with a song called "Klap Ya Handz," produced by Dexter James. They also had two other tunes, "They Want EFX" and "Looseys," which were joint efforts of Skoob and Derek. The remaining tracks for the ten-song album were the collaborative effort of Chris and Derek, who called their production team Solid Scheme.

Working out of Firehouse Studios in Brooklyn Heights and North Shore Soundworks in Long Island, Solid Scheme and Das EFX recorded the album between March and November of 1991. Sitting in Chris's house, a dreadlocked Derek says, "All the ideas for the songs were between us four—me, Skoob, Dray, Chris—you know, we did it all together, but EPMD was the executive producers. If we did a song they didn't like, they tell us, take that out or do this, but, you know, basically all the production stuff was between us." Chris, smoking a Newport, adds, "We had never done it before, done an album, so we didn't know that like, doin' an album means, yo, you in the studio like six days out of seven days a week." The last four months were especially demanding, says Chris. "One day off and ten days straight, full-time. Full-time. It's no joke—the process of doin' it. You get towards the end and it's really a serious thing."

Appropriately, the album is called *Dead Serious*, a title Dray explains as meaning, "This is our life we're lookin' at, you know. This is a career for us now. There's no more whining and all a that stuff. It's fun bein' a rapper and doin' what you want to do, but you gotta take your shit seriously.

"Yo, this shit, we look at it as, yo, this is our last chance—not our first chance—it's our last chance to make a record. We're not serious about this shit, ain't nobody gonna want to fuck with us next time, knowwhatimsayin? It's all about, yo, let's make sure this shit happens, you know?"

Dropping out of Virginia State to complete the album, Dray and Skoob had a lot riding on their musical venture—parental concern being the most obvious. But Dray's father, Alvin Weston, a former journalist and reggae producer from Jamaica, had confidence in the venture, saying, "My reaction was not like the regular parent. Education is paramount, but when Parrish showed enthusiasm, I said to him [Dray], 'Go ahead,' and gave him my full support."

Like Dray and Skoob, Parrish had sacrificed his senior year of college to make a bid for music. "If business is not straight," he says, "then all this is senseless. You drop one def album, the money's all messed up, you can't pay for this. Then next year, when it's time to step to the second album, you got too many problems to even think of Das EFX. And then what's gonna happen? You're gonna rush your album and it's gonna be garbage. When it's time to do concerts and rip shows, and write music, it's all fun, but it ain't no fun when you got massive headaches in the industry, which is ruining a lot of rappers today."

Though Parrish exudes the confidence of a multiplatinum-selling artist who has always taken care of business, he also speaks with the experience of someone who has charted a course through the perilous music industry successfully. He admits, "Sure we could pull, we could mess up, and we could go out, but we try to limit that. And the only way to limit that is to be in control, sum all that stuff up. 'Cause you ain't in control of your life and the whole shit be goin' down. What more could you ax for than being able to wake up every morning and make your own opportunities for yourself and make at least $100,000? For just sitting down, writin' lyrics, and makin' beats."

In the September 1991 issue of *The Source*, a pictorial entitled "Fat Rides of the Rich and Famous" features Erick Sermon and Parrish Smith posing beside their small fleet of luxury automobiles. Parrish leans against his desert-red 1989 Mercedes Benz 560 SEC while his onyx 1991 Corvette

ZR1 convertible looms in the background. Erick, opposite him, sits atop a modest midnight-blue 1989 Mercedes Benz 300E. Parrish flashes his typically stern look, but the small grin on Erick's face acknowledges that they truly are making dollars. With three gold albums behind them, they are selling more plastic than American Express.

Their career in rap music was launched during the summer of 1987 with a single called "It's My Thing / You're a Customer" (Sleeping Bag/Fresh), which was released while Erick was still in high school and Parrish was a sophomore in college. They were longtime friends, born and raised in the suburban town of Brentwood, Long Island (population 45,218), about an hour's commute by train from Manhattan. Parrish best relates his story in rhyme. In the song "It Wasn't Me, It Was the Fame," from EPMD's second album, *Unfinished Business*, he says:

> Before I cut records I had dreams of livin' large
> Runnin' crazy cash flow, the whole nine yards
> But when I told my college friends they kicked back
>   and laughed
> Said you better grab your books and take your behind to class
> They said you couldn't make a record and expect to get paid
> 'Cause there's too many def rappers in the world today
> I said, yo, my name is MD and my style is def
> They said your name is Parrish, son, and you're like all
>   the rest
> Frontin', you're gettin' a contract? You fess
> But when you heard my record playing your mouth was
>   wide open
> You're head was tilted back and you was almost choking
> But I just lounged and cooled with the fellas
> Like my roomie D. Wade, Tom Knox and James Ellis . . .
> My record started selling, then the P withdrew
> From the college Southern Conn. known as SCSU.

Parrish's roomate, Dennis B. Wade, was in football camp with him when they heard "It's My Thing" on the radio for the first time. "That's the day I'll never forget, you know," he says. "We just sittin' there, and we didn't have a big radio, and it was all staticky, but we heard it. I think that's when everything started rolling."

Erick and Parrish commenced work on the album, sometimes practicing rhymes over the phone. When *Strictly Business* was finally released in the summer of 1988, it took only six weeks to eclipse bestsellers such as Prince, Sade, and Michael Jackson and clinch the top spot on *Billboard's* black music charts. Roughly one month later, the album went gold, prompting Parrish to quit school in his junior year so that he and Erick could go on tour.

Since then, they have toured often and wide, even bringing their brand of smooth yet rough hardcore hip-hop to such obscure venues as Wichita, Kansas; Little Rock, Arkansas; and St. Paul, Minnesota. But hailing from Brentwood, they know that the "boondocks" can still be rugged. Like their music—tough talk over smooth funk tracks—their personas tread the line of contradiction. While EPMD embodies the image of the hardcore B-Boy, they are very laid-back. Always ready to get the job done, they are content to take it easy. Erick and Parrish combine work and play into the activity they have mastered: "chillin'."

On an evening in late February 1992, Erick and Parrish can be found chillin' at PowerPlay Studios, nestled amid the drab, working-class sprawl of Long Island City, Queens. Inside, the studio resembles the bridge of the starship *Enterprise*, glistening with high-technology sound equipment—the centerpiece of which is a fifteen-foot- by four-foot mixing console studded with hundreds of small knobs, dials, and meters. Sitting behind it, a boyish Ivan "Doc" Rodriguez, 32, with baseball cap worn backward, controls the 48 tracks. His fingers nimbly make adjustments as he consults coded instructions from a television monitor that hangs directly above. His assistant, Rob Curbelo, 21, makes some necessary connections with patch cords. Parrish, meanwhile, lounges at the back on a black leather couch, and Erick reclines in a chair.

EPMD is in the process of mixing their fourth album, *Business Never Personal* (culled from a Wesley Snipes line in the film *New Jack City*), which is slated for a summer release. They were supposed to be in the studio the previous night, too, but Doc was sick and, as Parrish explains, "We never work without Doc," who has been their studio engineer for the last two albums. He has also worked with practically every major act in hip-hop, including Boogie Down Productions, Eric B. & Rakim, and Biz Markie. As engineer, Doc sets recording levels and transfers the recording from two-inch reel-to-reel to digital audiotape. He also works out last-minute flaws before the master is sent to be equalized and finally duplicated and manufactured as CDs or cassettes.

As music booms from the seven-foot- by four-foot speakers that are built into the wall facing the console, Parrish's gaze is intent. He is not

PARRISH SMITH LOUNGES AT POWERPLAY STUDIOS.

satisfied with the opening lines to "Brother from Long Island" and tells Doc that he wants to rerecord them. Stepping into the vocal booth and donning headphones, he is visible through the thick glass window facing the mixing console.

"One, two," says Parrish into the mike, asking Doc, "You gonna put more bass in the music?" Then, nodding his head, he begins rhyming, "Peace to the posse / Yeah, O.K., ya got me / Another rap junky, about to O.D. / Beat fanatic, straight from the hard scene" before trailing off.

"One more time, Doc," says Parrish. Doc rewinds the reel-to-reel, saying, "You don't think you sound too laid-back?"

They run through it again, the level meters on the reel-to-reel bouncing into the red. "Yo, E.," says Parrish. "Yo, Erick, did that sound cool?" Erick, who is having some trouble staying awake says, "Yeah, it sounds the same."

"One more time D.," says Parrish. They redo the same part three more times. After the last try Parrish says, "Whaddaya think E.?"

"It was pretty cool," responds Erick, coming to life suddenly. It's a take. As Parrish rejoins the others in the main studio, he says to no one in particular, "One little glitch and you'll be pissed off when you play it in the jeep."

They listen to "Brother from Long Island," which begins with a scream courtesy of James Brown. Like a tongue twister, the song's chorus repeats, "Brother from Brentwood, Long Island, Brother from Brentwood, Long Island" over a hard cymbal slam and EPMD's trademark subterranean bass sound. "So Doc, the speakers got room to breathe, right," says Parrish. "The bass is gonna be throwin' in the cars." Doc responds by playing the song on just the high- and midrange speakers, before clicking in the bass. Heads nod. With his clients satisfied, he records it from the reel to the DAT. Despite the time and trouble they put into this tune, it will not even appear on the completed album, but as the B-side on the first single.

Weeks later, with their studio work completed, Erick and Parrish reminisce about their early days in the almost bucolic surroundings of Brent-

wood. At the beginning of high school, Erick had just moved from Regis Park, which he describes as "strictly hardcore, yunno, kinda rough," to the next block over from Parrish. With a lisp that is accentuated by an occasional stammer, Erick explains, "We met in school, where the first day, I'm on the bus and stuff, and my mother had shaved my head, she gave me a bald head and everything," breaking into a chuckle. "And I had on some fake sneakers," he continues, "I thought they was real Pumas, but they wasn't the real ones. And, you know, Parrish and them was snappin' on me and everything like that."

From this adolescent hazing developed a friendship that was strengthened through the common bond of music. Erick was into rhyming and body popping, a form of break-dancing, while Parrish deejayed. Parrish's family was also known for the huge block parties they threw for his older brother and sister's high school graduations. No ordinary fetes, these events featured the legendary Afrika Bambaataa and the Zulu Nation.

With such exposure to the burgeoning Bronx hip-hop scene, Erick and Parrish started making their own demo tapes, but with no thoughts of actually making a record themselves. "And then, when the radio came on and there were some fake brothers on the microphone," says Erick, "we had to say, 'Yo, hold on. This can be done.' "

Parrish, who had entered college by this time, working summers in a bakery to earn his tuition, diverted these funds toward time at North Shore Studios in Long Island, where the duo cut their demo. "We took our chance," says Erick, "and, you know, there's nothing else out there, and you try to make it, and the world is hard, and you gonna spend your college money? We knew we was better than some guys on the radio, that we would get heard." Parrish adds, "The music sounded like it was ready to go. Because there's a difference between spendin' your money for a fuckin' demo and comin' home with 'It's My Thing' and 'You're a Customer.' We liked the shit."

They applied this same confidence and drive toward getting a recording contract, a difficult proposition for young, unproven artists with no acclimation to the music industry. "We didn't even know nothin' about Manhattan," says Parrish. "We just jumped in the vehicle and rode to the big city, and we was like, yo, we in this to win it. Walked the pavement and the whole nine."

Topping a list of prospective record labels they had made was Sleeping Bag/Fresh, a hungry, independent dance label that had also developed an interest in rap. Upon hearing the demo, label president Will Socolov recalls, "I said, 'Sign them immediately." I could tell it was slammin'. I knew it was great." *Strictly Business* eventually became Sleeping Bag's top-selling album of all time. Featuring the slow, laid-back rapping style of Erick and Parrish, and samples showcasing the seventies hits of Bob Marley, Steve Miller, Rick James, Kool & the Gang, and Zapp, Socolov says, "I think that first album was an absolute classic." Few in the industry would dispute him.

Initially signing to Sleeping Bag/Fresh for $15,000, EPMD got a six-figure advance for their second album, *Unfinished Business*, which continued their agenda of "snappin" necks and cashin' large checks." Tracks such as "So Wat Cha Sayin'," "The Big Payback," and "Get the Bozack" forged a new, deadly sound and created a huge underground following for EPMD. This sophomore effort also featured the turntable wizardry of DJ Scratch (George Spivey), a local star from Brooklyn's Albany projects who became a permanent fixture in the group. With their Timberlands comfortably in the door and their stars on the rise, Erick and Parrish found themselves in a position to bring some of their friends along on the musical odyssey.

The track "Knick Knack Patty Wack," for example, debuted the lyrical skills of Kevin "K-Solo" Madison, from neighboring Central Islip, Long Island, whom Parrish had known through their association in a group called the Rock Squad. After his guest appearance on *Unfinished Business*, Erick and Parrish produced Solo's album *Tell the World My Name* (Atlantic), which was released in 1990.

A one-time contender for the Empire State boxing championship, Solo came to the Hit Squad through a circuitous path that included a 16-month jail term for aggravated assault and battery. He recalls the incident that put him there—which occurred on his birthday, April 17, in 1985—in the hit song, "Fugitive":

> Here I was walking down the block
> I seen these two big bikers standin' by the bikers' shop
> They seen it was me, and to make themselves feel bigger
> One pointed at me, and he called me a nigger
> I stuck my finger up, said his mother, and kept steppin'
> His friend told his other friend, Korky, Hey let's get him
> I looked to my back, to my surprise
> One had a chain, and the devil in his eyes
> I said, I'm in trouble, let me think real quick
> I looked down on the ground and got this big, fat brick
> With no time to waste I put the brick in my hand
> And hit the biker till the chain fell out of his hand.

Today, this unfortunate biker has a steel plate in his head from the damage sustained after Solo's fury. "I was fed up that day," says Solo, 27. "It was my birthday, I had nothing to be proud of. I had nothing to be happy with, and now I'm being called 'nigger.' And it could have been my little brother." A racist attack in Howard Beach had only recently left a black youth dead. "So with that in mind," says Solo, "I did what I did, and I would do it again tomorrow."

Of his time behind bars, he says, "It was hell. It was my worst nightmare. I didn't want to be there. But God works in mysterious ways, because when I went to jail, I didn't have any urge to sit back and listen to inmates talk about crack or girls or cars. I sat and wrote *Tell the World My Name*," as well as his latest release, *Time's Up* (Atlantic, 1992). Keeping to himself, he earned the nickname, K-Solo, a self-proclaimed acronym for Kevin Self Organization Left Others. After being released in 1988, he worked various odd jobs before a mutual friend brought him to Parrish's attention. Solo says, "He [Parrish] felt strong with it, like I did, and it happened. We got busy, and everything else, yunno, fell in place."

Reggie Noble (a.k.a. Redman) came to the Hit Squad through an equally roundabout route, which is confirmed by his own admission that "I wasn't even supposed to be here, youknowwhatimsayin.' " It all began one night at Sensations, a Newark, New Jersey, nightclub where MC Lyte was scheduled to perform. When she canceled at the last minute, however, her spot was filled by EPMD. At the time, Redman deejayed for a friend who rapped, and they were all hanging out at the club with Erick, kicking verses. Despite having only one rhyme, Redman was goaded into rapping, and Erick was so impressed that he gave him his number. "I think my man got jealous and shit," says Redman. "And when Erick was passing me his phone number, my man took it."

But this move did not prevent Redman from finally contacting Erick, and rapping some newly written rhymes over the phone to him. He also journeyed to Brentwood twice before Erick put him up indefinitely after he was kicked out of his mother's house. In repeated trouble with the law for dealing drugs, Redman's involvement with the Hit Squad saved him from the streets. "I ain't even gonna front," he says. "I'd probably be locked up. I was selling everything from weed to rock, youknowwhatimsayin'?"

A hip-hop junkie since the age of 16, Redman, now 22, got his first chance to unleash his rough rhyme style on "Hardcore" and "Brothers on My Jock" from EPMD's *Business As Usual* in 1991. On their most recent *Business Never Personal* LP, he also appears with K-Solo on the song "Headbanger." His own scorching debut, *Whut? Thee Album* (Def Jam, 1992), was produced in collaboration with Erick.

"It's a whole bunch of shit, man," says Redman about making an album. "Muthafuckas is gonna be lookin' at you like, oh, you makin' a record, so you chillin', you in a jacuzzi, you over there with EPMD. But see, muthafuckas don't know, man." Having learned about the industry through Erick and Parrish, he echoes the familiar wisdom: "If you don't have the business, no matter what you say, you ain't goin' nowhere."

Despite the abundance of talent in the Hit Squad, Solo concedes, "It's so hard to say that if you're good, then you'll make it. That's not true. There's a lot of guys that are good that don't make it, yunno. You gotta be around somebody that knows the flavor, and P. knows a lot of flavor. P. knows a lot of shit that's goin' on in the industry." But the combination of business savvy and street smarts that characterizes the Hit Squad comes not only from Erick and Parrish.

**ERICK AND PARRISH
MAKE DOLLARS
AT THE MUSE.**

"Erick and Parrish can do shit on their own," says Redman, "and I love them brothers, but to the fact that they got brothers like us hangin' around them, it's like, yo, 'cause I'm strictly nigro." This connection to the streets is consistently reflected in EPMD's music, bass heavy, villainous funk, which has tremendous appeal to the underground core of hip-hop. No other group brings to life the image of the hand-on-his-crotch, hardcore street soldier as effectively as EPMD.

"Every time we bring in a new group, like Das EFX or Redman," says Parrish, "these guys are really from the street, so we can't be naive to the fact that we gonna put our stuff in jeopardy. So we be out there in the street."

"That's the main reason we're still here," adds Erick. "When something is goin' on you always have to stay focussed to what's goin' on, 'cause if not, you're gonna lose."

For EPMD, the music is a constant, driving force. "We still in there making the music," says Parrish. "And we in there for the music." He shuns the complacency that success often brings, saying, "The minute you sit back and you go to that big restaurant, you're sittin' back in there in the nice big house and the vacation and the girl, you away from all that, man. We don't give a fuck about none of that."

"This is your job," reminds Erick. "And without your job there ain't gonna be no house, and there ain't gonna be all type of stuff happening, restaurants and big vacations, and stuff like that."

On March 5, the eve of their first New York performance, Dray and Skoob once again trundle into the $55-per-hour rehearsal space at SIR for one last look in the mirrors. Blitz, their road manager, carries a Das EFX twelve-inch single, newly purchased from Tower Records. "They Want EFX" is already ruling the airwaves and getting serious play on MTV. Blitz does not have the DAT tonight, but a copy of it, dubbed over a cassette of *Vulgar Display of Power* (Atco, 1992), by heavy-metal rockers Pantera. He cues up the tape before adjusting levels on the Soundcraft mixing board. Dray and Skoob, meanwhile, throw their belongings—knapsacks, some photo albums from their recent West Coast promotional tour, and a red-striped box of Kentucky Fried Chicken—on the couch, and slide out of sleek, black Das EFX–logo jackets. Embroidered in gold on the sleeve is "Da Yung and Da Restless."

Both rappers wear their dreads, which have been growing since January 1989, in matching, black wool tams. They limber up onstage as the instrumental of "Straight from the Sewer" booms over the JBLs. Skoob mimics a beat box in between saying, "Yeah, turn the shit up . . . Yeah . . . Turn it, turn it up, yeah." Blitz pushes up the volume slowly. Dray joins with, "We want to know who want EFX. My nigger Books is gonna start one off like this . . ." They run through the entire show tape once before discussing staging and how they will make their entrance. Then they rehearse into the night.

As the tape rolls, the duo are animated by the music. Blitz goes over to the light switch and starts flicking it on and off to simulate a strobe. Dray comes in with an ad-libbed introduction: "Straight from the muthafuckin' sewer, from the land of the lost, it's the young and the, uh, restless." Skoob delivers his lines with sweeping hand motions. Dray dances around his

DAS EFX
REHEARSE FOR
THEIR FIRST
NEW YORK
APPEARANCE.

microphone wire, strutting around the stage as if he's having an epileptic seizure. When the music ends, however, Blitz is not there to cut it off and a barrage of Pantera's acidic guitar riffs shatters everyone's eardrums. Dashing over to stop it, he discovers that they have lost sound in one of the JBLs. "Shit is thick," says Blitz, shaking his head.

After deciding to not immediately inform the SIR staff about the mishap, Das EFX practice at half volume. The mood is one of trepidation and disbelief. "Shit, rock bands must play louder than this," says Dray. Toward the end of their two-hour session, Erick Sermon, accompanied by K-Solo and Solo's cousin, R. Kim, troop in to liven up the atmosphere. Erick, sporting bright yellow denims, takes the mike to perform his own garbled version of "Straight from the Sewer," which is almost unintelligible because he doesn't know the words. Then Dray and Skoob do "They Want EFX" for their new audience, joined onstage by K-Solo and Erick, who primp and pose in front of the mirrors.

After tinkering with the soundboard, Blitz discovers, to everyone's relief, that they have not damaged the speaker. But the rest of the session is spent hanging out. Solo shadowboxes onstage as he discusses an upcoming celebrity boxing event. Erick, meanwhile, shares stories about trouble on tour, relating an incident when a hostile crew pulled guns on EPMD and they had to run for cover. Then he discovers the photo albums, and everyone gathers around to gawk at photos of ripe California beauties. There is even one of Dray and Skoob, sans dreadlocks, during their early days of college.

The following night at Manhattan's Muse club, Das EFX are introduced to their first New York crowd. Before they perform, a hooded Dray and Skoob casually eye the packed house from the V.I.P. area above the main floor. Any anxiety is hidden behind poker faces. "Jus' chillin'," says Dray in his usual deadpan. The whole V.I.P. section is a slalom course of photographers, film crews, profiling homeboys, glamorous women, and other rappers, and the duo are swept up in a storm of activity.

Down on the floor, where there is little room to breathe, the crowd is slightly on edge because the evening's entertainment has been moving slowly. A disturbance in the back sends everyone fleeing in a mad rush in all directions. Apparently, people in line who are still attempting to get inside, caused this stampede, prompting DJ Clark Kent, the show's promoter, to try to calm the crowd down. Standing on the stage, he says, "Check this out. Black people only understand one language y'all. I can't say nothin' like a human being 'cause niggas outside gotta act like fuckin' fools. Was y'all havin' a good time?" The crowd cheers. "If somethin' was wrong, please tell me, man, I would have closed this shit down. Do you all want the show to go on?" Once again the crowd roars. "Well, all these niggas on this fuckin' stage gotta get off the fuckin' stage, and niggas cannot flip. If niggas flip, you go the fuck home. I already got your money. Now think about it like that." Muffled laughter runs through the crowd. "Y'all want to see the rest of the show?" A universal roar. "Let me see the peace sign in the air one time. Everybody just chill." With crowd control taken care of, a group called Original Flavor comes on to do two songs. People clearly want EFX, however, and a chant begins at about 2:00 A.M.

Dr. Dre, the rotund host of *Yo! MTV Raps*, asks that the spiral staircase leading from the V.I.P. area to the stage be cleared so that Das EFX can descend. Dray and Skoob arrive onstage saying, "Yeah, yeah," "word is bond, check it out. Yo, kick the funk, G." When the music hits, they start bouncing around in a frenzy and, feeding off their energy, practically everyone in the house begins to pogo in tandem. Behind the duo, the extended Hit Squad family crowds the stage, lending their support. After the show, admist cheers, they all come forward and acknowledge the crowd.

The last track on EPMD's *Business As Usual* LP is a stick-up fantasy set to a funked-up beat that sounds like a ticking time bomb. Fittingly titled "Hit Squad Heist," the perpetrators are none other than Erick, Parrish, K-Solo, Redman, Tom J., and other Squad members, including Albie (Alvin Toney) and D. Wade. This aural adventure features lyrics such as, "Freeze, put your hands up, don't make a move" and the sound of screeching tires and explosions. With the crime reference implicit in the name

"Hit Squad," Tom J. explains that they are, in fact, "like a Mafia." He adds, "It's like a crime family, but we're not doin' crime." The Hit Squad are terrorists on wax who snatch up the funds and churn out hits. But their business is completely legitimate.

After years of getting into fights, joyriding, and generally causing havoc, Steve Leonard, 20, who along with Tom comprises the Knucklehedz, says, "Finally, you know, we're a part of something that's positive. 'Cause everyone who's out here now, you could be a part of a gang, but a gang ain't positive. We're a part of the Hit Squad, and the Hit Squad is strictly positive—gettin' what you want out of life, you know, and helpin' each other."

According to Parrish, the Hit Squad is "sort of like a whole mode. It's a feeling, yunno. Guys come in there and they have to understand what's goin' on. Basically just serious brothers who want to do for themselves. And doing for yourself don't mean a big gold chain and money in your pocket. It's longevity—can you sit around a pool at 35 or 40. That's what the Hit Squad is, 'cause there's no wild Indians out there flauntin', 'cause if they look bad, they gonna make us look bad."

At a memorable show at New York's Marquee, featuring EPMD and Run-D.M.C., shots were fired backstage, and people pointed the finger at Tom J., whose reputation has gotten him into trouble on many occasions. He says he had nothing to do with the incident, however, and further concedes that he has changed a lot since being around Erick, Parrish, and the rest of the Hit Squad. "I've learned how to block a lot of shit out, man," he says. "Lot of things used to bother us, you know. We used to take care of it the way we have to take care of it, but now it's like, you just learn to brush shit off, and just concentrate on what you gotta do." Music has opened new horizons for Tom and Steve, who says, "If you have a goal, and you focus on it hard enough, you can do it." Knucklehedz is currently at work on an album, which will feature tracks produced by Erick, Parrish, and Solid Scheme.

While the Hit Squad encompasses many flavors of rap, there exists a basic unity within the crew. "We're into each other's music, man, yunno," says Solo. Redman adds, "It ain't like we lookin' at each other, oh, he got a better album, O.K., we gotta go back in here. We ain't really schemin' on each other and shit, it's just like, yo, that shit is slammin'. We all learn from each other so, boom. By that, we all come out with the slammin' shit."

From Erick's perspective, "Everybody coincides with everybody. Everybody's out here trying to make it, trying to live comfortably. There's no rule, yunno, everybody know what time it is. Rap is in here for we don't know how long, and we gonna try to fuckin' capitalize and try to get paid. And let everybody come correct, man."

EPMD are obviously doing something right, as they sell records without the kind of publicity that surrounds more commercial rappers whose appeal is measured by the pop charts. Though chart-toppers themselves, EPMD's fan base comes from the street. Parrish credits the group's longevity to "the music and the fans. You see a lot of rappers lose their base with the business. The business messes them up and pulls that connection from the fans. But with Erick and I, man, no matter what, man, we always want to drop the def cassette because we loyal to our fans."

The music is strictly for a hardcore audience, and as for the preponderance of gun lyrics, Erick explains, "Guns is just a way of expression," something that the kids on the street understand. "Plus, some of the lyrics we write, we compare to some of the powerfullest weapons out there." Potent images of street culture are represented in such songs as "Hardcore," from the album *Business As Usual*:

> Flowin' to avoid the caps and blows
> By the gangbangers, at the B-Boy shows
> With the cops, try to control the crowd
> But they can't, system's cranked, so what choo sayin'
> Pump it loud
> Blows are thrown, heads are flown like Pan Am
> Brothers lickin' off like the Son of Sam and
> The bass continues to pump, some brothers hit the parking
> lot, to go pop trunks
> Hoes are slapped, jewels are snatched

Brothers are caught in the cross fire without no caps
And on my way out, I heard a sucker scream and shout
"Niggas!" Go turn the party out.

One of their biggest fans, Dennis Wade, who runs the day-to-day affairs of the Hit Squad from Shuma Management, says, "They got the funk music, they got the rugged stuff. Other people do the crossover, but they gonna keep the funk and the underground stuff. There won't be none of that crossin' over."

A calm, sunny afternoon in mid May finds EPMD on a rubble-strewn lot in Manhattan's Lower East Side. Dominated by a crumbling, gutted building, the gritty locale serves as the backdrop for the video "Crossover," the first single from *Business Never Personal* (Def Jam, 1992). Two members of the film crew hold up speakers, which belt out the song, as director Jim Swaffield motions the camera in for a close-up of Erick and Parrish, who are dressed for the occasion in B-Boy formal wear: matching oversize black denim jackets and jeans, topped with black baseball caps. DJ Scratch stands with them, his name written in rhinestones on a baseball cap that glints in the sunlight. Over a chunky funk groove, Parrish raps, "The rap era's out of control, brothers sellin' their souls to go gold / going, going gone, another rapper sold / to pop and r&b, not the MD / I'm strictly hip-hop, I stick to to Kid Capri."

Perched on the hood of a parked car, Tom J., K-Solo, Redman, and Albie look on, joking among themselves. Despite the balmy spring weather they are outfitted for a snowstorm, wearing heavy jackets, baggy jeans, sweats, and woolen hats. Others, including D. Wade and Sandy Griffen from Shuma, and Emperor Russell Simmons, also observe.

The hooded duo of Das EFX make their entrance like the stars they have become. With sales of *Dead Serious* surpassing 250,000 (and still counting), Dray and Skoob, cloaked in all-black and wearing wraparound shades, have a mellow assuredness in their gait. Greeting people as they go, they finally stroll over to their crew and heartily embrace the other members of the Hit Squad. A massive grin spreads across Redman's face as he shakes his head at Dray and simply says, "Muthafuckas," in awe. On MTV, on the boom boxes, the jeeps, and on the radio, "They Want EFX" is getting people off like a hit of crack. Capitalizing on their success, Das EFX are touring rigorously, having just returned from the West Coast for a few days before they head south for dates in Florida.

Meanwhile, Parrish, holding a 16-millimeter Bolex camera at arms length, films himself, moving the camera up and around his head at various angles as he raps. When the shot is over, Dennis shouts, "Yo P., throw that shit here, man," as if they were back at football practice at SCSU. Parrish smiles—and feigns a toss. Then Erick gets his chance as cameraman, freestyling at the end of the take when the music ends.

The Squad then retire to a rented trailer to take a break. Before filming starts again, Russell Simmons must send someone to move his white Rolls

ERICK AND PARRISH SCOWL FOR THE CAMERA AT THE "CROSSOVER" VIDEO SHOOT.

Royce Silver Spur so that Erick's black Forerunner, Solo's Pathfinder, and another red jeep can be moved in front of the delapidated building. A gang of about 30 brothers gather before the shiny vehicles to take part in the next shot. Standing front and center, Erick and Parrish slide and glide to the music as they go through various takes. Director Swaffield collaborates closely with EPMD, who want to see all the camera angles before the actual shot. "Yo, Jim lets shoot another one," says Parrish. With $60,000 invested in this video, EPMD want to make sure the funds are well spent.

Miles away from the madness of Manhattan, the boondocks of Brentwood represent another world. Replacing the concrete and corrosion are modest houses, green lawns, and air that is free of pollution and traffic noise. "People come out to Long Island and be like, yo, how can you live out here," says Erick. "There's no noise here whatsoever, and the little noise we do have and stuff, it still don't sound like nothin' to people. It's too quiet. You know, we like it like that. We like the land, the trees and grass, and just chillin'."

Brentwood serves as the headquarters of the Hit Squad, and even though its various members are moving around constantly—whether on tour, in the studio, or taking care of business—Shuma Management provides the base of daily operations. Located in the cramped basement of 114 Alkier Street, a smart, gray dwelling (one of several owned by Parrish), Shuma abounds in the suburban splendor of dogwoods, chain-link fences, basketball courts, swimming pools, and friendly neighborhood dogs. The kid next door is even riding around on a big wheel.

Started by Parrish to serve EPMD's needs, Shuma (a nickname given to Parrish by his parents) now exclusively manages all the groups in the Hit Squad. Its staff consists of Dennis Wade, Jeff Stewart, and Sandy Griffen, a former vice president of Rush Management who now works as an independent consultant. Dennis, 23, joined the organization on the day after his graduation from Southern Connecticut in 1991, first touring with EPMD. Jeff, 28, a Brentwood native and friend of Parrish's older brother and sisters, also came to Shuma after recently earning his degree. With no real experience, both were simply thrown "in the mix," as they describe it, and learned by doing.

Their responsibilities, according to Jeff, include "every aspect that involves getting someone's album out—publicity, booking shows, clearing samples, everything." With all the busy work taken care of, the artists have peace of mind as well as more time to focus on creativity. "Now, for the first time," says Dennis, "they're really able to get into their music and not worry about all of the business work—even though they're very much involved in it, you know. They make the big calls and they push the big buttons."

Currently, much of the work involves booking shows for Das EFX, whom Sandy describes as "an overnight success." They are doing consecutive dates at such places as Buffalo State, Drexel, and the Jersey Boys Club, and making about $4,500 per performance, as opposed to the $1,500 they got for their first show at the Muse. Sandy argues with one promoter over the phone about Shuma's policy of getting the money up front. Then she gets a call from Blitz, who is on the road with Das EFX in D.C., and tells him about their accommodations there.

Management is important, says Sandy, "to help them and direct them in every direction of their career." She adds, "EPMD are definitely one of the rare examples of good businessmen in this business. As far as taking care of business and being dedicated to their job, to their music, they're totally responsible, and you don't see that a lot, and it's really refreshing. It's one of the main reasons why I'm here."

Since Dennis and Jeff are close friends of Erick and Parrish, management has the added personal touch. "It's all about doing everything right, making sure everything's on time, having people take care of you 'cause you take care of them," says Dennis. "That's one thing about the crew. If there's any problems, you know, they can go see Parrish and Erick. Parrish and Erick will take care of them. That's one thing I must say:

They take care of you with money, and they have feelings for the people."

This loyalty has gone a long way in shaping the success of EPMD, who came up through the ranks by watching and learning from the mistakes of others. Their knowledge and experience is now passed on to their crew, and what they get in return is support. "We so to the point now that we got a big posse, a whole camp of positive people," says Parrish. "So every time we check to the left and we do start slippin', we keep it in." As Erick raps in "It's Goin' Down": "If there's a problem, the Hit Squad rolls mad deep, so I can rest my head and get some sleep."

"State to state, stage to stage, as I clock loot."

You would never know it was morning rush hour in Babylon, Long Island. Deerpark Avenue, a main thoroughfare, remains peaceful. Instead of blaring horns and curses, a lone pedestrian greets a road repair crew. Down an alley beside the bingo hall—the biggest building on the street, and a quick step from the pizza parlor, the record store, and the bank—a small crowd forms outside an unmarked glass storefront. Sandwiched between a hairdresser and a seafood restaurant is the new headquarters of Shuma Management.

Inside, the reception area becomes gridlocked with bulky vinyl cases and stuffed duffels, not to mention their owners, who pass the time playing cards atop a lone speaker. In the next room, Shuma's staff of three are on the phones perpetually. As the rendevous point for the Hit Squad World Tour—featuring Redman, Das EFX, K-Solo, and EPMD—the three small offices of Shuma double as mission control and the Greyhound lounge.

By early afternoon, it's bright and balmy outside, and people flow in and out of the building. A surly assembly of crew members, clad mostly in black, wait in the parking lot for the tour buses that were supposed to have picked us up at 10:00 A.M. Nothing in the rap business, however, goes off on schedule. Beats pounding from Dray's new, black Mitsubishi Diamante fill up the slack time.

Meanwhile, Parrish, Dray, Skoob, and Tom J. do some last-minute shopping at Loman's, a camping store across the street. Though Dray's Timberland boots look as though he got them yesterday, he buys another pair without deliberation. Parrish settles on a duffel, and Tom J. hovers over a glass cabinet that displays a sinister collection of hunting blades. On the way back to Shuma, four teenage girls, who have been running around the alley all day, approach them for autographs.

As the sun dips, so does the temperature, and the waiting game grows tedious. All the magazines have been read, the levity and good humor spent, and most members of the crew are slouched over on chairs or dozing off on the floor. Craig Mack, formerly of the Long Island rap crew JVC Force, works on some rhymes. There is no relief from the bright fluorescent lights overhead or syrupy r&b tunes playing from a small stereo.

A welcome burst of activity accompanies the entrance of Redman, K-Solo, and their respective crews at 11:00 P.M. A scowling Redman with balled-up Kleenex stuffed in his left nostril and a white aluminum baseball bat in hand, says, "Niggas is gonna catch shit if they mess with me on this tour." Alvin Toney, or "Albie," the head of EPMD's touring crew, cannot resist the challenge, and he and Redman lock horns. They wrestle around the room—Albie's linebacker physique against Redman's reckless energy—and just before desks start toppling, Shuma staffer James Ellis, a former prison guard, breaks up the melee.

At about 1:15 A.M. word arrives of the buses' approach. Assembling everyone outside, Parrish and Albie give a pep talk to the troops, who gather around 26 deep. Initial remarks about respecting the bus drivers and giving road managers D. Wade and Ellis room to operate, give way to warnings about sexual encounters with groupies—specifically regarding AIDS and statutory rape—and fights.

"If you out there strictly to stomp shit," says Albie, a veteran of all of EPMD's tour, "don't even go."

"The object of the game is to get home. Some niggas don't get home," says Parrish.

"Just go out there to have fun," adds Albie. "Take advantage of the opportunity."

"Fuck the bullshit," says Parrish, in summation. "There shouldn't be no bullshit at all." DJ Scratch, who has been with EPMD since 1988, adds another cautionary word, saying, "All them niggas want a rep, so we gotta watch out."

The first bus—a sleek, white behemouth called "Genesis" that will carry the artists—growls as the crew loads its baggage bays. The second one, a more standard-looking version, pulls in and is similarly attended to before the crew pile in. Equipped with sound systems, TV, and VCR in both the front and back lounge areas, each bus also sleeps 18. Boots are pulled off, clothes shoved in closets, and curtains drawn on the coffinlike bunks, which are stacked three high. Finally, at 2:06 A.M.—about 16 hours behind schedule—the show is on the road.

Though the tour officially opens at Albany's Palace Theatre, a rehearsal show is scheduled first for the Chance in Poughkeepsie, a club that holds about 650. This venue is small compared to the arenas and concert halls in which the tour is booked. Arriving in town at 6:20 A.M., there is barely a chance to rub the sleep from our drooping eyes and unload the buses at the Edison Motel before it's time to leave for the soundcheck. Assembling in the lobby, however, the crew seems ready, taking full advantage of the complimentary coffee and donuts.

It's cold and sunny as we ride through Poughkeepsie on the second bus, reaching the venue by about 11. The stage door literally opens onto the small stage, which faces a sunken floor area and a wood-paneled balcony. Aside from some tinted windows high above, the place is lit by stage lights, and the air is musty and cool. James Ellis, whom everyone simply calls Ellis, sizes up the surroundings as the crew set up the turntables and hoist the Hit Squad banner—on which all the groups' logos appear beneath "Shuma Management"—into position.

First up for the soundcheck is DJ Scratch, who carefully unpacks his Technics 1200s from their yellow, metal housing and sets them up beside a

Numark Digital Sampler. Pulling an album from his yellow record case, he samples and loops it and commences scratching over the newly created beat. Over the next 45 minutes, Scratch conducts a break-beat seminar, creating loops with the sampler and deftly cutting and scratching between turntables. The long fingernails of his right hand barely glide over the vinyl as his left hand teases the cross fader to produce high-pitched squeaks and scratches from the grooves. Several crew members stand around transfixed.

During the rest of the afternoon, Das EFX, K-Solo, Redman, and EPMD arrive and go through their shows as the crew watches on. Some of them go out and buy lunch while Ellis sets up shop in a room beneath the stage, making tour laminates (all-access passes).

Back at Southern Connecticut State, he, Dennis, and Parrish met through the football team. A year ahead of the other two, Ellis had met Dennis when he was a high school senior recruit, and was told by a mutual friend to keep his eye out for Parrish, who would also be attending in the fall. Dennis and Parrish ended up as roommates, and as one of the first people they met upon their arrival at school, Ellis became a close friend.

Once while watching an Eric B. & Rakim video on MTV, "Parrish had come up to me," says Ellis, "and he said, 'Yo, Ellis, I'm tellin' you. One day, I'm gonna be larger than them niggas. Watch, man, watch.' " Breaking into laughter, Ellis continues, "And I was like, yo, man, go back in your fucking room. He said, 'Watch, man, you think I'm playing. I know how to do this shit, man. I know how to do it.' " That summer after his freshman year, Parrish stepped into the studio with Erick, and returning to football camp that fall, he told Ellis, " 'Yo, it's coming out Saturday.' "

"And I turn on the radio, and I'm listening," says Ellis. "Then I heard Parrish's voice. I was bugging out, and that was it." Ellis joined EPMD on their first tour, working security and lugging baggage before returning to his regular position as a guard at Rikers Island and the Tombs in Manhattan. Then, two months before the current tour, Parrish persuaded him to sign onto Shuma full time. "I'm just honored," says Ellis of his new role as road manager. "I'm glad he looked out like that, 'cause usually people forget about the little things you did. But he didn't forget any of that.

That's how I know he's true. And I know he wouldn't call me unless he knew it was there for me, you know what I mean. So I'm comfortable."

Upstairs, the building shakes as EPMD do their soundcheck, with Parrish asking the soundman for full volume. Unlike the usual live rap set, which lasts about fifteen minutes, EPMD take their time, doing such classics as "You Got's to Chill," "It's My Thing," "Jane," and "So Wat Cha Sayin'?" as well as cuts from the newest album. Although Scratch is one of the few remaining deejays who provides the backing track from the turntables, they must coordinate the prerecorded intros with Tom J., who operates the DAT from the side of the stage. As the afternoon winds down, we head back to the hotel, change, and return for the show.

At about 8:00 P.M. the first half of the tour—Redman, Solo, and crew—arrives at the venue, which is already packed with a mostly teen crowd. Greeted by screaming girls at the stage entrance, they step from the van, inside, and then quickly upstairs to the cramped dressing rooms. Two large pepperoni pizzas and a bucket of Kentucky Fried Chicken sit invitingly on the table in one room, but Dennis has instructed that no one eat until all the artists arrive.

With his debut single, "Blow Your Mind," just out, Redman leads off, stepping onstage at 8:45. Bundled in a white parka, colored, wool-knit cap, black sweats, and Timberlands, he also carries a baseball bat, waving it around as he stalks the stage. With him are Richard and Raymond Grant, interchangeably referred to as "Twin," who at 19 are veterans of Madonna's Blonde Ambition Tour, where they performed with openers Technotronic. One deejays while the other backs up Redman on the mike, getting the crowd revved for their short set.

As the curtain drops, 20 hands scurry around changing deejay sets and preparing for K-Solo. Sam "Sneed" Anderson, who produced most of the tracks on Solo's *Time's Up* LP (Atlantic, 1992), readies the DAT, while DJ Flair from Brooklyn sets up the records that he will scratch. Now standard at live hip-hop shows, DATs insure against skipping needles when there is a lot of movement onstage. At about 9:15 K-Solo casually walks out to do work. The stairway leading up to the dressing rooms is crowded with onlookers, as is one of the rooms above, which has a window onto the stage. Solo, too, does a short set, but sets the crowd off. He returns shirtless to do an encore, "The Formula."

Following another brief intermission, the stage is set for Das EFX, whose second single, "Mic Checka," has inched out EPMD's "Crossover" to claim the number-one spot on the *Billboard* rap charts. When the dreadlocked duo walk out and proceed to get busy, they raise havoc. Jumping up and down in unison, the audience raps along to the lyrics of "They Want EFX" and "Mic Checka." Young girls in the front row longingly make grabs for Dray and Skoob, who move back and forth across the small stage like ducks at a shooting gallery. Despite having only one album's worth of material, they perform for 30 solid minutes before saying "Peace," and telling the crowd to stay tuned for EPMD.

Five minutes later the curtain opens on DJ Scratch, who stands behind his turntables in the spotlight. Erick and Parrish wait at the top of the steps as their intro, a sampled loop of Rare Earth, fills the club. As this mellow break segues into more ominous music from the DAT, Parrish makes his entrance to the song "Boondox." Cloaked in black hoody and jeans, he is soon joined by Erick, whose voice is slightly raw due to a sore throat. After going through most of their older material, Erick and Parrish take a break, leaving the crowd in the able hands of Scratch.

EPMD's show has included Scratch's intermission ever since he debuted as their deejay on November 18, 1988, at the Mecca in Milwaukee. Before going on that night, Scratch told Erick and Parrish to stop the DAT in the middle of the show. When asked what he was going to do, he replied, " 'Yunno, I'ma take off my shirt, I'm gonna cut with my ass, shit like that.' They thought I was joking when I was sayin' this shit. They was lookin' at each other like, this mufucka's crazy.

"So in the middle of the show," he continues, "I started doing all that shit, and they wasn't even lookin' at me. They was, like, paying attention to the crowd. And when the crowd started screaming, they turned around and looked at what I was doing, and they was just standing there shocked like the crowd." Ever since then, Erick and Parrish have made sure to give

Scratch the spotlight so that they too can check out his latest tricks. Tonight, he starts out cutting up "Scenario" by A Tribe Called Quest and Leaders of the New School. While cutting the line "My pants are sagging," Scratch walks to the other side of the turntables, and with his back to the crowd, slowly pulls his pants down as he cuts. The highlight of his session occurs when he gets up on chair, straddles the turntables, and moves the cross fader with his butt while scratching with his hands.

At 10:45, EPMD return for part two, during which they perform mostly newer material. Das EFX joins them for "Cummin at Ya," and then Solo and Redman return for the finale, an all–Hit Squad jam called "Headbanger." Even the crew crowds the stage for this one, and the place becomes a free-for-all. As the song ends, the curtain drops and all the artists are whisked immediately onto a waiting van, which takes them back to the hotel. The rest of the crew, meanwhile, gather the turntables and equipment and socialize with the crowd that mills around outside the

DJ SCRATCH "CATCHES WRECK" AS GETO BOY BUSHWICK BILL LOOKS ON.

club. A horde of teens, mostly female, assemble near the stage entrance in hope of seeing the artists, but they are equally excited about talking to those with "all-access" Hit Squad laminates around their necks. Two girls, who claim to be 17, are invited for the van ride back to the motel. Several others follow in cabs.

The next morning everyone begins appearing in the lobby at about 10:00 A.M., once again decimating the complimentary supply of coffee and donuts. *Love Connection* airs on the lobby TV, but the crew have their own, far more interesting, tales. Scratch, Solo, Jamel (Erick's cousin and security man), and R. Kim (Solo's cousin and road manager) hold an animated powwow about the previous night's activities, when the hallways were filled with females roaming from room to room. Some of these girls show up in the lobby somewhat rumpled in appearance and call cabs.

At 11:10, the tour buses roll out of Poughkeepsie for the short trip to Albany. Having partied well into the morning, most of the crew take refuge in the bunks. Some nod off in the front lounge with Redman's new album pumping on the system. The next stop is the Ramada Albany, where the entourage raises quite a stir in the lobby as the bags are unloaded. A group of black women excitedly ask who the rappers are so that they can get autographs for their kids. Shawn, one of Das EFX's crew, walks in carrying five pairs of Timberlands by the laces. As always, his dreads cause others to mistake him for a member of the group. Another roadie with dreads, Marquest, puffs on a Newport in the lobby. A nearby woman tells her companion, "Can't you ask him to put his cigarette out?" He replies, "He's not gonna listen to me. He's probably got a lot of money. He's a rapper; they do what they want." Marquest puts out the cigarette on his own.

With the soundcheck later that afternoon, some rare downtime allows for a real meal at the hotel restaurant to supplement the standard road fare of fast food. Once at the 2,800-seat Palace Theatre, however, brown, recyclable McDonalds bags almost seem to clone themselves as the crew check DATs, microphone levels, and lighting, hang backdrops, and wait. Erick sips a cup of tea with honey and lemon for his recently developed laryngitis. In a hoarse whisper he says, "I love my backdrop. It's so dope," motioning to the orange on black EPMD logo commanding the stage. Outside a blushing sun signals that it's time to return to the hotel before show time.

In Manhattan, people wouldn't step into a club before ten, with the show beginning a couple of hours after that. But when the crew returns at 8:15, the blonde lady in charge says that things are already running late. A disturbed Redman, bat in hand, growls about the treatment he is receiving. By 8:25, though, the twins are onstage pumping up the mostly teen crowd, and Redman joins them with a real tiger in his tank. The rest of the Hit Squad also tear the paint off the walls, on this, the official opening gig of the 1992 world tour.

The next night in Rochester, EPMD and Das EFX's custom stages are used for the first time. The sets travel with their own crew of four, who arrive in advance of the rest of the tour. It takes them roughly four hours to assemble the wooden facades, which add theatrical flavor to the live performances. Das EFX's set resembles a sewer, complete with exposed piping, gray stone, and two barred drainpipes that face the audience. Behind it, EPMD's set consists of a wall of fake speakers with Scratch's deejay platform on top.

The War Memorial in Rochester plays host to the NHL's Amerks, but tonight the ice lies beneath sections of wide wooden planks. From the rear of the 7,000-seat arena, the stage is dwarfed on either side by two vertical billboards for Genesee Cream Ale and Wendy's. At show time, the floor, as well as half the arena's bleachers all the way around, are filled. Redman and Solo perform in front of a closed curtain, which rises for Das EFX to reveal the sewer set. As suspenseful intro music and the sound of dripping water fill the darkened arena, a green beacon shines through the mock drainpipe, creating an eerie glow. Shrouded by a cloud of smoke, Skoob kicks open the grate and emerges before the cheering crowd. Dray appears from the other one, dreads flying free. Both lug sledgehammers until they start rapping, and their energy drives the crowd on.

EPMD's entrance does not disappoint either. Perched atop the wall of speakers, Scratch stands behind the turntables playing the Rare Earth intro groove. Beneath the wail of an air-raid siren, Albie—wearing a blue bandanna, gypsy-style; rhinestone-encrusted, wraparound shades; Carhartt vest; and Tims—rears his head to the ceiling shouting, "Are you ready for Mutha Fuckin EPMD?" As if signaling impending chaos, an oversize, red, police siren spins wildly. Parrish rises from behind the speaker stacks on a motorized hoist, rapping "Boondox" over a slamming backbeat. Smoke and bright lights gush forth as twin stairs unfold from the middle of the set, allowing Parrish access to the stage. Then he leads the audience in a chant of "C'mon E double E, E double E, go!" as Erick rises from the hoist and joins his partner onstage. Complete mayhem breaks loose in the arena as EPMD charge through their 45-minute set.

The tour leaves Rochester at 3:00 A.M., and we have hardly made use of our rooms at the Days Inn. The groupie scene in the hallways, however, is thick, and while some seek only autographs or T-shirts, others want stories to tell. One attractive 15-year-old boasts that her girlfriend

gave Sen Dog (from Cypress Hill) a blow job when the group passed through town. Every once in a while a girl leaves a room zipping up the back of her dress or fixing disheveled hair. The constant flow of females even sends one of the bus drivers dashing madly for his condoms.

Rolling into Manhattan shortly after 11:00 A.M. on a sun-drenched Saturday, our first stop is Harlem's Apollo Theatre. The Hit Squad holds court here for two performances, and although Parrish jokes that "niggas be buying new clothes for the show tonight," he and the rest of the crew know that this is where it really counts. In hip-hop's hometown, at the mecca of black entertainment, the Apollo crowd promises to be no joke.

On Harlem's main strip of 125th Street, the Apollo is lost in a swirl of activity that includes everything from street vendors selling produce, sweatshirts, bootleg cassettes, and incense to drug dealers peddling crack. At 6:00 P.M., an hour before the first show, a calm prevails, and most of the crew linger outside the stage door enjoying the October Indian summer. Barricades are set up in anticipation of the throngs claiming to be "down" with the Hit Squad who will soon clog the area trying to get backstage.

Inside the theater a shimmering red curtain hides the stage sets and backdrops. With people still arriving and running the gauntlet of airport metal detectors and body searches, Redman begins the first show at 7:10, tossing Philly Blunts cigars into the crowd as he performs "How to Roll a Blunt." About half of the Apollo's 1,500 comfortable, red seats are filled, and not even Redman can bring the crowd to their feet. Albie, watching backstage, says, "These niggas is a bunch of stand-still Stanleys. Shit, we rocked those country niggas in Rochester." The multiplying masses only begin to show some life when Das EFX comes on at 8:00 P.M., followed by EPMD at 9:00. Although Parrish suddenly loses his voice after the third song, the crowd still appreciates their performance. Even the security guard by the stage bounces his head to "So Wat Cha Sayin' " as he raps along. With the whole Hit Squad onstage for "Headbanger," the finale, the others are able to cover for Erick and Parrish, who beeline to the dressing rooms afterward and try to save their voices.

When Redman opens the second show at 11:25, he faces a completely different crowd. They are up out of their seats, waving fists in the air, and responding loudly as he leads them in chants of "Fuck You, Redman." Solo has them all put gun signs in the air as he struts around menacingly during his set, while guest deejay Ron G. supplies the scratches. Solo's one-year-old son, wearing a tiny fisherman's hat, watches below on a TV in the green room.

On the screen, Das EFX's theatrical entrance from the manholes resembles a horror movie scene. Even scarier, however, is the huge knot of flying fists that begins right in front of the stage when Dray and Skoob are only 45 seconds into their set. The screen goes blank, and an uncomfortable moment of silence and confusion ensues. Three minutes later a voice comes over the sound system telling everyone to go back to their seats so the show can begin again, and a troop of police run around rounding up the perpetrators. Someone jokingly says, "Brooklyn in the house," referring to that borough's roughneck reputation. With the situation soon under control, Das EFX incite a riot of their own, making people in the balcony jump so frantically that the Apollo literally feels as if it's about to come tumbling down.

Limping through their second set on strained vocal cords, Erick and Parrish really cannot follow this act, yet they command respect just from their powerful presence. EPMD, after all, is no Milli Vanilli, and their huge black parkas inscribed with the "No Crossover" insignia say it all. They have been on the scene for years, consistent in what they do—which is making some of the hardest and funkiest hip-hop around. As the finale, "Headbanger," kicks off with Redman's familiar shout of "Nigroes!" Erick and Parrish's verses are covered by the rest of the Hit Squad—Solo, Redman, Dray, and Skoob. The Apollo seems ready to blast off into outer space. Total chaos and mass confusion.

Following the highly successful 1992 Hit Squad Tour, which worked its way around the country concluding in Los Angeles, Parrish Smith suddenly disbanded EPMD, citing personal reasons: Although for rap fans the breakup of one of the most influential, organized, and hard-hitting rap acts seemed to come out of the blue, there was a lot going on behind-the-scenes that most people were unaware of. Months earlier, in December 1991, according to sources within the Hit Squad, armed men had broken into Parrish's home in Long Island apparently intending to do some harm. Though Parrish was absent at the time, he pulled up to the house just as they were leaving and was able to get their license plate numbers, eventually leading to their capture and arrest. It was subsequently discovered that these men were acting not on their own, but on behalf of Erick Sermon, Parrish's long-time friend and partner. For the sake of the rest of the Hit Squad (especially Das EFX and Redman, who would be going out on their first major tour) Parrish sat on this news, going through with the tour as well as with the fourth EPMD album, ironically titled Business, Never Personal.

What ultimately set the stage for this situation, causing a rift between two men who were practically brothers? Only Erick and Parrish know for sure, but it is safe to say that business, the keystone of EPMD, did become personal. Clearly, the more business-minded Parrish, as sole owner of Shuma Management, was benefitting directly from all Hit Squad acts, not just EPMD. Parrish was also the more vocal of the two, leading many to believe that maybe the group was not the equal partnership they made it out to be. In the entertainment industry, especially, matters of money and respect (i.e. fame, egos, credit) do not mix well with friendship, and these forces have pulled apart many groups, not just EPMD. This situation is symptomatic of the larger forces operative within the industry of which the creative artist must always be aware. As hip-hop today is just as much a business as an art form, artists seeking to have longevity must constantly strike the crucial balance between their art and commerce. This can often prove to be problematic—even for consummate professionals like EPMD.

recommended
listening

1. EPMD, *Strictly Business* (Sleeping Bag/Fresh, 1988).
   Unfinished Business (Sleeping Bag/Fresh, 1989).
   Business As Usual (Def Jam/Columbia, 1991).
   Business Never Personal (Def Jam/Columbia, 1992).
2. K-Solo, *Tell the World My Name* (Atlantic, 1990).
   Time's Up (Atlantic, 1992).
3. Das EFX, *Dead Serious* (East-West, 1992).
   Das EFX, *Straight up Sewacide* (East-West, 1993).
4. Redman, *Whut? Thee Album* (RAL, 1992).
5. Knucklehedz, *Strictly Savage* (East-West, 1994).

ChApTeR 8

In the Mix

With the digital age of compact discs and computer-based recording technology upon us, the good old long-playing record—better known as "wax," "vinyl," or "the platter"—is on its way to becoming a museum piece. Outside of the odd promotional copy, major labels rarely manufacture vinyl anymore, and most consumers have adjusted to the times quite easily—just as they did when the eight-track cassette format was made obsolete. Hip-hop deejays in this respect represent a rare breed of traditionalists, as their very existence traces back through the grooves of vintage vinyl. Before anyone even touched a microphone, early turntable technicians such as Kool Herc, Afrika Bambaataa, and Grandmaster Flash provided the main attraction at parties, creating continuous break beats from a few seconds of a song and pushing the capabilities of their equipment in feats such as scratching. This humanization of technology is one of the great triumphs of the art form, whose development has always stretched the barriers of sound.

But ironically, as science propels us rapidly into the future, technology threatens to eclipse the vital human element of hip-hop. Deejays, after all, cannot scratch with a compact disc. Also, outside of such groups as EPMD and Gang Starr, who still perform to special instrumental pressings of their songs, cut up by their deejays, most rappers favor the "canned" music of digital audiotapes (DATs) due to their cleaner sound and the fact that, unlike a needle, they don't jump or skip when there is movement onstage. Both trends do not bode well for a music based on spontaneity, rawness, and the ability to manipulate sound. Though the digital sampler has proved itself an essential tool, revolutionizing the music and paving the way for complex sonic collages, hip-hop still remains the realm of the deejay. As rap's original innovator, manipulator, sound arranger, and, ultimately, producer, he conducts an invisible symphony with twin turntables and a mixer.

Today, deejaying lies in the able hands of people like the X-Men, a crew of underground turntable assassins whose sole purpose is to perfect, and wreck, the art form as we know it. They build and progress by keeping each other abreast of the latest techniques, and sharpening their skills through competition. They destroy conventions as they enter into areas where no deejay has ventured before, propelled by the notion that there are no rules. The X-Men consists of Rob Aguilar (a.k.a. "Rob Swift"), 20; Andrew Venable (a.k.a. "Dr. Butcher"), 23; Chris Forte (a.k.a. "Grandmaster Spin"), 23; and Joe Wright (a.k.a. "Sinister"), 23—who are all from Queens; Sean Matthews (a.k.a. "Sean C."), 22; Anthony Williams (a.k.a. "Roc Raider"), 20; and John Rolle (a.k.a. "Johnny Cash") 22, from Harlem; and Diamond J., 23, from Long Island. Influenced by such legendary spinners as Grandmaster Flash, Charlie Chase, Grandmixer D. ST., Cash Money, and Aladdin, they have all been deejaying since their preteens and met through such competitions as the DMC (Deejay Mixing Competition).

On a Friday night, prime-time hours for deejays who spin at clubs and parties, the X-Men convene in the renovated basement of Chris Forte's house, located on Farmer's Boulevard in Queens (around the corner from L.L. Cool J.'s house). While the Celtics and Knicks wage war on TV in the main room, a small room to the side plays host to some ferocious battles on the Technics 1200s, the hip-hop deejays' weapons of choice. Separated by a Gemini Scratchmaster mixer, the turntables sit lengthwise beside each other to be closer together and to prevent someone from hitting the needle arm when executing a backspin (spinning a record backward). Surrounded by sound equipment and crates of records, Rob Swift still has enough elbow room to cut up two copies of "Nobody Beats the Biz," by Biz Markie.

Demonstrating the X-Men's specialty, Rob makes new beats by scratching certain segments of records and cutting between turntables with blurring speed and precision. Without headphones, he cuts by sound, sight, and feel, his fingertips gliding alternately over each platter as the free hand slides the cross fader. Teasing the fader back and forth rapidly while deftly massaging the record produces fluid chirping sounds, which he improvises into a melody as his hand dances over the revolving disc. Sometimes Rob also moves the pitch control up and down, changing the speed of the record as it revolves. He coaxes sounds from the wax that the

turntable, left alone, would never have produced, creating something uniquely his own. In this respect Rob and his crew are musicians, playing the turntables as one would play the saxophone, drums, or guitar.

As the other X-Men take turns in the small, blue room, everyone else watches from outside, letting out an appreciative "Ho!" whenever an especially nice move is executed. Each have their own favorite records to cut, and their own special tricks, and they all make it seem so easy. Dr. Butcher, who has deejayed for Kool G. Rap, doesn't even look at the turntables as his hands move with the dexterity of a concert pianist. But you almost expect to see sparks flying from the grooves as he lets loose a cacophony of scratching. No cut is premeditated, it all just flows. "Whenever I scratch, I'm just doing it for the moment," he says, speaking like a jazz improviser. "I never sit down and try to make up a pattern; things always just come out." Roc Raider, on the other hand, who deejays for Showbiz & A.G., seems to be the most acrobatic of the group, moving the cross fader with his chest and scratching behind his back. He puts the Technics warranty to the test, propping the turntables up at ridiculous angles while keeping a rhythm running back and forth between them.

After witnessing the collective talents of the X-Men, it is difficult to imagine why current trends have favored a DAT to an able-handed deejay cutting and scratching at live shows. The only time deejays really get to showcase their skills these days is at competitions. Still, Sean C. says, "I don't think deejaying can ever die out because it started rap, yunno. Deejaying is rap."

While today's deejays have clearly advanced turntable trickery to an art form, the pioneers were more concerned with the records themselves, isolating funky segments as break beats and cutting between turntables in the earliest form of sampling. Keeping a continuous beat still required precision, but a deejay was only as good as the wax he was spinning. He had to be creative and open-minded when it came to finding beats on records, and the more obscure and funkier his collection, the better.

It was his skill in finding the rare grooves that no one else had, for example, that earned Afrika Bambaataa the title of "Master of Records." Most of Bam's favorite break records—including "Funky Drummer" by James Brown, "Take Me to the Mardi Gras" by Bob James, "Think" by Lynn Collins, and "Dance to the Drummer's Beat" by the Herman Kelly Band—have gone on to become the foundation for numerous hip-hop tracks.

Diamond, 24, a Bronx native who attended the early hip-hop parties, grew up on such beats and was inspired to become a deejay himself. In 1992 he released his self-produced debut *Stunts, Blunts, and Hip-Hop* (Mercury), on which he also raps. "There's an art to finding a break that somebody else doesn't know about, you know," he says. "It makes people go, 'Oh, shit, where'd he get that beat from?' That's part of the mystique." In the tradition of the early Bronx deejays, Diamond, who owns approximately 5,000 old records—mostly funk and jazz—still combs record stores for beats but refuses to say exactly where he shops.

"A beat man never reveals his spots," says Paul Mitchell, laughing, when asked about where he goes record shopping. Mitchell, 20, better known as the Large Professor, another producer/rapper extraordinaire, constantly hunts for vinyl, which he scours for beats to use in his own productions. "All the people that I know who was successful with beats—you know, this is just from the New York side—they know about the [Greenwich] Village, they know about all the spots. You know you gotta know your spots, all that shit."

People like the Large Professor and Diamond illustrate the dual nature of the deejay as someone who is not only adept on two turntables but also possesses a critical ear for music as well as a creative flair for collecting and mixing sounds. This innate skill carries over to the process of actually making new tracks from existing records. It is also responsible for the gradual transformation of the deejay from sound provider to groove creator.

"Hip-hop started because muthafuckas didn't have no money for no instruments, so they said, alright, fuck it, we gonna get two turntables and play records," says Diamond. "We don't have a drum set for the guy to

**BOY WONDER:
THE LARGE
PROFESSOR.**

rhyme over, so now we gotta go out and look through some old records and see which ones have drum sounds on 'em. So hip-hop was based on the idea of taking somebody else's music, and everybody who knows hip-hop will know that." He hastens to add, however, "I would defend it because it's a form of—even though, yes, we are taking a piece of somebody else's work—we are altering it, chopping it, making new sounds out of it. This is the whole thing with hip-hop."

Without more sophisticated technology—in the form of samplers and drum machines—this manipulation of sound would have been impossible. Drum machines, which originated in the accompaniment section of home organs in the fifties, first became standard studio equipment around 1980 with the introduction of Roger Linn's LM 1, which retailed for $5,000. This machine was soon replaced by less costly models—the Linn Drum and Oberheim DMX—available for around $3,000, but still beyond the reach of most consumers. Grandmaster Flash, the first deejay to introduce the electronic percussion machine, or "beat box," to hip-hop, would clear the turntables in the middle of a show and take a few steps back while a programmed beat from the DMX would keep the party rocking and the crowd amazed. Roland, a company that specialized in drum machines, deserves special mention for its contribution of the TR-808, whose heavy "kick" remains a staple sound in rap music today.

The California-based E-mu Systems was another company that played a pivotal role in the development of hip-hop. Started in 1971 to make modular analog synthesizers, they introduced the Emulator in 1981, the first machine dedicated to digital sampling. Accomplishing electronically what deejays were doing with their hands, the sampler copies sound from another source, making it possible to slow down, speed up, or loop it (repeat endlessly). "Before there were samplers," says Diamond, "you had to go out and try to get doubles of something to cut so the rapper could rhyme over it. Now we don't need that, we just loop it, yunno." For other aspiring producers, who painstakingly made loops using the pause button on their cassette deck, the advent of the digital sampler made life a lot easier.

The only problem was still cost. Less expensive versions of the Emulator—the Emulator 2 and the Drumulator—were developed subsequently, but in 1985, E-mu's SP-12 hit the market. Certainly no steal at $2995, this compact drum machine allowed ten seconds of sampling time and proved to be simple to use. The SP-12 and its counterpart, the SP-1200 (exactly the same except for an internal, as opposed to external, disk drive), released in 1987, became the essential tool of the hip-hop producer.

"The 1200 got that sound that just bring it home and shit," says Large Professor, who learned to make beats on the user-friendly machine in only one night. "Shit be sounding real good." While the Akai MPC-60 is also a popular sampler today, most rap producers agree that it has a clean sound compared to the rawness embodied by the SP-1200. In hip-hop, especially, it is that abstract "raw" quality that everyone strives for. "Like Pete Rock & C.L. Smooth, 'Reminisce,' you know what I'm saying?" says Large Professor. "That shit makes you feel a certain way. That's what it is, it's a feeling. You gotta get with that shit, you know."

Combining the capabilities of this new technology and a certain intuitive feeling for music that all deejays, record collectors, and music fanatics share, nonmusicians were finally given the opportunity to isolate a favorite sound or part of a song—a bassline, drum break, or horn riff—and combine it with other sounds to create something completely new. Thus was born the rap producer, a kind of composer, arranger, writer, and director who is responsible for the backing track of rap.

Hip-hop, more than any other music (except dub), is the producer's medium. Transcending the role of a musician, the producer is a sonic technician who is responsible for combining and mixing layers of sound into a rhythmic format over which the rapper practices his/her art. Though he does not actually pluck the guitar strings or beat on the drums, the entire realm of sound, musical or otherwise, provides the raw materials with which he creates. This highly innovative art form is filled with talented individuals—both known and undiscovered—who have pushed, and continue to push, the creative threshold further and further into the stratosphere. Some of the best include Prince Paul, Eric "Vietnam" Sadler, and Dr. Dre.

In 1989, Tommy Boy Records released the debut of an Amityville, Long Island, trio called De La Soul. Coming completely out of left field with its quirky funk sound, abstract rapping (overflowing with humor and inside jokes), and game show format, *3 Feet High & Rising* quickly climbed the *Billboard* charts on its way to selling over a million copies. It also introduced rap to the D.A.I.S.Y. Age—not some hip-hop hippiedom but an acronym for "Da Inner Sound Y'all." This exciting new sound emanated from the heads of group members Pos, Trugoy, and Mase and their mentor, producer Prince Paul.

Born Paul Houston, he started his career in music as a deejay for another Tommy Boy act called Stetsasonic—one of the first rap groups, incidentally, to use a live drummer. But Paul was intrigued with the turntables from the first time he attended an outdoor party in Amityville in 1978. Since his father, an avid jazz fan, collected records, it was also easy for him to get into deejaying. Reflecting on those days, at his friend Don Newkirk's house in Queens, he says, "Back then it was a lifestyle. It gave you a little recognition among your peers and girls, but you never see no money." After Paul hooked up with Stet in 1984, subsequently going on tour with them and doing six shows a week for $800 per week, he was more than happy. Still, Stet did not allow him the kind of creative input he would have liked, and after three albums the group went their separate ways.

While at Amityville Memorial High, Paul knew another deejay named Mase, three years younger, with whom he sometimes worked. In October of 1987, Mase approached him with a demo for a song called "Plug Tunin' " that he had done with two other friends from school—Trugoy and Pos. After hearing the tape, Paul says, "I kinda freaked, I said, 'Yo, this is kinda fly. Let me sit at home and work on it, and kinda tune it up a little

PRINCE PAUL IN THE STUDIO.

bit, you know.' So I did that, called 'em in for a little meeting, and
you know, we got together to know each other a little better." After
scraping together about $1,000 between them, they went to Calliope, a
24-track studio in Manhattan, and recorded "Plug Tunin' " and another
song called "Freedom of Speech." Then they proceeded to shop for a
record deal.

"This is what happened," says Paul. "It's always been printed wrong. I
made the demo up. I gave it to Daddy O. [of Stetsasonic] 'cause he was
shopping some guy named Frankie J. at the time, to bring along with his
stuff, 'cause he knew all the people. I lived in Long Island, so he knew
everybody in the industry. He shopped it along. Some people picked up
on it, like Profile and I think Geffen had liked it. I personally brought it to
Tommy Boy and let Monica Lynch [president of the label] listen to it, and
I played 'Plug Tunin',' me and Pos. They liked the way Tommy Boy
responded, more or less, to the music and everything. They showed more
interest, so they chose Tommy Boy."

Made for under $20,000, De La's first album featured an eclectic blend
of influences—Ben E. King, The Turtles, Steely Dan, French-language
instructional records—by an eccentric group of people. "Aside from me
being a deejay and everything, I was still kinda nerdy," Paul explains,
flashing his metallic nameplate belt buckle as proof. "That's how De La
Soul was. So we did what we did, we didn't try to front off all that hard
stuff, so that's how it came out. It wasn't like, O.K., we're trying to be
different or whatever, we just more or less manifested what was in our-
selves, you know what I'm saying.

"That's why I made 'Me, Myself, and I,' more or less meaning, do stuff
on your own, but people took that out of context. Instead of, like, us
stressin' be your own person, be your own thing, they just copied what De
La Soul did, whether it was the dress code, whether it was the dreads, and
they kinda got it backwards, you know what I'm saying," he says, exposing
two rows of Osmond-like teeth as he laughs. The project's originality
came through in the poetic rhymes, diverse samples, and, of course, the
first-time use of "skits" (now, almost standard on rap albums) connecting
the songs, which brought the total number of titles up to 23.

"I despise skits now," says Paul. "It was cool when I initially had the idea to do it, know what I'm sayin', so I was like, ah, you know, let's find a way to link an album together as opposed to cut, stop, cut, stop, you know. Let's make it interesting, so as you listen to it, it's like visual. 'Cause there wasn't, I think, any rap albums at the time that were visual, where you sat down and you could actually picture everything that's goin' on, like a game show and everything else." The album starts out with MC Don Newkirk quizzing the contestants—Pos, Trugoy, Mase, and Paul—about the number of feathers on a Perdue chicken, the number of fibers intertwined in a shredded wheat, and the amount of times the Batmobile caught a flat. "We worked on it and it came out like that," says Paul. "It's just from listening to a lot of Parliament Funkadelic. George Clinton does all that visual, underwater stuff."

Paul, who was as much a fan of P-Funk as he was of hip-hop while growing up, says, "I envied a lot of George Clinton, he really bugged me out. He dogged my mentality as a child, you know what I'm saying." Reading and rereading the message-filled album covers, and inspired by the conceptual nature of the music itself, Paul adds, "I loved George Clinton and Parliament Funkadelic, and for me to have the opportunity to have somebody to do the same thing like that, which was De La Soul, it was like heaven, you know what I'm saying? 'Cause you try to tell a hardcore B-Boy, 'Yeah, I got this idea to do a game show. Let's do this,' they'll laugh at you, and they [De La] were just as nerdy as me, so it kinda helped."

Of the creative process on that first, ground-breaking, De La album, Paul says, "They would come with some loops and some rhymes as well as some stuff I had. I would take it, listen to it, and more or less help them arrange it, you know what I'm saying? Just make it the sound that we have. And that's what it really boiled down to." While working with Stet's six very different members proved to be difficult, Paul says, "I tried to make De La Soul an equal effort and everybody a part of it, yunno? 'Cause it's kind of hard when somebody's tellin' you to do something, and you don't really want to participate. You kind of rebel against it. So my theory was, everybody throw in something—if you got a sample or hear something, it doesn't hurt to try it to see what it sounds like. If it's whack we'll take it out, but at least I gave you the chance to listen to it yourself. So I just polished everything up." Laughing, he adds, "Anything you hear silly on all these records, is what I put in, you know what I'm saying. Point-blank, that's what I do."

De La Soul is not the only innovative rap act to have emerged from the backwaters of Long Island. "Strong" Island, as the "sixth" borough is also known, has also produced the likes of EPMD, Rakim, Leaders of the New School, and, of course, Public Enemy. "You gotta remember, out in Long Island, muthafuckers have shit to prove 'cause they wasn't from the city," says Eric "Vietnam" Sadler, who was born and raised in Hempstead. Sadler, along with Hank and Keith Shocklee and Carl Ryder (better known as Chuck D.), comprised one of the most legendary and cutting-edge production teams in all of rap—the Bomb Squad—responsible for detonating the musical explosions behind PE's first three albums.

Sadler first met his collaborators around 1982, when they moved into an upstairs space at 510 South Franklin Street, a building owned by Sadler's neighbor. Hank Shocklee and company, who ran Long Island's popular Spectrum City mobile deejay unit, needed a headquarters in which to store their records and equipment. At the time, Sadler and a partner rented the basement, where they ran a small rehearsal space for bands. Though an accomplished musician himself, Sadler spent most of his time down there—always dressed in his father's army fatigue jacket, black cap, and mirrored shades (thus the name "Vietnam")—learning to master a DMX drum machine that had been left in his care by friend and future superstar Eddie Murphy.

One day Chuck invited Sadler upstairs to hang out and work on some songs, and they produced "Five Funk" and "College Collegiate Jam" with Keith Shocklee. Meanwhile, the whole Public Enemy concept was slowly coming together, and when it came time to do the first album, Chuck wanted Sadler to be involved. " 'Cause at the time, I was the only musician. I was the only one who could do all the drum machines, do all the sampling, nobody knew how to work anything. Hank couldn't turn on the equipment. Chuck was just a genius at finding stuff, whatever, but none of them knew how to do anything technically," says Sadler from his spacious, sky-lit Soho studio, furnished with oriental rugs and couches, and filled with crates of records and state-of-the-art recording equipment.

His current location is not far from INS on Murray Street, where *Yo! Bum Rush the Show* (Def Jam) was put together in 1986 for under $17,000. In a faded blue sweatshirt, jeans, Fila's, and a black baseball cap turned backward, Sadler, 33, who could easily pass for one of the legions of kids who buy his music, recalls, "On the first one, it was basically Chuck and Hank who came up, yunno, with ideas for certain grooves and certain things. On a couple of songs I came up with certain things, but the majority was basically them on the first." Chuck would even sometimes hum a phrase to Sadler, who then translated it into a groove or a beat, as well as arranging samples that were selected by Hank and Chuck.

"We had mad different opinions," admits Sadler. "I had a musician's mentality. They were, like, fuck timing, fuck notes, fuck all that shit. So they were basically teaching me. There were no rules for them. It was ignorance to music, which was great. Basically, they were teaching me, that, fuck all the bullshit, it just gotta be funky, it gotta be soulful, and I was, like, alright, it's gotta be soulful, but it's gotta be relative, you know what I'm saying?" Sadler acted as the interface between the creative and the technical, making way-out ideas a reality. " 'Cause Chuck and Hank, they wanted certain things that were just unheard of. They had no rules. Fuck it, if it was distorted, fucked up, that's the way they wanted it, and it was, like, I had to be a communicator to explain to the engineer what everybody wanted."

Sometimes Sadler also had to link up several different drum machines and play them together to achieve the sound that Hank and Chuck wanted. "A lot of times, with the [drum] programming," he says, "I would do what nobody else was doing at the time. You know, in programming r&b, most people would have one beat or two beats playing through the whole thing. At the time, I had been programming jazz, so I was, like, alright, this beat's gonna play when Chuck says this, and in the beat, little things were just constantly moving. I had like 20, 30 patterns in a song, just doing, like, tat-ta-ta-tat, boom, yunno, just a little bit different as Chuck would go along. 'Cause when Chuck would do his rap, you would feel different things as he got to a certain point—even if it was just an extra kick or high-hat—it would make it feel like the song was doing something else." These complex percussive arrangements contributed to the busy sound of Public Enemy.

But what really made their sound unique was the concept of using pure noise (or coarseness) as music, an innovation introduced by Hank, and exemplified by 1988's "Rebel Without a Pause." The song features a whiney, almost sirenlike sound—actually a doctored Maceo Parker horn loop—that caught the rap world completely off guard. Following the first album's lagging sales and radio play, Sadler explains, "We were in that mode of just rebellious, you know, our motto was, fuck the music industry, fuck everything, fuck motherfuckers, you know what I'm saying? Fuck 'em. We just want to destroy shit, we want to fuck music up, yunno."

Starting with that caustic horn loop, the various elements of the song fell into place at Chung King Studios in Chinatown. Using a DDD1 drum machine, Hank Shocklee had Sadler program completely opposite beats for the changes, almost as if two unrelated songs had been fused together. "It was not something that had been done, but like, alright, cool, fine," says Sadler. "It just gave it, like, tension. It gave it drops and tension. It's like, yo, that shit is fat, so once Chuck dropped the lyrics down, it was like hype.

"I remember sitting at a bus stop waiting for the bus, and I heard this shit screaming by in a car. Muthafucking people was like, 'What the fuck is that?' Niggers didn't know what it was. They was listening to it, but it was too far gone. Today it's nothing, but at the time it was insane. You got this high-pitched scream going on, mufuckas just didn't understand it. A week went by, yunno, muthafuckers started picking up on it, started hearing it in the club, and then, like, within a day, it was God."

By that time, the complete Bomb Squad—including Keith Shocklee, this time—were working on *It Takes a Nation of Millions to Hold Us Back*, which they hammered out in 30 days of nonstop work at Greene Street Studios. Sadler, who had been denied production credit on the first album, says that everyone contributed equally to this one. While he focused on foundational beats, Hank, Chuck, and Keith provided samples, embellishments, and ideas that added to the project's experimental nature. Accommodating all those ideas also used up a lot of tracks. "I remember engineers used to come from other rooms to look at our track sheet, 'cause it was incredible to them," says Sadler. "We would have, like, a little list of 15 things on one track that came in at different times, but you have a whole bunch of tracks like that, of things coming in at totally different times. The track sheet looked like a book." He estimates using 70 tracks for some songs, which even today is unheard of in hip-hop.

The success of *It Takes a Nation of Millions . . .* , coupled with the controversy created by group member Professor Griff's anti-Semitic remarks to the press, created serious tensions for and within PE, which manifested themselves in the third album, *Fear of a Black Planet*. The making of "Welcome to the Terrordome," that album's first single, provides some insight into how creative artists channel their feelings into their work. "We went into the studio and we really didn't know what Chuck was going to do. We had the track, we laid stuff down or whatever, and when Chuck does his vocals I'm usually his guide," explains Sadler. "So the track comes on and he just starts ranting and raving, you know what I'm saying, he just keeps going. He was thinking about this Griff shit, he was thinking about a whole bunch of shit, and it just all came out, and it was so incredible. He just spewed it out of his guts, and it was there on record for mufuckas to either judge or not to judge."

Keith, who programmed the song, had made it too short, but since the vocals were already laid down they left it alone. As a result, Chuck only comes in at certain parts, and during other times, he raps over the sampled voices ("Will you join me please") that were supposed to be a break. "It works 'cause it makes it feel like shit is out of control, like this is the Terrordome," says Sadler. "Chuck is rapping and shit is coming in and it worked." Nick Sansano, an engineer at Greene Street, also suggested enhancing the track with a stereo panning effect. "We were listening to it and it was swirling. It's like panning, but panning around in a circle—like if you're in the middle, things are going around you to give it, like, a swirling effect." With no organized structure, chorus, hook, or anything to really latch onto, "Terrordome" further wrecked any preconceived notions of rap and music in general.

In addition to Public Enemy, the Bomb Squad has injected their volatile funk into r&b albums by Vanessa Williams and Bell, Biv, Devoe, as well as working with rappers Slick Rick and Ice Cube. This last project bridged the significant gaps between the East and West Coast sounds, pairing the Bomb Squad—represented mainly by Sadler and Keith Shocklee—with Ice Cube and his longtime associate, producer Sir Jinx. "Eric Sadler and Keith Shocklee played a really big part in it," explains Jinx, while tinkering with a radio-controlled model car at Paramount Studios in L.A. "Eric Sadler did, like, the beats, the bottom beat, and Keith Shocklee, he did some of the bottom beats, and then, yunno, we all just worked together to put it together. That gangster flavor was still in there, 'cause I'm pretty sure they weren't introduced to gangster music until we came down there."

Though gangster (or O.G.) music, the ruling sound on the West Coast, is defined differently depending on who you ask, most agree that it is music that sounds best when booming from a car—preferably a 1964 Chevy Impala, the gangster's ride of choice. Gangster music, which also includes oldies like P-Funk, Zapp, Slave, Cameo, and Lakeside, is slow and low funk, both bass heavy and somewhat moody. Jinx, whose other production credits include L.A.'s Yo-Yo as well as Kool G. Rap from Queens, has a unique perspective on the difference between the East and West Coast sounds. "The New York style is a little more rougher," he says, "and the L.A. style is smoother. It's a lot smoother, kicked back, with

PRODUCER
SIR JINX
TAKES A BREAK
OUTSIDE OF
PARAMOUNT
STUDIOS IN L.A.

just the bassline and the beat, yunno, and New York, from working with G. Rap, I learned that, like, New York likes drums. They like real tough drums, and maybe one bassline, but the bassline don't even have to be fat. Fat meaning big, like, boom-ba-doo-ba-doom. Yunno, it could be like that, and they'll love it. But L.A., you gotta have some BASS."

Jinx also offers an interesting spin on the rap producer, saying, "I figure all of us right now that do beats and stuff, we're good coordinators and good arrangers, but ain't too many real producers out there, know what I'm sayin'? You could produce a record, but sampling is not really producing a track, you know what I'm sayin, you just taking some other shit, and putting it together, and putting it here and there. And you putting some stuff together, that's cool, that's good arranging, but you arranging some other music, you know what I'm saying?

"But now to where [Dr.] Dre's album came out," he continues. "It's gonna revolutionize, just change everything, because he didn't use samples. He might have used one or two or three, but as of a whole album, no. And that's gonna change up everything, because that's showing that we don't need the samples. We can do this stuff on our own." Live musicianship is certainly nothing new to hip-hop, extending all the way back to the Sugar Hill house band of Doug Wimbish, Skip MacDonald, and Keith Le Blanc, who played the backing track for "Rapper's Delight" and other hits. But 1992's *The Chronic* (Interscope), produced by Jinx's cousin, Dr. Dre, takes the concept of "live" hip-hop to new levels.

Twenty-seven-year-old Andre Young, the mastermind behind N.W.A.'s gangsta grooves, has the platinum touch. In addition to producing their classic debut *Straight Outta Compton* that sold over one million copies, *NIGGAZ4LIFE*, the follow-up, and *The Chronic* each sold more than two million copies. Not many L.A.-based artists would find their music pumping in New York's hip-hop mecca, but Dre is one of them. His sound, in fact, transcends all regional boundaries within rap, while still preserving L.A.'s "gangster" vibe.

"My first exposure to hip-hop was *The Adventures of Grandmaster Flash on the Wheels of Steel*," says Dre, taking a break from doing some remixes at

Track Record Studios in North Hollywood. "That was my favorite shit. That's what started me to deejaying. I think I was about 15." Spinning at high schools and proms with a crew called the High Powered Boys, Dre's first big break came when he challenged and beat Yella, the deejay at a Compton club called Eve After Dark. He was offered a job on the spot, and eventually joined Yella in a group called the World Class Wrecking Cru, one of the West Coast's first r&b/rap groups to gain some notoriety. Wearing a doctor's suit and stethoscope, Dre would cut up such hits as "Juice," "Surgery," and the balladlike "Turn Out the Lights," as the Wrecking Cru took their show as far as London's Wembley Stadium.

"I mean, it was cool," says Dre of those days, "but I still wasn't able to do what I wanted to do. You know we had another guy who was running things, and I was a kid, I was the youngest one, you know. Just pushed my ideas to the side like that, you know, but I was making a little bit of money, so I said, fuck it." After Eazy-E, whom he's known since he was 13, started Ruthless Records, Dre finally had a chance to develop as a producer, and one of his first tracks, "Boyz N Tha Hood," reached number one on L.A.'s all-rap KDAY. That song set the precedent for all of his work to date.

While Dre has gotten much mileage out of sampling—especially from the records of his all-time favorites, George Clinton and Bootsy Collins—his technique has evolved to the point where his studio time these days resembles something of a live jam session. "I start fucking with the drum machine," he says, "have people in there, somebody's fucking around with the bass keyboards, I'm fucking with the drum machine, somebody's fucking around on the guitar or something, and we have a tape rolling all the time in case somebody hits a note or something. 'Cause a lot of times I'm in the studio, and somebody hits some shit, and I'm like, 'Yo, what was that?' And they don't remember what the fuck it was. So we'll just rewind the tape, and we'll get something out of that. One note sometimes, we'll get a whole song, yunno."

While his basic equipment includes the Akai MPC-60 drum machine sampler, the Yamaha SY-77 keyboard, and a Mini Moog—the same type of keyboard used by Bernie Worrell of P-Funk (which Dre bought secondhand for $300)—Dre also employs live horn players and a versatile young musician named Colin Wolfe, who plays bass, guitar, and keyboards. Wolfe, 25, whom Dre first saw performing a bass solo onstage at L.A.'s China Club, was soon drafted to go on tour with Michel'le, Dre's sole r&b act (and girlfriend). He has been working with Dre ever since.

DR. DRE IN DEEP CONCENTRATION BEHIND THE BOARDS AT HOLLYWOOD'S TRACK RECORD STUDIOS.

Sunk comfortably into one of the studio's black leather couches, Wolfe describes the creative process: "They just have a drum loop going, and I'm just coming up with about 50 different basslines, trying everything. And then we just finally come up with something. We hear something and it just clicks and we'll know that's the one." Sometimes, however, some of the best sounds result from accidents. Laughing, he explains, "Dre and I was writing this song once, and I had messed up, and he said, nah, nah, keep that part. So then, you know, we'll keep parts like that. This is on a song we wrote for Immature." A musician of 13 years, Wolfe's deep, heavy basslines propel many of Dre's tracks. Though normally he favors a Charvell electric bass or a Fender jazz bass, which is known for its crispness and precision, Wolfe played the acoustic Clevinger Jr. for the hit song "Deep Cover," whose four-note bassline creeps along dangerously like the soundtrack to a slasher movie. Wolfe also plays the high-pitched, demonic-sounding keyboards on many cuts from *The Chronic*.

In addition to the album's superb musicality, the whole format of *The Chronic* represents something different for rap because it is a compilation rather than a solo release. Joining Dre on the mike are a slew of new artists—Snoop Doggy Dogg, Daz, Kurupt, Emmage, RBX, Jewell, and Rage—who are signed to independent projects on Dre's new Death Row label. "Originally, Snoop was gonna be the first act," explains Dre, "but they were telling me, 'yo, man, you got the name, you coming off the whole N.W.A. thing, you know,' I'd be the perfect thing to set the foundation for Death Row. We'll just make my album like one big commercial, yunno, for all the acts on Death Row. I'm figuring, everybody that's on my album is gonna get crazy juice."

On this record, as well as on a lot of other Dre-produced albums, there are also inserts or commercials, actually little skits similar to the ones that Prince Paul introduced on De La Soul's debut. "When I go buy a record at the record store, what do I want to hear? That's what I put on my records," says Dre. "And I want to be entertained—not just the record coming on, and yunno, it fades out and the next record comes on, yunno? You want to be entertained." Skits like "The $20 Sack Pyramid," a takeoff on the TV game show *$20,000 Pyramid*, and "The Doctor's Office" definitely add some humor and unexpected twists to the flow of the album.

Though his vocal cords were injured in a car accident soon after the release of his gold-selling, Dre-produced debut, *No One Can Do It Better* (Ruthless) in 1989, the D.O.C. performs on some of these skits. He's the gruff, gravelly voice you can't miss. Wearing a red Karl Kani jeans suit and sipping from a flask of Remi Martin, D.O.C. adds a little personal footnote about Dre, whom he has known since coming to L.A. from Texas around 1986. "Me and Dre's homies. Me and Dre is like brothers, you know what I'm saying. I trust him, I got faith in him, so I'll follow him, like, into almost anything," he says in that unmistakable voice. "Like, if he said he wanted to do a rock 'n' roll group or some shit like that, then I'd follow him into some way-out shit like that, 'cause he could probably pull it off. He could do anything, man. Dre know, he know everything. In the studio, you can't tell him shit, man."

Certainly one thing that producers like Dre, Eric Sadler, Jinx, and Prince Paul have in common is consummate professionalism about their work and the desire to take the art form to new areas. Conceivably, anyone with a knowledge of music and a good ear could produce a rap song, but it also takes much more than that. Rap music thrives on originality and newness, and thus, the ability to break away from the pack, delve into the unexplored, and create visionary sounds are the hallmarks of rap's best producers—people like Marley Marl, EPMD, DJ Premier, Mixmaster Muggs, Pete Rock, Diamond, Large Professor, 45 King, Beatnuts, and the list goes on and on. Their new approaches to making and presenting music makes rap one of the most dynamic art forms of our time.

DJ Mark the 45 King (Mark James) sums it up best when he says, "There's no rules to it. I don't know how anybody could tell you it needs more, when it's like—it's like drawing a painting, you know what I'm saying? And somebody gonna come in and say it needs red, yunno, their opinion. There's no fucking rules. Whoever thought somebody was gonna go 'boom-chaka-boom' on a microphone with their mouth. Or gonna take a turntable and go 'zig-a-zig-a-zig,' whatever. There's no rules to the shit, whatever's clever."

———

THE PRACTICE OF SAMPLING—electronically copying bits of sound from another artist's recordings—is a prime element in rap music. But recent lawsuits against sampling have raised concerns that rap records in their present form will become too expensive to produce.

The challenges have some recording company lawyers thinking anew about what constitutes fair use of artists' material. Others in the music business are worried that a clampdown on sampling would adversely affect the creativity of rap artists.

New York Times, April 21, 1992

Back when rap was still an underground art form confined to the streets, no one cared what old records deejays were mixing and cutting up to create the earliest sonic collages. Today, of course, with the heaping profits generated by rap, artists are sued regularly for appropriating snippets of someone else's music without permission. The simple threat of a lawsuit, in fact, has initiated a whole painstaking process whereby rights must be obtained—or samples "cleared," in industry lingo—in a monetary agreement prior to an album's release. Rap artists who have disregarded this process wish they hadn't, many settling out of court for huge sums. The legal implications of sampling has created a subsidiary industry within rap, fattening the pockets of lawyers, older artists, defunct labels, and sample clearinghouses, who conduct the actual busywork of acquiring rights and negotiating fees. It has also meant that, in the studio, artists do not have the carte blanche to create as freely as they once did. But this constraint, in itself, is opening up whole new avenues of creativity. Meanwhile, sampling's uncharted legal territory continues to be mapped out with each new court case.

Most lawsuits have originated over the issue of copyright infringement, in which the original owner of a work that was sampled has been denied credit or compensation for the use of his piece. Under the Copyright Act of 1976 (an amendment of earlier copyright acts), a musical recording embodies the written composition (a song's words and music, usually referred to as the "publishing") as well as the sound recording itself. Aside from fair use—which authorizes the use of a copyrighted work for criticism, teaching, research, or reporting—and not-for-profit exemptions, permission must be obtained from the copyright owners (plural, because an artist usually shares the publishing rights with a record company or music publisher such as ASCAP or BMI in exchange for an advance and royalty rate) before a specific work may be reproduced. Establishing infringement is as simple as comparing the two compositions, so most offending parties have been reluctant to let the courts decide their fate, opting instead for an outside settlement. As a result, the official line on sampling remains fuzzy.

One of the first cases of sampling as copyright infringement occurred with *Castor versus Def Jam Records* filed on August 25, 1987. In the suit, singer Jimmy Castor sued the Beastie Boys's label over unauthorized use of drum beats and the phrase "Yo, Leroy" from Castor's 1977 hit, "The Return of Leroy (Part 1)" incorporated in the Beasties' song "Hold It Now, Hit It." As with the July 1989 suit filed against De La Soul for unauthorized use of a few seconds of the Turtles 1969 hit "You Showed Me," on De La's "Transmitting Live from Mars," the case was settled out of court for an undisclosed amount. The same holds true for "Ice, Ice Baby" by Vanilla Ice (which sampled Queen and David Bowie's "Under Pressure") and Hammer's "U Can't Touch This" (which used Rick James' "Superfreak"), which have netted substantial sums for the original artists.

The only case to date, in fact, that has actually gone all the way to a judge's ruling was *Grand Upright Music Ltd. versus Warner Brothers Records*, in which seventies' British pop star Gilbert O'Sullivan sued rapper Biz Markie's label over illegal use of Sullivan's 1972 hit "Alone Again (Naturally)." Not only did Biz lift the title of that song, but he sampled and looped the first eight bars, including the refrain, "alone again, naturally." In his ruling of December 16, 1991, Judge Kevin Thomas Duffy invoked the moral codes of the Bible, quoting the Seventh Commandment: "Thou shalt not steal." So unfamiliar with black music that he apparently asked one witness what r&b was, the hard-nosed Duffy ordered all copies of Biz's album *I Need a Haircut* (Warner/Cold Chillin', 1988), on which the song appears, pulled from the shelves after only a few months in circulation (with sales at about 300,000). The case was also referred to the U.S. District Attorney for possible criminal prosecution, though no charges were brought.

The irony of this situation was that just prior to the album's release on August 26, an attorney representing Cold Chillin' had attempted to clear the sample—usually a routine process—through Gilbert's brother Terry, who handles his business affairs in the United States. By the release date they had not received a definitive response from O'Sullivan but, in a sloppy procedural move, still went ahead and shipped the album anyway (expecting to reach an agreement imminently). Biz, 29, who has built a career on his humorous brand of rap—including many parodies and takeoffs of popular songs and jingles—says, "I never had no trouble [clearing samples] until the time that happened with the lawsuit. I felt that I was made an example of." In defense of sampling other artists' works, he adds, "We just bringing it back to life. They ain't doin' nothing with it anyway, so why just let it sit?" Biz's next album is appropriately titled *All Samples Cleared*. Though legal experts downplay the case's relative significance, as the first concrete decision of its kind to equate sampling with stealing the outcome does not bode well for rappers. Major labels currently take great pains to ensure that similar situations are avoided in the future.

As a result, sample clearance houses such as Clearance 13'-8", Sample Doctor, and Diamond Time are doing a brisk business. For Diamond Time, an international company specializing in copyright clearance work, a rap roster that includes Das EFX, EPMD, L.L. Cool J., Kool G. Rap, Big Daddy Kane, Jungle Brothers, and the Biz, among others, accounts for most of its business. After the client submits a tape of his work along with a list of the songs sampled on each of the new compositions, as well as any information about the originals, Diamond Time initiates a two-phase process:

1. Investigating a song; confirming writers, publishers, and owners of the copyright and master recording; submitting letters of request to those parties along with an audiotape of the song and a description of the sample used, and then negotiating terms.
2. OK'ing quotes with clients; securing final written agreements.

For each sample to be cleared, two fees must be negotiated: one for publishing and another for use of the master. Thus, permission to use ten samples would require twenty individual clearances.

Fees are determined on the basis of a statutory royalty rate set by Congress. For a recording of under five minutes, an artist sampling (or wishing to purchase the mechanical license of) another artist's work must pay $0.0625 per composition or $0.012 per minute of playing time. These figures represent guidelines, and could be higher or lower, quickly adding up when several samples are used in a song and when the sampled work has more than one publisher (thus splitting the pie into more pieces, so that everyone will want a bigger share). Master use, which is determined more by a nominal fee per unit, can also add up, depending upon the number of units sold. Often, however, Diamond Time negotiates a one-time flat fee for the master use.

To bypass paying for master use, producers such as Marley Marl sometimes bring in live musicians to re-create a sample, but they must still pay for the publishing rights on that sample. Despite being used over and over by many different groups, drum tracks like those featured in the popular *Ultimate Breaks and Beats* series technically must also be cleared, though usually they are not—another one of the strange ambiguities that exists in the "rules" of sampling. While some of the clearances Diamond Time negotiates are for free—such as in reciprocal agreements between rap labels, who might sample each other's artists—the most one of their clients has ever paid for a sample is $20,000 (paid by Heavy D. to Hamilton Bohannon). Deborah Mannis-Gardner, the director of Diamond Time, estimates that, on average, sample clearances for a rap album usually run about $30,000 (of which about $2,000 is Diamond Time's fee).

A staunch supporter of her clients, Mannis-Gardner says, "I always ask people, 'Is a collage a piece of art?' And the answer is, 'Yes.' Well, sampling is like a collage. You're just taking different pieces of different songs and creating a new piece of art. And I don't think there's anything malicious, I don't think there's any theft intended or nastiness." Aside from such glaring rip-offs as Biz's rendition of "Alone Again (Naturally)" and Hammer's "U Can't Touch This," which appropriated Rick James' "Superfreak," sampling tends toward the more subtle and original.

Producers such as DJ Mark the 45 King ingeniously combine layers of different sound like a painter mixing colors on a palette. "It's an art form because it's a collage," says Mark. "I'm not stealing all their music, I'm using your drum track, I'm using this little 'bip' from him, I'm using your bassline that you don't even like no fucking more, you know what I'm saying?" Mark also uses live horn players on many of his compositions. While he believes in paying for the use of recognizable loops, he also sees a skill in disguising sounds, "like putting glasses and a fake nose over your drum track."

"If you're slick enough, you can hide your samples," agrees Prince Paul. "In the days of De La Soul, *3 Feet High & Rising*, it was strictly straight up loops. I mean, now it's to a point where I take stuff, chop it up, filter it, you know what I'm sayin', take little bits and pieces, you know, you have to." Rap producers are also using more obscure sounds instead of the recognizable hits from the past. "Everyone's going back in the crates and finding real, real abstract stuff, which even now the record labels and publishers are starting to get hip to," says Paul. "But a lot of producers are a lot more skillful than they were back then. They, like, see more now, and there's more technology than there was back in the days. I mean, you can do a lot more stuff with sampling than you could do like even five years ago, yunno? It just got a little better, so you're able to do more. So that's how people can disguise stuff."

Even George Clinton, who has been sampled to no end (also benefiting from income received from the publishing), expresses amazement at the sophistication of the art form. "I mean, 'cause Public Enemy got hip-hop production down like Holland-Dozier-Holland had Supremes and the Four Tops down," he says. "Those guys mix that shit for a college degree. It ain't just no loops, 'cause they will take a loop and turn that into something that don't sound like it should be able to be done."

One of the guys he was referring to, Eric Sadler, who has spoken on panels and addressed seminars on sampling, says, "A lot of people are very creative with it. You take things, you turn 'em backwards, forwards, you slow 'em down, you turn it into something new, yunno, that's not recognizable. To me it's like this really: If somebody out there can recognize their shit in your shit, you should pay 'em. That's it." Today, however, Sadler says he doesn't even sample because the whole issue of lawsuits and clearance costs has gone out of control. "When we were doing PE and other groups," he says, "we just went and were free and created. We tried not to blatantly use anything because we had respect for those who were taken from. I think Hank said it best because Hank's not a musician. Sampling records was making him a musician—a bassline from here, a guitar from here, drums from here, and organ from here slapped all together created another piece. It created another piece of music."

The unsung hero of hip-hop is the studio engineer. While a good deejay, producer, or rapper always gets his share of the fame, money, and groupies, the engineer receives an hourly wage for services rendered, and maybe, if he/she is lucky, credit on the CD or cassette jacket. But as rap music has evolved into a complex studio art form, the engineer has become indispensable. He/she supervises the technical aspects of recording—usually operating most of the equipment and adding an opinion on creative decisions whenever necessary. "An engineer's job is to translate what you have in your mind to the tape machine," says Ivan "Doc" Rodriguez, 32. "He's basically the record button, the guy that records everything to tape." In his six years behind the boards at PowerPlay Studios in Long Island City, Queens, Doc has worked with some of the biggest names in the industry, including Grandmaster Flash and the Furious Five, Eric B. & Rakim, Boogie Down Productions, MC Lyte, Real Roxanne, Big Daddy Kane, Biz Markie, Kool G. Rap, EPMD, Ultramagnetic, and L.L. Cool J.

"I could easily call a lot of what I do coproduction," says Doc, "because I feel that I want to make the record sound the best possible—you know, get the best possible sound out of it, and I put my extra effort in, you know, but I don't have to." Doc knows the ins and outs behind every piece of high-tech hardware that surrounds him in the studio. If need be he can also play several instruments, add a cut or scratch from the turntable, and even come up with a crucial sample from his massive library of sounds.

From the time he was a kid, tinkering with electrical equipment and getting shocked, Doc has been sharpening his technical skills. Born in Puerto Rico, he grew up in Hell's Kitchen on the West Side of Manhattan, and first got involved in music as a mobile deejay. In high school he excelled on the basketball court but decided to put that on the back burner to study electrical engineering at New York City Technical College in Brooklyn. After only a year, however, he gave that up to enroll in the Center for Media Arts in Manhattan to study audio engineering.

Outside of his classes, Doc deejayed at house parties, while also helping his friend Speedy put together a demo. It opened the doors to PowerPlay, where he and his friend met the well-known producer/artist Spyder D., who was working out of there. "So he was doing something, and the engineer couldn't seem to get it together, so I said, 'Listen, you know, I don't want to interfere, but I might be able to do this for you,' and I got it done really fast," recalls Doc. "And we kept working, and I kept helping him and making certain things happen faster than normal. So I guess he felt I could be an asset to him." A week later, Spyder D. called up Doc and asked him to go on tour with him.

"We hit the road, and that was it, you know, I was official, with the program, and I started learning more through Spyder as I went to the studio with him," says Doc. "The studio owner got interested in my skills as an engineer, 'cause I wasn't a producer, but I was very good technically."

Doc juggled engineering school with dates on the road while getting practical experience at PowerPlay. His skills improved rapidly.

One day he got a call from Gary Salzman, former general manager of PowerPlay. "And I sat down with him in the office, and he gives me a very serious look, and he goes, 'Listen, I need your help,' 'cause usually when they would need equipment or anything, I always knew who to go to or who to speak to, 'cause I love equipment," says Doc. "So I said, 'Well, what can I get you?' And he goes, 'Well, I need an engineer.' And I said, 'Well, I can't buy that, I don't have any friends who have connections for that.' And he goes, 'No, I mean you.' So I was really shocked." Though still in engineering school, Doc began assisting at PowerPlay for two weeks before he was assigned his first official engineering project—Eric B. & Rakim's *Paid In Full* (4th & Broadway, 1987).

That project was followed by BDP's *By All Means Necessary*, (Jive, 1988), after which Doc devoted a lot of his time to the group, eventually touring with them as their deejay. DJ Doc recorded BDP's show on a reel-to-reel tape so that they would not have to worry about their records skipping on stage—the first time this was done in hip-hop. "They had some tapes with really nice intros and special edits, and I did all that shit myself with blades," explains Doc. "Then you scratch on top of it. But the tapes were, like, shit you couldn't do with turntables." When DATs (digital audio-tapes) were introduced, he used them to record show instrumentals and intros, and many other rap acts started coming to him to prepare their live-show tapes in the same way.

But Doc's real skills lay behind the boards at PowerPlay. While he learned his way around the studio in just two months, he also says, "It took me a solid two years before I knew what I was hearing properly. You know, your ears may tell you one thing, but that's not really what's happening, so you have to train yourself, and say, O.K., and you look deeper." The ears, according to Doc, are probably the engineer's most valuable asset in setting the sound levels during the mixdown. "Balance is important, and a lot of people don't have that," he explains. "I mean, how could they? They're drinking and smoking, and, you know, their head isn't straight when we're in this, so how do they know that they're actually hearing what they're hearing? Their ears could be shot 'cause they've been playing headphones in their ears for so long—things of that nature. So I would say balance is very important, you know, hearing. You have to have good hearing and you can't over Eq [equalize] things—that's a part of hearing—'cause things get distorted and you can't go back and fix it."

After the recording and mix down, for which Doc is responsible, the tapes—whether analog, reel-to-reel, RDAT, or DAT—are sent to be mastered. "Mastering adjusts all the levels," says Doc. "If you have too much bass or you put two things in the mix that are out of phase, they try to rephase it so your stereo mix sounds like a stereo mix. A lot of these things engineers are supposed to know, but they really don't—some don't. Basically, what they are doing is preparing it to hit wax, and then it goes to the manufacturer, and they make the records and the label." As the mediator between the producer and the equipment, however, the engineer plays the crucial role of translating basic concepts and ideas into actual finished songs.

As with anyone associated with the music industry, Doc has many negative impressions about the thievery and back-stabbing that goes on. Like any professional, though, when at work in the studio he is concentration personified. Doc has trained scores of younger engineers coming up at PowerPlay, who have gone on to their own degrees of success, and more recently he has branched out into more producing. He does acknowledge that music has been good to him, saying, "I came from a street full of junkies and crackheads and murderers, and I always tell people one thing. I always tell interns and assistants at PowerPlay, to give them a little support, I tell them when I walked into PowerPlay, I had a token in my pocket. A year later I had a new car."

Rap music creates not only endless possibilities, but opportunities. After all, who would have thought that youths from the ghetto, denied access to musical instruments, could ever make their own music? The process of putting together a rap record—from choosing the samples to actually laying down the tracks in the studio—is hardly as simplistic or unoriginal as some would make it out to be. In fact, it requires a knowledge of music and an intuition far beyond the realm of notes, chord structures, and any other formal elements that we usually associate with music. Rap bridges the gap between the present and the past, between different kinds of music, and between human beings and technology, making it a universal medium. It refuses to get stale and die because it is always turning the corner in search of the newest thing.

recommended
listening

1. Main Source, *Breaking Atoms* (Wild Pitch, 1991).
2. Diamond and the Psychotic Neurotics, *Stunts, Blunts, & Hip-Hop* (Polygram, 1992).
3. DJ Mark the 45 King, *45 Kingdom* (Tuff City, 1990).
4. Eric B. & Rakim, *Paid In Full* (4th & Broadway/Island, 1987).
5. De La Soul, *3 Feet High and Rising* (Tommy Boy, 1989).
6. Public Enemy, *It Takes a Nation of Millions to Hold Us Back* (Def Jam/Columbia, 1988).
7. Ice Cube, *Amerikkka's Most Wanted* (Priority, 1990).
8. Dr. Dre, *The Chronic* (Interscope, 1992).
9. Pete Rock & C.L. Smooth, *Mecca and the Soul Brother* (Elektra, 1991).
10. The Brand New Heavies, *Heavy Rhyme Experience, Vol. 1* (Delicious Vinyl/Atlantic, 1992).

ChApTeR 9

Oral Funk
Journalism

Language not only helps to define a culture, but it provides the vital link that binds a community together. As a primary conduit for information, ideas, and emotions, it fulfills our basic need for communication and expression. It is no wonder, then, that Chuck D. has referred to rap alternately as the "black CNN" and the "black American folktale." Though the term "rap" has long been synonymous with "talk," today rap represents the language of the urban, primarily black culture of hip-hop. It describes the lifestyle of the youths who comprise this culture, mostly in very candid terms. Though some take offense at the crude ghetto sensibilities that rap reflects, as well as its frank depictions of violence and sex, these negative elements go with the turf. In general, however, rap resists simple classification. As Jon Pareles observes in the *New York Times*, "It's time to recognize what rap is: a huge, varied symbolic realm, too big to be stereotyped. There are smart rappers and idiotic ones, rappers who want to teach and rappers who want to pander and rappers who just want to make people laugh."[1] Rap is simply as unadulterated a form of expression as you can get. As spoken poetry it is an art form. As the world seen through the eyes of a young black male or female it captures life as vividly as a photograph and as precisely as any other form of reportage—backed, of course, by the beat of the street.

Though the newest form of music since rock 'n' roll, rap has a firm foundation in the black experience. Author David Toop writes, "Rap's forbears stretch back through disco, street funk, radio DJ's, Bo Diddley, the bebop singers, Cab Calloway, Pigmeat Markham, the tap dancers and comics, The Last Poets, Gil Scott-Heron, Muhammad Ali, a cappella and doo-wop groups, ring games, skip-rope rhymes, prison and army songs, signifying, and the dozens all the way to the *griots* of Nigeria and Gambia."[2] If you add to this list black preachers, Jamaican deejays, and the soulful monologues of such singers as Barry White, Isaac Hayes, and Millie Jackson, rap, as we know it may be seen as the latest extension of a healthy tradition of black music traceable all the way back to Africa.

Today's rappers bear a striking similarity to the *griots* (or *gewel*, the Senegalese term), West African bards who played an especially important role in precolonial society, orally passing on the cultural history of their people. Dr. Pearl E. Primus writes, "The art of the *griot* requires music and song skill and also an unerring memory. The spiritual life of the citizens of the community, past, present, and future, rest in the virtuosity and unerring exactness of the *griot*. The songs of the *griot* are more precise than any history book."[3] Endowed with this much prized oral skill, the *griot* enjoyed a very respected position within his community, just like many modern-day microphone personalities.

Unfortunately, a knowledge of such indigenous African languages as Yoruba, Igbo, Twi, and Kikongo was largely wiped out during the Middle Passage, which brought Africans to the New World. As the slaves were dispersed among different Southern states and plantations, they lost the ability to communicate in their own tongues, thus severing the crucial link with their native cultures. While reprogrammed in the ways of their new land, they were also, with few exceptions, kept illiterate, but this was precisely what the slave owners wanted. Any link to their Africanness—even the drum, a vital tool of communication—was taken away, in the hopes of fashioning them into drones who had no concept of their true identity.

Despite the best efforts to wipe out their culture, the slaves preserved many of the musical and oral traditions of Africa, merging them with elements of their new culture to create something distinctly African American. As Henry Louis Gates, Jr., writes, "This African-American culture was a veritable 'underground' culture, shared surreptitiously, as it were, by word of mouth. African Americans nurtured a private but collective oral culture, one they could not 'write down,' but one they created, crafted, shared with each other and preserved for subsequent generations out loud, but outside of the hearing of white people who enslaved them, and, later, discriminated against them. It was in this isolated and protected black cultural space that African-American vernacular culture was born and thrived."[4] There are many terms for this vernacular in America and the Caribbean—including patois, creole, pidgin, or jive. What mainstream society often perceives as slang, however, is actually a cleverly coded language within a language that those unfamiliar with black culture would have a difficult time trying to understand. But that is the whole point.

As an expression of young blacks, rap speaks directly to and from a black point of view. Using the ever changing idiom of the streets, it captures and epitomizes contemporary black culture as nothing else. "It's like a way of life," says rapper/producer Showbiz. "This is a culture, so look at us. See how we are? It's the way we dress, the way we talk, the way our state of mind is, the things we do. This is how we can relate."

Today, rap is the voice of reality, fable, humor, entertainment, education, protest, and, above all, opinion and personal style. But back in the day, it was all about freestyle—basically "talking shit" in simple rhymes and flowing with the beat. Early MCs such as Busy Bee Starski and Melle Mel, who started off talking about his deejay, Grandmaster Flash, per-fected boasting to such a level of entertainment that microphone skills earned instant ghetto stardom. Every Bronx youth who ever witnessed an MC control a crowd has dreamed of basking in those frenzied cheers of approval as well. But competition was stiff, and reputations were built on the charred remains of "sucker MCs" who were reduced to dust with scathing disses (insults). "Back in the day," says Lord Finesse (Robert Hall), 22, "you wasn't thinking about no props or no dancers. It was all about coming into a party and ripping shit up with your lyrics, youknowwhatimsayin'?" MCs either wrote and memorized books of lyrics or were blessed with the talent to ad-lib off the head-top in rhyming couplets.

Today, freestyle has evolved into more of a stream-of-consciousness flow incorporating varied rhyme patterns, endless pop culture references, and highly imaginative metaphors that keep progressing from punchline to punchline. Diamond demonstrates how it's done in the song "Check One, Two":

I get hype when I kick the ballistics
And get paid from the use of my linguistics
The style is dope even though it's simplistic
Soda breaks me out, so now I drink Mistic
At the res I listen to the Stylistics
Break down rappers as if they had cystic
fibrosis, never snackin' on a Hostess
Or pork rinds—none of that swine
Word got around that my shit was boomin'
It ran through the Bronx just like Paul Newman
Now everyone can get a sample of the skills
That won't trample when I build
an example of the will
That's stronger than Sampson,
see I'm the champ, son
When I relax, I'm off to the Hamptons
Compare the sound to another and let's see
I slam shit up like Wayne Gretsky
Sing a simple song like Sylvester Stone
And catch ya out there like Rick Cerone . . .
So grab a chair and sip on some Jacobazzi
I stimulate your brain like a game of Yahtzee . . .

**BUSTA RHYMES OF
LEADERS OF THE
NEW SCHOOL AND
PHIFE OF A TRIBE
CALLED QUEST
PERFORM
"SCENARIO" AT
THE RITZ.**

Substituting slang for stilted verse, and striking a mental chord through cleverness, freestyle represents poetry in motion. Though substance is not a requisite, style, imagination, originality, and an unfettered tongue are, and such rappers as Lord Finesse, Showbiz & A.G., Das EFX, and Leaders of the New School have made their mark with a distinctive freestyle flavor on the mike.

When you get several artists in the studio together, some of the most eye-popping, jaw-dropping freestyle spews out onto tape as the mike passes through many eager hands. Memorable crew cuts include "The Symphony," conducted by Juice Crew members Masta Ace, Craig G., Big Daddy Kane, and Kool G. Rap; the collaboration of A Tribe Called Quest and Leaders of the New School on "Scenario"; "Stranded on Death Row," featuring various talent signed to Dr. Dre's Death Row label; and "Protect Ya Neck," which includes eight underground MCs known as the Wu-Tang Clan. Passing the mike is always in order at shows, and "Live at the BBQ," a hardcore, lyrical romp from Main Source's first album, *Breaking Atoms* (Wild Pitch, 1991), re-creates the fast and furious spontaneity of these verbal gymnastic meets. Queens rapper Nasty Nas sets off the chain:

> My troops roll up with a strange force
> I was trapped in a cage and let out by the Main Source
> Swimmin' in women like a lifeguard
> Put on the bulletproof, nigga I strike hard
> Kidnapped the president's wife without a plan
> And hangin' niggas like the Ku Klux Klan
> I melt mikes till the soundwaves over
> Before steppin' to me you'd better step to Jehovah
> Slammin' MCs on cement
> 'Cause verbally, I'm iller than an AIDS patient
> I move swift and uplift your mind
> Shoot the gift when I rip and rhyme

Rappin' sniper, speaking real words
My thoughts react like Steven Spielberg's
Poetry and text
paragraphs punch hard my brain is insane
I'm out to lunch God . . .

As the other verses unfold—each in a unique style—the rappers on the track weave a continuous verbal tapestry. Freestyle is rap's bread and butter, and dedicated MCs usually have a catalog of rhymes absorbed in their heads ready to spit out at the drop of a beat.

While freestyle meanders from topic to topic, liberally doused with boasting and dissing, story rhymes are more geared toward specific concepts, running the gamut from serious issues to pure entertainment. Sometimes they cover both bases, as in Slick Rick's "Children Story." Presented in the form of a dramatic bedtime story as told by "Uncle" Ricky (in his inimitable English brogue), the song tells of the unfortunate fate that befalls a kid who turns to a life of crime. As problems common to the ghetto, crime and violence, in fact, provide the basis for numerous songs, and while groups like the Parents Music Resource Center (PMRC) suggest that rap promotes or glorifies negativity, they often miss the point.

In "Soliloquy of Chaos," for example, Gang Starr's Guru (Keith Elam) tells a very gripping tale about violence at a hip-hop show. At the song's conclusion he says, "This can happen often and it's really fucked up/So I ask you to your face homeboy, what's up?/Did you come to see my show or to the stupid nigger playoffs/Killing you and killing me, it's the soliloquy of chaos." Though Compton's Most Wanted does not send an overtly antiviolent message in "Driveby Miss Daisy," they provide an insider's perspective on the anatomy of a drive-by. This highly cinematic gangsta rap about an innocent bystander who accidentally gets shot in a retaliatory drive-by between rival gang members reflects the reality of an all too common scenario in which innocent lives are claimed. Understanding the root of the problem is the first step in working toward a solution.

Even on the far left of rap's spectrum of violence, epitomized by a group like the Geto Boys, the shocking nature of the material does not belie the fact that there are valuable insights to be gained. Like twisted horror movies, "Mind of a Lunatic" and "Mind Playing Tricks on Me" both explore the psyche of the criminally insane as adeptly as an advanced psychology text. On his solo album, Geto Boy Mr. Scarface also penned the unforgettable "Diary of a Madman":

> Dear diary, today I hit a nigger with a torch
> Shot him in his face and watched him die on the front porch
> Left his family heartbroken
> Flashbacks of him lyin' there bleedin' with his eyes open

The experience of taking a life catches up to Scarface, the narrator, who initially undergoes mental anguish, grappling with his actions before becoming a hardened killer.

> It used to be hard but now it ain't nothin' to me
> To go to a nigga's house
> Put a pistol in his mouth and blow his fuckin' brains out

In real life, Scarface says, "I'm not a fuckin' gangster, I'm a realist, but I've been in every situation." While songs such as "Diary of a Madman" reflect harshness and brutality beyond measure, they take us into the twisted mind of a killer, shedding light on his motivations. They also express a very specific point of view in the bluntest manner possible, as is one of rap's strengths.

"Rap is one of the only music forms where you can express yourself any way you want to. You can say what you want as clear as you can," observes Andre the Giant of Showbiz & A.G. Whether it is explicit sex or violence or explicit humor, such as Biz Markie's "Pickin' Boogers," rap encompasses all views. Analyzing a contemporary's work, Wise Intelligent of PRT says, "When Ice Cube do his songs, he put the message out there, but he put it on his level. Like, for instance, the song that he just did, 'It Was a Good Day,' yunno, that's gonna send people in pursuit of having a good day—just subconsciously gonna plant that in you, youknowwhatimsayin? Like today, I didn't even have to use my A.K., I gotta say, today has been a good day."

RAKIM ALLAH ONSTAGE AT THE RITZ WITH A JUNIOR MEMBER OF HIS CREW.

His partner Culture Freedom adds, "To teach anybody anything, you gotta be able to speak the language, you knowwhatimsayin, and that's how I see Ice Cube, in a way. He puts his message out there, but he puts it in a language that people can understand. You gotta know the language before you can talk. You gotta walk like the people and talk like the people before you can be accepted by those people sometimes. Because people be like, 'How the hell you gonna try to tell me something, for one, you ain't never been in the ghetto, for two you ain't never had shit stolen, you ain't never had any welfare cheese, how can you come in here and tell me.' "

For this reason, the rappers who get the most respect are those who speak from the heart and are true to the art form. Hip-hop audiences know when someone is faking it, and they have no tolerance for "sucker MCs." On the other hand, they revere such skilled lyricists as Big Daddy Kane, Grand Puba, and Rakim. Thus, when Kane strayed from his hard-core roots, delving into more r&b-inspired rap, he lost many of his loyal following (but he seems to be reverting back to his former self with the 1993 release of *Looks Like a Job for* . . . on Warner/Cold Chillin'). With his cold monotonal delivery, Rakim, on the other hand, has consistently proven his skills on the mike while writing some of the most progressive rhymes in hip-hop. In "Follow the Leader" he says:

> In this journey you're the journal I'm the journalist
> Am I eternal or on an eternal list
> I'm about to flow long as I can possibly go
> Keep ya movin' 'cause the crowd said so
> Dance, cuts rip your pants
> Eric B. on the blades, bleedin' to death
> Call the ambulance
> Pull at my weapon and start to squeeze
> A magnum as a microphone, murderin' MCs
> Let's quote a rhyme from a record I wrote
> "Follow the leader"
> Yeah, dope

Rakim is neither the first nor the last MC to compare his mike to a weapon, which recalls the days of serious rhyme battles. But breaking the mold of ordinary freestyle, which depends on instant audience recognition of cultural references and punchlines, he belongs more to the school of abstract rap, which initially sails right over the head. The cleverness of abstract rhymes and concepts usually sinks in over time, but when it does one is left utterly amazed.

Abstract rap encompasses many styles, from the rootsy rhymes of such groups as A Tribe Called Quest and the Jungle Brothers, to the fractured rhyme scheme and delivery of PE's Chuck D., to the completely erratic free association of Kool Keith of Ultramagnetic. A former patient at Creedmore and Bellevue hospitals, Keith is a singular character, who if he played for the Yankees would be out in deep left field. Though he credits Special K of the Treachcrous Three and K's brother T LA Rock with pioneering the abstract style, Keith, and his alter ego Rhythm X, are masters of the game, spinning dusted science fantasies with an offbeat cadence. He puts his mouth where his mind is on "Traveling at the Speed of Thought":

> I go 1, 2, 3, 4, 5, 6,
> 7, 8, 9, as I take your mind off
> and on to a new track
> to train ducks how to act
> respect me, when I whip your brain
> skip your brain and dip your brain
> in a lotion, while I tap your skull
> I'm like a bird when I'm pecking your skull . . .
> But I'm traveling on to Bellvue
> 'cause I'm sick
> Traveling hard at the speed of thought.

In other songs, Keith uses SAT vocabulary and shares a fresh perspective on most things: He would never say "sucker MC" when he could call the competition ducks, germs, or parasites.

Another group much underrated for their lyrical complexity and sophistication is the Queens-based Organized Konfusion, consisting of The Pharoahe Monch and Prince Poetry. On the song "Prisoners of War" from their self-titled debut on Hollywood Basic, the Pharoahe raps:

> Wake up to the mathematics of an erratic rap
> Rejuvenator of rhyme that sort of come automatic
> Poetical medical medicine for the cerebellum
> I divert 'em and flirt 'em insert 'em then I repel 'em . . .
> I'm mathematical, acrobatical
> Attack the wack take rap to the maximum . . .
> Pickin' 'em, stickin' 'em, breakin'
> shakin' 'em up and bashin' them
> Lyric dictator the aviator of antonym
> On beware so prepare for the guillotine
> Rhymes go express, expert, extreme
> Be up to par with wisdom and intellect
> Detaching one's head directly from the neck
> Still I've been illin' and drillin' your brain
> Like a villain I came in the darkness to spark
> the literature for sure
> When I rhyme for the prisoners of war.

Abstract rhymes take expression to new galaxies maximizing the potential of language by twisting it, stretching it, turning it on its head, obeying no conventions, and, of course, being as creative as possible.

Another abstract realm in which rap delves is that of pure feeling. Like the best poetry, some rap lyrics resonate with greater meaning, able to express thoughts of love, anger, and hate or an endless spectrum of moods with uncanny accuracy and depth. When such lyrics are matched with the appropriate beat, the combination can be powerful. "They Reminisce

Over You (T.R.O.Y.)" by Pete Rock & C.L. Smooth is a particularly poignant song dedicated to the memory of Trouble T. Roy, a dancer for rapper Heavy D. who met an untimely death. Over the song's penetrating Tom Scott horn loop, C.L. Smooth not only recalls his friend, but talks about the roles various members of his own family played while he was growing up.

"Personally, Pete Rock and I wanted to formulate a song so that his family and friends and our family and friends could understand the power of death," he explains. "And when you understand the power of death, then you could understand the power of life, and the power of life that's going on now, and that gave me life, and gave you life, and gave him life. This is the family, and the way the family is structured to raise you. When I was helpless, when I couldn't feed myself or clothe myself, my uncles and my aunts and my grandparents and my mother and father were there to basically help me get to the state I'm at now. Because statistics show that I

PETE ROCK (right) & C.L. SMOOTH (left) GET DOWN TO BUSINESS.

could be anywhere in society—jail, dead, I could be a mugger, a rapist, anything." The song unlocks precious memories as a means of celebrating life.

The diversity of rap songs is matched only by the diversity of the people making them. Rap, in itself, represents only a mode of expression—the vehicle in which to convey thoughts. Using slang and sophisticated vocabulary; techniques such as repetition, alliteration, and onomatopoeia (using words whose sound implies their meaning, i.e., crash); and vocal inflections that could be as natural as Erick Sermon or Kool G. Rap's lisp or B-Real's nasal whine, rap simultaneously unites the premeditated art of writing with the spontaneous skill of performance. While other types of poetry assume the printed form or are meant to be recited, rap is meant to be experienced along with its rhythmic backtrack. In this respect it is an art form in and of itself, a new form of "beat" poetry.

> I want the right to speak
> I want the right to walk where I wanna
> Yell and I'm gonna
> Tell and rebel every time I'm on a
> Microphone on a stage cold illin'
> The knowledge I drop will be heard by millions
> We ain't the problems, we ain't the villains
> It's the suckers deprivin' the truth from our children
> You can't hide the fact, Jack
> There's violence in the streets every day
> Any fool can recognize that
> But you try to lie and lie
> And say America's some motherfuckin' apple pie
> Yo, you gotta be high to believe
> That you gonna change the world by a sticker on a
>   record sleeve.

> "Freedom of Speech"
> Ice-T

Controversy and rap go together like Smith & Wesson. Any mention of rap in the mainstream media usually involves the latest antipolice rap song, yet another attempt to link rap with violence, or a politician or prominent figure (like Dan Quayle or Bill Clinton) taking issue with something a rapper says. As Ice-T observes in the above song's chorus, there is "freedom of speech—just watch what you say." Ever since Tipper Gore, wife of the current vice president of the United States, organized the PMRC in 1985, instigating the now familiar "Parental advisory— Explicit lyrics" stickering that appears on many rap albums, the issue of censorship has commanded the attention of the music industry. Despite a wealth of so-called "offensive" material out there—in all areas of enter- tainment and media—rap continues to shoulder the bum rap.

In a country based on such lofty ideals as "freedom," "equality," and "inalienable rights," censorship has reared its ugly head all too often since the much-publicized "Cop Killer" incident, in which the Texas Fraternal Order of Police threatened a boycott of Time Warner (parent company of the Warner Brothers record label that distributes Ice-T) unless they "voluntarily" removed that song from the debut album by Ice-T's rock group Body Count. After initially fighting this outright example of police harassment, the corporate giant suddenly stood to lose hundreds of mil- lions in the planned mass boycott. On July 28, 1992, Ice-T, supposedly acting on his own, relented, pulling the song from the album and causing a severe panic within the industry as record company executives scrambled to purge any other potentially offensive lyrics from their own rap releases. It didn't matter that Body Count was a heavy-metal band or that the grinding guitars of "Cop Killer" bore no likeness whatsoever to rap. Once the wheels of censorship were set in motion, labels employed draconian measures to determine if an album was appropriate for release. Even Warner, whom Ice-T had praised for their unwavering support in the matter, subsequently dropped him after refusing to distribute his next album, *Home Invasion* (Rhyme Syndicate, 1993), based on cover art they deemed offensive.

The Ice-T fiasco had repercussions that affected the works of many other rappers, as *The Source* reported in their November 1992 issue. A&M

artist Tragedy, a.k.a. the Intelligent Hoodlum, was forced to remove the song "Bullet" from his album because it expressed sentiments similar to "Cop Killer." Boo-Yah Tribe, who record for Hollywood Basic, dropped "Shoot 'Em Down" from their *Rumors of a Dead Man* EP as a direct result of corporate pressure. FU2, who were set for a promising debut with their single "Boomin' in Ya Jeep," was dropped from MCA over another song called "No Head, No Backstage Pass." And the list goes on: Juvenile Committee withdrew the cut "Justice for the Hood" from their album, and Boston's Almighty RSO was dropped from Tommy Boy after their first single "One in the Chamba" was construed as condoning killing police. The most stunning examples of censorship came from within Warner's own house, with such artists as Kool G. Rap and Paris.

G. Rap's album, titled *Live and Let Die* was released almost two years late as a result of the Biz Markie sampling case and the fallout over "Cop Killer." The number of samples and snippets of movie dialogue made it a clearance nightmare, and according to producer Sir Jinx, "Then the Ice-T shit came along. Whoa, whoa, whoa, they [Warner] gettin' spooked again. [They said] G. Rap, you have to take out everything you said about cops now. Now if you heard that record, G. Rap killed more cops, you know what I'm saying?" Even after making the appropriate changes, redoing tracks, and sitting on the album for so long, the album eventually was only distributed independently by Warner's Cold Chillin' subsidiary, reaching a significantly smaller audience than it would have had the project been fully supported by Warner.

The whole creative aspect of the album had also been compromised. "If you ever hear the first version of the record, you'll love it 'cause it was called *Live and Let Die—The Movie*, and we made everything like a movie. It was basically about G. Rap growing up, becoming a gangster. His pops used to be a gangster, his mom was a gangster, everybody's a gangster," says Jinx. "We had inserts in there, we had a movie review that was in there. It was dope." G. Rap adds, "We had to take out so much shit, like voices and everything which connected the songs with each other, that it fucked up the movie format, youknowhati'msayin'?"

Tommy Boy, which is distributed by Warner, also put the clamps down on Paris for the singles "Bush Killa" and "Coffee, Donuts & Death" from the *Sleeping With the Enemy* LP. In a press conference on November 24, 1992, the very articulate Paris highlighted the double standard in the industry, saying, "I might not mind all this censorship so much if it didn't seem that rappers were the targets of it to a much greater extent than any other type of recording artist. It's infuriating that Warner Music goes after me, but gives the green light and everything short of a big parade down Broadway to Madonna, whose work is surely as offensive to as many people as mine is. And as others have noted, Arnold Schwarzenegger has killed whole stations full of police in the *Terminator* movies and nobody's trying to shut him down. I am certainly not saying that Madonna and Schwarzenegger ought to be censored. I am absolutely anticensorship. But I do think it's worth noting that those artists are white and I am not."

Following a settlement with Warner, which held up the release of the record, Paris was eventually able to distribute it independently on his own Scarface label, but this was after Tommy Boy, 4th and Broadway, and Sex (an independent label run by Rick Rubin) all turned him down due to corporate pressure from above. While most of the recording industry showed no spine, Marjorie Heins, director of the American Civil Liberties Union's Arts Censorship Project supported "Bush Killa," a first-person, fantasy narrative about a man plotting to kill the president, "Because it is obviously fictitious, and because the song deals primarily with political issues such as racism, police violence, and the Persian Gulf War, it could not be considered a 'true threat' against the president under the case law construing the federal statute."

So why was Warner so intent on suppressing the album? The monetary threat from a boycott, for one, and "because the issues are real, I suppose," says Paris. "And because certain people in power are interested in preserving the power that they have, and that [the album] can be seen perhaps as being threatening because it washes away the smoke screen of what they're really about because it speaks the truth." The truth is that police and other authorities who are mandated to "serve and protect" have continually abused their power to harass and degrade—especially in countless instances involving black youths. The videotaped beating of Rodney King that brings home this point in a most graphic fashion is neither the first or the last incident of its kind. Amnesty International, in fact, has issued a report about the Los Angeles Police and Sheriff's departments specifically, saying that for years these organizations have used excessive force out of proportion with the threats posed by suspects.

The April 1993 issue of *The Source* also documents several cases of unwarranted harassment, physical abuse, and even death at the hands of police, involving members of Whodini and Gang Starr in New York, as well as DJ Pooh in California and Scarface in Louisiana. In most of these instances, the police justified their actions by calling their treatment of the rappers in question as a case of mistaken identity. Taking into account these incidents, as well as numerous experiences that happen every day in the 'hood, it is hardly surprising, then, that so many young, black youths who rap should release songs about killing cops. Real attention should be drawn to the reason behind such sentiments, and how the police can work with the community to improve relations between themselves and civilians. As it stands, there is no trust in either direction. Rappers will always call it as they see it, and though the powers that be may try to stifle their words, the music is a powerful medium for reaching the people.

> *Ice Cube*: This is a man's world, thank you very much
> *Yo-Yo*: But it wouldn't be a damn thing without a woman's
> touch

> "It's a Man's World"
> Ice Cube

Like so many other aspects of our society, rap is a man's world—as concentrated a mix of Clint Eastwood films, locker room lingo, Marlboro ads, Mike Tyson, and back issues of *Hustler* as you can squeeze together.

But as man's biggest preoccupation, women have always figured prominently in the scheme of things—even if they have been used, abused, and left quite unamused. Weathering an endless litany of "bitch," "hoe," "trick," "stunt," and "gold digger" in rap songs, women have a right to be rabid. They also have the right to pick up the mike and set the record straight, which is exactly what they have done. Rap, after all, is a form of verbal combat, and from the beginning female rappers—including Sha Rock (of Funky Four Plus One), Sparky D., Sweet Tee, and Jazzy Joyce—have added their voices to the battle of the sexes. These pioneers set the stage for such talent as Roxanne Shanté, the Real Roxanne, MC Lyte, Antoinette, Salt-N-Pepa, Queen Latifah, and Yo-Yo, who further defined themselves as strong and able women. Today's bumper crop of female MCs includes many hard-edged personalities including Boss, Nikki D., Le Shaun, Rage, and Hurricane Gloria, who appeal to the "strictly street" audience as much as any of their male counterparts. They also add an important perspective in a male-dominated world where "life ain't nothing but bitches and money."

From the start, sex was a hot topic with MCs such as Spoonie G. down the line bluntly boasting about their sexual prowess or sheer animal instinct toward women. Ice-T dispensed with formalities, flattery, and foreplay on "G.L.G.B.N.A.F. (Girls Let's Get Buck Naked and Fuck)," manifesting the behavior of George Clinton's "Atomic Dog" ("Why must I chase the cat, it's nothing but the dog in me"). Without apology, this is the nature of the beast. Meanwhile, Kool G. Rap takes crassness to new depths in "Talk Like Sex," where he says, "Swingin' with this here stud, you need practice/I'm leaving floods of blood on your mattress/I'll leave you holdin' your swollen backside and rollin'/Fillin' all three holes, just like bowlin'." Others, such as Too Short, AMG, and the 2 Live Crew, have built careers on being as nasty as they wanted. As sex rules most young peoples' thoughts, rappers will always tap the subject, exploring new ways to make it more exciting and explicit in their X-rated rhymes.

But the ladies have made the issue more of a dialogue. Confronting claims as fantastic as porn movie escapades, BWP (Bytches With Problems) penned "Two Minute Brother," for those men who didn't have the stamina to match their words. Roxanne Shanté aimed straight for the head with "Brothers Ain't Shit," in which she says, "Brother's ain't shit/They're lookin' for the next big ass they can stick/But this here chick's not on your dick." Ice Cube, who easily qualifies as one of these brothers—especially after having written "A Bitch Is a Bitch" in his N.W.A. days—did something surprisingly different on his solo debut. On "It's a Man's World," he introduces Yo-Yo (Yolanda Whittaker), who strong-arms his sexist outlook in a head-to-head rhyme duel that plays out the problems between men and women.

Twenty-two-year-old Yo-Yo, a native of South Central L.A., has been rocking the mike since the age of 14, when she started winning talent shows and gaining a local reputation. After mutual friends introduced her to Ice Cube, who was planning on leaving N.W.A. and going solo, the two immediately developed a business relationship (Yo-Yo is adamant about the fact that she has never been romantically involved with Cube). In October of 1989, around the same time she was planning to attend San Diego State University, she ended up working on her 1991 debut *Make Way for the Motherlode* (East-West). Selling about 400,000 copies, this successful album was followed by *Black Pearl* and *You Better Ask Somebody*. In addition to being musically thumping, all three albums share the ideology of the independent, confident, self-respecting, and strong yet feminine black woman that Yo-Yo epitomizes.

As a female in a man's game and a spokesperson for her gender's perspective, Yo-Yo realized early on that she would be a role model, a position she takes very seriously. Consequently, she and Cube's manager Pat Charbonnet organized the Intelligent Black Women's Coalition (IBWC), a support group that organizes meetings and benefit concerts and now has nine chapters nationwide. Yo-Yo explains, "We had said that we would get a coalition started with women to really just confide in Yo-Yo. You know, Yo-Yo don't take no shit, this is the type of woman Yo-Yo is, she ain't gonna let a man hit her. You know,

**NIKKI D. (far left)
AND
APACHE (right)
POSE WITH
A FRIEND.**

just that self-esteem—encouraging her." Soon, she was getting calls from university professors and receiving more mail than even Ice Cube, even though she had not yet released her first album. All this attention brought home the fact that she was as much a role model/counselor as an entertainer.

The reason, she suggests, for so much disrespect toward women in rap songs is "because the way the guys have been raised. I think men who have been trained to respect women respect them." On the other hand, she observes, "Rap is strictly street to me. The way guys talk among themselves on the street is the way they write their music. Yunno, my everyday language, I'm not an angel, I curse, yunno, I'm a homegirl. When I get around my homegirls and they talking shit, and if they saying, yunno, whatever it is, I'm blending along wit' 'em 'cause those are my buddies. And yunno, it's just a thing, and we're young."

Rappers such as Yo-Yo, MC Lyte, Queen Latifah, and Roxanne Shanté show that girls can play the same games as guys—and provide competent challengers. One of the rawest male-female confrontations on record, "Who Freaked Who," from Apache's self-titled debut on Tommy Boy, is one session of the dozens on bedroom politics. Apache starts out telling Def Jam artist Nikki D. (his girlfriend):

> Who freaked who?
> That's a stupid-ass question
> I freaked you and taught that pussy a lesson

Then he goes into a more explicit discussion of just how it was done. Nikki D. gets her own back describing how she was really doing all of the teaching:

> Layin' me, you lose your mind
> Don't know what to do
> Who freaked who? I fuckin' freaked you

While women are on the receiving end more often than not in rap songs, Nikki D. shows that they can dish it out, too, verbally and otherwise. Representing the voice of the strong female, she also displays a more serious side on her own album with such songs as "Daddy's Little Girl," a firsthand account of teen pregnancy. As different as these songs are, they mirror real attitudes and situations, speaking point-blank on life in the community that produced them.

While talk can get quite racy, concepts are often couched in metaphors. Black Sheep, a duo not exactly known for political correctness or sensitivity when it comes to women, coined such terms as "Similak Child," to describe the ideal girl, and "Strobelight Honey," for females at clubs who only look good in bad lighting: Both are from their debut album *A Wolf in Sheep's Clothing* (Mercury, 1991). Discussing the latter song, Dres (Andres Titus) of the Black Sheep says, "That came straight from this, that, and the other, 'I was with honey, the strobe light had her looking good. I'm tellin you.'

"I went away up to Jersey to see this girl—long-ass ride into the heart of Jersey, somewhere where smog don't even be," he continues. "And I had met her the night before, she was like, 'Yo, I'm cookin' you dinner.' And my friend was visiting from uptown, she said, 'Bring your friend.' Yo, I got to her crib and it was like a shack. The door was, like, on one hinge, like 'errrrrr.' She came in wearing, like, a sweater made out of, like, a blanket, yo, that was like from the 1800s. And I was looking for anything that resembled the girl I saw last night. 'It's me,' " he says in falsetto, mimicking the girl's voice. "I was like, oh shit. My man, just started laughing. I was like, yo. We walked in, she's like, 'Dinner's almost ready.' I was like, 'Yo, I gotta go get something to drink—I seen a store right down the street, I'll be right back.' My man was like, 'I'll wait here.' I was like 'Nah, nah, come on.' We was outta there. Got back on the train. It was a long ride home, but, yo, she was busted," he says laughing.

With all the focus on sex and the turbid relations between men and women, rap's love songs are often overlooked. Quite surprisingly, this is a realm where the men hold their own, transcending the usual machismo to produce some very poignant material. L.L. Cool J., who claimed to be "hard as hell" on his first album, is responsible for rap's first ballad, "I Need Love," a slow, sexy paean to that one special girl that smacks with sincerity. Along these lines are also such songs as A Tribe Called Quest's "Bonita Applebaum," Pete Rock & C.L. Smooth's "Lots of Lovin'," and the Jungle Brothers respectful tribute, "Black Woman." Completely by-passing all rap stereotypes, however, is the sensitive man, as exemplified in such songs as Pharcyde's "Passin' Me By," about the pursuit of an unattainable girl, and Main Source's "Looking at the Front Door," where a

WOLVES IN SHEEP'S CLOTHING: MR. LAWNGE AND DRES OF BLACK SHEEP.

guy threatens to leave a girl who is not treating him well. Speaking straight from the heart, Large Professor raps:

> And when you're with your friends, I glide to the side
> Until the spotlight is mine and never sabotage a good time
> But when they're not around the fights commence
> I'm the one you're against and it doesn't make sense
> 'Cause I'm the one that you claim to love for life
> But all I get is gray hairs and strife
> And I can play some ole stuck-up rapper role
> And get foul every time you lose control
> But that's not my order of operations
> So I should win an award for lots of patience
> 'Cause that's all a fella can have
> With a girl who's shootin' up his world like Shaft
> And I don't think that I can take it anymore
> I'm lookin' at the front door.

Clearly not all rap is sexist. While it would be folly to justify material that does degrade women, it suffices to say that such attitudes are rooted deeply in the culture of their origin. Since most cultures worldwide exhibit some degree of sexism, it is also unfair to single out hip-hop as a target for criticism. There are as many opinions and outlooks on male-female relations as there are people and, while there will always be tall tales that belong in *Penthouse Forum*, rappers, like most writers, base much of their songs on personal experience or what they see happening around them.

Rap simultaneously reflects and defines hip-hop, a culture whose fashion, slang, dance, and visual art are in constant flux. Just as graffiti writing evolved from a simple name "tag" on a project wall to full-blown, intricate murals covering whole sides of subway cars, to canvases displayed in galleries from SoHo to Paris, rap has progressed from hollow boasting to expressing all the subtleties of the lives of young blacks. It connects the hip-hop nation, telling homegirls and homeboys from Detroit to Dallas, New York to L.A., about the attitudes, styles, latest slang, and general lifestyle of their contemporaries.

Speaking of the material on his debut album *Represent* (Relativity, 1993) Fat Joe Da Gangsta says, "I try to talk about basic, common sense shit we live, day-by-day experiences I have had in the past, and all that which made me a much better person and a wiser person. Like 'I'm a Bad, Bad Man,' all that shit is true. I got a song called 'Shorty Got a Fat Ass,' it's catchy, you know. That's what niggas say everyday when they're chillin' on the corner drinking a 40. They see a girl go by and they say, 'Shorty got a fat ass.' You know, common shit, nothing too complex, you know, just everyday, daily life things that everybody can relate to." Such real life scenes compose the essence of the art form.

As a medium created by youth for youth, rap also reaches its audience often more effectively than the educational system. "So many people are just so content to be in front of the building just chilling," says Masta Ase, who grew up in the Howard Houses of Brownsville, Brooklyn. "Nobody wants to be viewed as, like, a sucker or whatever. If you go to school, if you actually go to class to learn something, you like a punk or some shit like that, and that's the scariest thing—that black people have that mentality." Ase, who did well in school, escaped his surroundings and earned a degree in marketing from the University of Rhode Island before embarking on his career in rap. He recalls, "Like, my whole thing was to do good in school, but don't necessarily promote it. Just try to act like you got an 80 when you really got a 90 and shit like that. So I was, like, a brainiac fronting like a dum-dum, and it's, like, a lot of kids like that. Everybody feels like they got to walk around and front. It's not fashionable to be smart, and that's the stupidest thing I ever heard of, man."

On his 1993 release *Slaughta House* (Delicious Vinyl) he challenges this mentality, as well as simply describing how he lives. Just as "My Adidas" celebrated Run-D.M.C.'s favorite footwear, "Jeep Ass Niguh" pays tribute to Ase's stolen Blazer, which was equipped with dual twelve- and fifteen-inch woofers. The jeep is such a vital part of hip-hop culture, he says, " 'Cause hip-hop, man, the only way to hear hip-hop is loud, and a lot of times you can't really blast it in the house like you want to for whatever reason—other people in the house or neighbors or whatever. But when you in your car, it's like, closed in. Your, like, in your zone, and you just driving real fast, and boom." As the best possible way to hear rap, the "boomin' system" also finds itself the subject of many rap songs.

Another kind of "boom" popular among hip-hoppers is the kind you smoke. In fact, there are almost as many slang words for marijuana—sess, blunts, Buddha, indo, ism, the Chronic—as there are for sex. While many rappers brazenly flaunt the fact that they smoke the illegal herb (distinguished from all other drugs, which are looked down upon in rap circles),

MASTA ASE (far right) AND HIS CREW IN BROWNSVILLE.

it took Cypress Hill to really bring that mentality out of the closet. "Because, man, we're the real fuckin' marijuana smokin' dudes here, man. We're the one's that said, 'fuck it,' yunno?" says Sen Dog, explaining this trend as he takes a pull off a fat joint. "The reason is, we're no fuckin' hypocrites, man, yunno? We're not gonna be embarrassed to smoke our fuckin' joint in the park just because people don't know we smoke. I'd rather just take my shit out and blaze it and feel happy, yunno?"

Both their self-titled debut and *Black Sunday* (Ruffhouse/Columbia) are laced with explicit references to the herb—"Stoned Is the Way of the Walk," "Light Another," "Hits from the Bong" "Legalize It"—and the group also serve as spokesmen for NORML (National Organization for the Reform of Marijuana Laws). "We're like anybody else, and that's the way people want to hear the shit," says an afro-headed B-Real as he lights another filled with the green, aromatic bounty of Southern California. "They don't want to hear it all watered down. They want to hear it the way they'd be talking about it with their homeboys. The other day I was down by the fucking weed spot, these motherfuckers came around the corner and started lighting that shit up blah, blah, blah. That's reality.

BROOKLYN'S OWN GURU KEITHY E. OF GANG STARR.

Motherfuckers talk like that, and if you can't say what you would say to your homeboy on the street in a song, what the fuck is that good for, yunno? So we say it the way they'd be talking about it."

In this respect, rappers fulfill a role as oral journalists, documenting their culture, environment, and society in much the same terms as the *griots* of Africa. But they also wear many other hats, from entertainer to role model to political leader. According to the Guru from Gang Starr, rappers are "all of those you just mentioned—an entertainer, I could talk politics, I could talk philosophy, I could talk all that. But, I mean, I see what everybody else is doin' and, like, my stuff, our stuff is just another piece of the puzzle." Rap, he says, is "music with an atmosphere, with a message that'll put you in the mood, whether the message is, I'll bust your shit, or whether the message is to combat the conspiracy against blacks and the conspiracy in society against good people."

Among rappers there are many different views on the art form and how they perceive themselves. "Being a rapper to me means you gotta be a role model," says 15-year-old Chi-Ali, who has one record behind him—*The Fabulous Chi-Ali* (Relativity, released in 1992). "Like right now, almost all black kids are listening to rap. If you don't want to be a role model you don't want to be a rapper, 'cause there's more to being a rapper than just rapping. It's a career, a business, it's like a job. If you get hired for a job, you're not going to like everything you're gonna do, you know what I'm sayin'? But you gotta do it, 'cause it's your job. And though you can't get fired, you start not wanting to be a role model and diss your fans, sooner or later it'll come back to haunt you."

Kool G. Rap, on the other hand, says, "I ain't trying to be a role model, youknowwhatimsayin'? I'm like everybody who listen to my shit. I just want them to feel like I'm one of them, youknowwhatimsayin'? We all the same, came from the same fuckin' place, youknowwhatimsayin'? All we doin' is seein' the same fucked up shit, youknowwahtimsayin'? We just makin' records about the shit we seein." Sitting beside him in the conference room of Set To Run Public Relations in midtown Manhattan, DJ Polo observes, "To me, I think rap gives us a way to express ourself throughout the community, throughout the world. Send a message to everybody—not just the kids—but send a message to everybody." G. Rap adds, "I think it's how you look at life, youknowwhatimsayin? A person's rap is how he looks at life, the way he sees shit. The way he grew up and all a that—a person's aspect on life."

Yo-Yo agrees. "Rap to me is a way of expressing myself," she says, while a girlfriend braids her long auburn extensions. "Rap has done something major to young blacks, I feel, although there's so much negativity. You have people really down on rap so much, but I think it's done so much for the black community because all these rappers that you do see were underprivileged kids who might not have had the chance unless rap came about. When rap came about, it was rhyming and everyone could rhyme.

"Rap to me is for my people—it's like black music," she continues. "When I say rap is for my people I'm talking about my neighborhood, blacks in general, although I know other different races get involved, but not where I grew up. Rap to me is something that we can all relate to and get involved in that is self-esteem to my people—although I'm not a racist person."

But Black Sheep don't share these thoughts. "The whole pack is stereotyped as strictly black," says Dres. "You have to be black to be def, knowwhati'msayin? Whereas, it's music and music is for everybody." Mr. Lawnge adds, "When you say that, you tell white America that it's a black thing, they look at it as, oh, only black people listen to it, nawimsayin? Sometimes they mean only a black person can do it well, but that's not necessarily true either." Certainly, rap is becoming more multicultural as funky Caucasians such as the Beastie Boys, House of Pain, Prime Minister Pete Nice, and MC Serch, and Latinos such as Cypress Hill, Kid Frost, the Beatnuts, and Fat Joe add their own flavors to the simmering stew of styles. But at its heart, the genre and its whole mode of expression originates deep from within black culture.

"I see hip-hop as being ghetto media, man, media for the poor kids," says Wise Intelligent of PRT. "I see it as a black business, man, hip-hop is black business, word up, it's black business, man. Yunno, that's the way the poor kids got they food on the table, man. We found a way to get some food on the table for a change." PRT's third album, in fact, is aptly titled *Black Business* (Profile, 1993).

PRT's labelmate, DJ Quik, best sums up these views on the art form by saying, "Hip-hop has given me a voice to say that you can do whatever the fuck you want to do, you just have to want to do it. You have to have a desire, and motivation, and drive, and a lot of faith, yunno, and a lot of

DJ QUIK WORKS ON HIS NEXT HIT AT MANAGER GREG JESSIE'S STUDIO.

patience. I mean, it ain't easy getting what you want if it's worth havin', yunno? 'Cause anything worth having don't come easy. So, yunno, it gave me a voice to talk to my people."

This voice is one that has been suppressed and ignored for a long time, then dismissed, trivialized, and criticized. But through the sheer power of persistence and continuous innovation and improvement, rap has risen to a position where it cannot be ignored. Encompassing many different views and feelings, it is the art and life of a new generation of poets, claiming respect and recognition as they speak over the drum.

recommended
listening

1. Grand Puba, *Reel to Reel* (Elektra, 1992).
2. Big Daddy Kane, *Long Live the Kane* (Cold Chillin'/Warner, 1988).
3. Queen Latifah, *All Hail the Queen* (Tommy Boy, 1989).
4. Digital Underground, *Sex Packets* (Tommy Boy, 1990).
5. Yo-Yo, *Make Way for the Motherlode* (East-West, 1991).
6. Black Sheep, *A Wolf in Sheep's Clothing* (Mercury/Polygram, 1991).
7. Gang Starr, *Daily Operation* (Chrysalis, 1992).
8. Lord Finesse & DJ Mike Smooth, *Funky Technician* (Wild Pitch, 1989).
9. A Tribe Called Quest, *The Low End Theory* (Jive/RCA, 1991).
10. Leaders of the New School, *Future Without A Past* (Elektra, 1991).

ChApTeR 10

Notes from the Underground

Despite the millions of dollars currently tied up in rap, despite sales demographics that say rap is now more popular among teens in the vanilla suburbs than in chocolate cities, despite all the bad press, and hype, despite DATs and CDs, sample clearances, and $25 concert tickets, hip-hop is alive and well and thriving in the underground—a place far removed from the pop charts, commercial radio, executive suites, malls, and MTV. Real creativity, as well as the soul of hip-hop, dwells in the underground, where rap music originated. Though mainstream and underground sensibilities occasionally collide (as in the universal acclaim surrounding Dr. Dre's double-platinum-selling *The Chronic*), these two distinct entities are constantly at odds as they shape the art form.

Rap, like rock 'n' roll, may already have had its reign in the sun, but true hip-hop shows no signs of overexposure. As the Large Professor (Paul Mitchell)—one of the few artists I didn't need a publicist to get in touch with—told me, "Rap, first of all, is Vanilla Ice and M.C. Hammer. That's the title they put on rap. Now with hip-hop, I see a lovely bright future for hip-hop, and I see rap going down the fuckin' tubes, you know what I'm sayin? 'Cause a lot of people just gonna start saying, damn, this rap shit that we looking at is real synthetic. You know, it's like somebody sat down and they had a whole plan—we're gonna be hard—you know, shit like that, and there's a whole plan to it and a gimmick, and all of that shit. But hip-hop is just how you feel."

Though he has made his name as a producer, the 20-year-old Mitchell does it all. No slack as a rapper, he also demonstrates his deejaying skills on the equipment that is the centerpiece of his sparsely furnished highrise in Queens. Describing the thrill of freestyling at a live show, he says, "That's hip-hop, you know what I'm saying, when you could just feel it. You could feel that shit running through you, man. And a lot of people be thinking that's some drug shit, man, but you can feel the beat flow through you, man, where you just know every lyric gonna come on time, and half the words gonna rhyme. I could do that shit all night."

In addition to the innovators and artists whose love and commitment to the art form shines as brightly as their talent, the spectrum of rap includes imitators, gimmick acts, seasoned veterans striving for longevity, mediocre kids trying to get over, and those who are just plain "faking the funk." But this state of affairs was inevitable—especially under the sway of the music industry that brought rap into the mainstream but flooded the market with a lot of lackluster product. As a result, rap today is more a job than an adventure. Proven formulas, like the overexposed genre of "gangsta rap" are exploited to death, while innovation is not prized as highly. But we should not forget that originality and the desire to constantly go to the next level has made the art form what it is today. The impetus for such growth usually originates in the underground, which creates the newest styles in music and expression. While rap's progress has threatened to stall several times, a new crop of hungry unknowns has always surfaced to rejuvenate the scene once again.

As heirs to the old school, Run-D.M.C. rescued rap from the discofied sound that did not reflect what was going on at live hip-hop parties. Other saviors, down the line, included new school artists such as Boogie Down Productions, Eric B. & Rakim, Public Enemy, and EPMD. As a purist, I think not in terms of old or new schools, but true school—artists who really define what hip-hop is by the simple fact that they exist and make music. They simply do what they do exceedingly well. These groups are well represented throughout these pages, as are a host of other underground talent who focus on street credibility and winning the respect of their community. Their allegiance lies with the serious fans of hip-hop, and they are not necessarily concerned with trying to achieve the highest record sales. The fact that Public Enemy sells platinum or EPMD gold is incidental—they are in it for the music first and foremost. I have also heard KRS-ONE say on many occasions that people should steal his records and sneak into shows (though I'm sure he doesn't mean that literally, you get the idea).

As a supporter of progressive sounds who has reviewed a lot of newer, more avant-garde artists for *The Source*'s "Hip-hop Alternatives" section, I do not turn my nose up to the new frontier of rap. In fact, it makes me feel good to hear albums like Mary J. Blige's *What's the 411?* (Uptown, 1992), the Brand New Heavies' *Heavy Rhyme Experience Vol. 1* (Delicious Vinyl/ Atlantic, 1992), or saxophonist Greg Osby's *3-D Lifestyles*, which blends live jazz with break beats. Such projects show that musicians and singers from other musical backgrounds think enough of the art form to take it seriously and incorporate it into their own sound.

When rap employs background singers, tinges of r&b, reggae, or a live band instead of sampled loops, these represent different approaches to innovation within the art form. Sometimes these artists move into realms that are beyond even hip-hop itself. While groups like D.C.'s Basehead or San Francisco's Disposable Heroes of Hip-Hoprisy are clearly influenced by Public Enemy and BDP, I see them as being in a category all by themselves, which I wouldn't even want to label. As long as they are making music that people enjoy, it shouldn't really even matter. Calling it "alternative" rap would probably be as much a misnomer as alternative rock is.

Then there are immensely successful groups like Digable Planets and Arrested Development, who are more difficult to factor into the equation. Digable Planets, for example, fuses jazz and hip-hop with undisputed skill and finesse, but so does Gang Starr, who have been doing it longer (three albums, to be exact) and without any gold records to their credit. Without getting into a more subjective discussion about whether Digable Planet's music is better or worse (I personally prefer Gang Starr), they are obviously appealing to an audience above and beyond hip-hop's core following. A catchy single and aggressive promotion might lead to daytime radio play, which in turn attracts more mainstream listeners—and sells more records. But what is popular on the streets—the "raw" hip-hop—is more likely to be heard pumping from the jeeps than on radio. A few groups, such as A Tribe Called Quest, are able to walk the line between mainstream and underground appeal, but in these cases the mainstream finds them, and not vice versa.

Grammy Award winners Arrested Development won mainstream recognition instantly, becoming the darlings of radio, MTV, and the press. But their appeal on the streets was minimal. They took rap and reshaped it in their own image, adding more singing and a musicality that reflected their Southern roots and distinctly nonurban experience. While I always appreciate originality, and the fact that their music was different, it seemed odd that such a group was being hailed as the new saviors of rap by the mainstream media. Perhaps it was a result of the backlash against all the "gangsta" rap going around. Arrested Development, however, is no De La Soul—and certainly not a Run-D.M.C. They are simply a new group who have created their own niche within rap that has proven to be very popular with the mainstream. As far as real hip-hop goes, though, I doubt if they would win any awards.

Arrested Development represents how rap's progressive nature inspires different offshoots that take the art form in various directions. But groups who are truly committed to hip-hop would rather be the tree than a branch. Beyond simply rhymes or beats, hip-hop captures a feeling and has a certain edge that its fans can identify with immediately. Though high standards are set on the streets, where new sounds are either played or considered "whack," mainstream acceptance cannot be tossed aside easily. Because so many more people are interested in the art form than 20 years ago, the possibilities for rap have opened up that much more. One of the latest manifestations of this influence is a renewed interest in poetry.

Ever since KRS-ONE acknowledged "I am a poet," on his debut album, *Criminal Minded*, rappers have been aware that their craft is nothing short of urban, street poetry. All rap is also not necessarily simplistic or low-brow: Prince Poetry from Organized Konfusion is known for his sophisticated verse, as is Q-Tip from A Tribe Called Quest, who calls himself "the Abstract Poet." The art form has undeniably sparked a new interest in the use of language and the spoken word, which is finding an outlet in poetry readings similar to those of the fifties and sixties, when the original "Beats" started their scene. While this nineties revival of pure poetry is taking place at a grassroots level—in small performance spaces and clubs around the country—it has been observed by the media at large. *The Source*, MTV, which has featured short poetry "spots," as well as an "MTV Unplugged" special and films such as John Singleton's *Poetic Justice*, have all felt the vibrations of these "new Beats," young blacks who are taking it to the stage in a very different way. Rap, meanwhile, will still be here, continuing to grow and hopefully progress, spawning different offshoots as it unfolds ahead through the nineties.

notes

Introduction

1. Nelson George, *The Death of Rhythm and Blues*, p. 188.
2. Leroi Jones, *Blues People*, p. 65.
3. Phyllis Garland, *The Sound of Soul*, p. 76.
4. Ibid., p. 77.
5. Jerry Adler, "The Rap Attitude, " *Newsweek*, March 19, 1990, p. 56.
6. Janice C. Simpson, "Yo! Rap Gets on the Map," *Time*, February 5, 1990, p. 60.

Chapter One: Return of the Boogie Down

1. Sally Banes, "To the Beat Y'all: Breaking Is Hard to Do." *Village Voice*, April 28, 1981, p. 18.

Chapter Two: Rap's Raggamuffin Roots

1. Stephen Davis and Peter Simon, *Reggae International* (New York: R&B, 1982), pp. 105–6.
2. U. Roy interviewed by Sister Morri, "U. Roy: Words of Wisdom," *Reggae and African Beat*, January 1989.
3. Ibid.
4. Dick Hebdige, *Cut 'n' Mix* (London: Methuen, 1987), p. 62.
5. Howard Johnson and Jim Pines, *Reggae, Deep Roots Music* (New York: Proteus Books, 1987), p. 70.
6. Interview with Sir Lord Comic, Johnson and Pines, *Reggae, Deep Roots Music*, p. 72.
7. Hebdige, *Cut 'n' Mix*, p. 127.
8. Sly Dunbar interviewed by J. Poet, "Ryddim Killer," *Vinyl Propaganda*, January 1990.
9. Ibid.

Chapter Three: Ain't It Funky

1. Cynthia Rose, *Living in America: The Soul Saga of James Brown* (London: Serpent's Tail, 1990), p. 24.

2. Timothy White, "P-Funk's Acid Test: The Dark Side of Gettin' Down," *Crawdaddy*, January 1978, p. 14.

Chapter Four: Gettin' Paid

1. Dennis Wepman, Ronald B. Newman, Murray B. Binderman, *The Life: The Lore and Folk Poetry of the Black Hustler* (Los Angeles: Holloway House, 1976) pp. 170–71.
2. Bruce Jackson, *"Get Your Ass in the Water and Swim like Me," Narrative Poetry from the Black Oral Tradition* (Cambridge: Harvard University Press, 1974), p. 13.
3. Ronin Ro, "Behind Bars," *The Source*, May 1993, p. 52.
4. Gordon Witkin, "The Men Who Created Crack," *U.S. News & World Report*, August 19, 1991, pp. 44–48.
5. Jackson, *"Get Your Ass in the Water,"* p. 21.

Chapter Five: Rebirth of a Nation

1. David Mills, "The Hard Rap on Public Enemy," *Washington Times*, May 22, 1989, p. E1.
2. Robert Christgau and Greg Tate, "Chuck D: All Over the Map," *Village Voice, Rock & Roll Quarterly*, Fall 1991, p. 15.

Chapter Six: House of Jam

1. Bill Adler, *Tougher Than Leather* (New York: New American Library, 1987), p. 28.

Chapter Nine: Oral Funk Journalism

1. Jon Pareles, "On Rap, Symbolism and Fear," *New York Times*, February 2, 1992, p. 1.
2. David Toop, *Rap Attack 2: African Rap to Global Hip-Hop* (London: Pluto, 1991), p. 19.
3. Marian Barnes and Linda Goss, eds., *Talk that Talk: An Anthology of African American Storytelling* (New York: Simon & Schuster, 1989), p. 12.
4. Ibid., p. 17.

lyric permissions

index

about the author

S. H. FERNANDO JR., a graduate of Harvard and The Columbia School of Journalism, is a frequent contributor to *The Source: The Magazine of Hip-Hop Music, Culture, and Politics*. He lives in Brooklyn, New York.